THE COLLECTED POEMS OF IRVING LAYTON

D1481653

THE COLLECTED POEMS OF IRVING LAYTON

 McClelland and Stewart Limited

THE COLLECTED POEMS OF IRVING LAYTON

Toronto/Montreal

0-7710-4837-8

The Canadian Publishers
McClelland and Stewart Limited
25 Hollinger Road, Toronto 374

for Amos Saunders

FOREWORD

When I was six my family lived in a crowded rectangular box that was divided into four tiny compartments. One of them was the grocery store my mother had thriftily made out of the front parlour; another was the bedroom where my father and mother, four of their children and cousin Fanny slept. Or rather tried to. For above us the semi-brothel run by a husband-and-wife team filled up each night with roistering drunks whose screams, shouts, laughter and imprecations rained down like invisible hailstones on the immigrant family below, making sleep impossible. My father's groans followed by those of my mother, we'd sit up on our beds to wait for the next part of the scenario, inevitable in its coming: the start of a brawl, the sound of overturned chairs and tables; of plates, beer bottles and glasses being smashed.

Now my mother, her mournful whispers joined by those of her daughters and cousin Fanny, would beg me to get the broom and thump its handle into the ceiling. In the frosty winter nights – we couldn't afford to heat the bedroom and I dubbed it the North Pole after my first geography lesson – I was very loathe to leave the hard-earned warmth of my bed, run unslippered (slippers? who ever heard of them?) into the now cooled-off kitchen and make the same comfortless journey back. However, since I was the youngest, there was no help for it.

Broomstick tightly clutched in my hand I'd perch myself unsteadily on the dresser and make precarious upward sweeps with it, only the dull wooden sound I heard in the darkness telling me I'd found my wide target.

It was then a miracle took place. The loud cursings and clatterings would stop suddenly, and silence like some mysterious night flower would blossom from the tip of my broomstick. I sensed it spreading out with swift amazing luxuriance until it filled the whole bedroom. It was uncanny, and in my child's imagination I saw myself a boy Moses parting the filthy noise-filled blackness so that long-suffering Israelites might pass safely into a region of peace and slumber.

Of course in less than fifteen minutes the noise, the tumult, would start up again, requiring another grumbling application of the broomstick. Yet each time the mysterious flower of silence opened its invisible blossoms over my head I felt the same thrill of power, of exulting joy. The cold, the freezings and shiverings were forgotten, obliterated. I, I alone, had punched a rectangular space of quiet into the filthy drunken chaos and presented it to those older and stronger than myself.

My early childhood experiences in Montreal put a crease into my mind neither theology nor socialism has been able to straighten out. I see life as a Dionysian cock-and-cunt affair with time off, though precious little of it, for meditation and good works. Certainly the first whorehouse raid I saw on De Bullion Street has given me an ineffaceable picture of the human situation: people laughing at the humiliation of others, maliciously enjoying their helplessness and discomfiture. Sweet, sweet human beings. French-Canadians, English-Canadians, Jews, Bulgarians, Germans, Italians, Spaniards, Swedes – is sick, is pathetic and pathological humanity any different anywhere? A poet has his images and symbols handed to him very early in life; his later poems are largely explorations he makes into the depths of his unconscious to unravel their meanings. Incontrovertibly my earliest impressions have coloured everything I've ever written.

Elsewhere I've said the poet is someone whom life knocks on the head and makes ring like a tuning fork. The knocking begins very early.

The whores, drunks, negroes, peddlers; the hostile French-Canadians living on and beyond St. Denis street, the Italians on Demontigny, now spacious ungracious Maisonneuve Boulevard – how they filled my mind with terror. And, yes, with unreasonable delight. I looked forward to the nightly battles with the youthful Jew-hating Christians who descended on the tiny Maccabean band waiting for them with stones, bottles and bricks or anything else to make up for our inferiority in numbers or pugnacity. I was young Lochinvar come out of St. Elizabeth street; I was the Minstrel Boy and General Wolfe and all the other heroes my teachers in Alexandra School (now without much change a huge factory building) sometimes raved on about. And I was Napoleon, especially when I directed the artillery barrage of rocks and iron filings I had amassed for just this eventuality in the unpaved lanes of the neighbourhood.

The joy of battle, of routing our enemies, of seeing them turn the corner of Demontigny street and disappear into the cowardly fastnesses of their hovels. And afterwards returning with my older brothers and their friends, jubilant and unscathed, to the surprising stillness of the now deserted street. It was all so quiet now, the asphalt echoing dully and eerily under our feet while above us stretched the summery ribband of stars as we marched down St. Elizabeth.

So the world was not only cock-and-cunt. It was also battle. You broke someone's skull, anyway made a profound philosophical dent in it, or he broke yours. People were so made they hated one another at first sight and sought their injury. They conceptualized and tortured; out of the same taproot grew their creativity and evil. They were neurotics – even the best of them – with an ineradicable penchant for cruelty. The reasons they offered one another for its display and enjoyment varied from place to place and were as spurious as they were incredible. Religion and manners, especially Art, enabled them to conceal their enjoyment, chiefly from themselves. A few kind and sensitive souls might wring their hands at the resulting carnage, at the wars, massacres, pogroms, and death camps but their despair was the measure of their helplessness.

In Montreal the dominant ethnic groups stared at one another balefully across their self-erected ghetto walls. Three solitudes. I remember the feelings of anxiety I had as a boy whenever I crossed St. Denis street. This street marked the border between Jewish and French-Canadian territories. East of St. Denis was hostile Indian country densely populated with church-going Mohawks somewhat older than myself waiting to ambush me. From one of these ambushes I once returned minus the new cap my mother had bought me for the Passover holidays – and almost minus an eye or two.

Bleury street and beyond, walking westward, took me into that other ghetto, the one in which the Anglo-saxons lived in tree-lined and privileged aloofness. Was it Miss Fairlawn and Miss Mc-Ildouie or the school principal, Mr. Spinney, and his spinsterish assistant whose dark eyes seemed to spit fire at the trembling boy before her that distilled, O ever so subtly, those first drops of

English superiority into my mind? So that when I found myself in Westmount, that once-upon-a-time enclave of unbelievably fatuous, unbelievably dull and self-complacent Bourbons, I'd feel a different kind of menace. One that was internal rather than external in its threat, its thrust. I felt weak, helpless, as if all strength was leaving me through the pores of my skin. Here I always felt myself to be a trespasser, not a warrior as I did when I crossed St. Denis street. At any moment huge mastiffs would be loosed on me or someone with a healthily tanned face would say to me with cold but perfect English diction, 'Get away from here.'

These are all gibbering shadows of the past now, absurdly melting snowmen under the maturing sun of a tolerant wisdom. And Miss Cook and her fat, jovial friend, coincidentally also named Miss Cook, didn't they teach me to play dominoes, feed me ginger-bread, and tell my mother what a bright and engaging lad her son was? They had rented the upstairs dwelling when complaints of other neighbours had become too insistent for the bribed police to ignore and the entourage of the semi-brothel had been forced to locate itself farther down the street towards the waterfront. They were goodness itself and also real English just landed from Sussex, England. Ever since the name Sussex has chimed tenderly in my mind and cast a spell over me. I loved those two spinsters with all my heart and God knows what portion of sanity and good humour I owe them. Surely they too had blossomed from the end of my broomstick, a miraculous flower of tranquil love in the frothing slum where I froze and blistered with the changing seasons of the Canadian year.

And Death, hadn't he also flowered from my extraordinary, mir-acle-working broomstick?

For one day in February, two months after the decease of my father, the father of two of our most virulent enemies, Henri and Gaston Labelle, also died. I still have a vivid image of the black satiny robe pinned to the door of their house and lifting, Catholic and disconsolate, in the biting winds. The family were neighbours, practically living next door to us. The two brothers found di-version from the study of the Cathecism in hurling refuse, ice and frozen horsebuns into our passageway so that my mother would have to leave the customer she was serving to sweep the mess out.

I don't know how many times she would have to do this but more than two or three times daily, certainly. And then suddenly her persecution stopped. The deaths of the heads of our two families, the one following so soon the other, as though needles in the hands of some vastly amused deity, began to knit, first a truce to our enmity, later a friendship. So that widow Labelle was shortly to be seen entering my mother's grocery shop and the brothers Henri and Gaston now always gave me a friendly greeting whenever I passed them.

Is it any wonder that I haunt cemeteries as if I were some kin of Dracula, some ghoul? Or that I've written in one of my poems about the 'fraternal graves of cemeteries'? And in a recent composition hailed death as the Messiah 'who alone brings peace, redemption from lies and murder'?

Am I a Canadian poet? Let others use abstractions and thick evasive words; they are welcome to them. With the other end of my broomstick I sweep them all generously towards their corner. God, History, Dialectical Materialism, Free Enterprise, Canadian Identity, all the 'isms' and 'ities' along with the murderous bad temper they evoke – they can have them. My country is wherever I can use my broomstick to bring a momentary grace, a blessed peace and stillness, into my life. It is wherever I can find a sheltered plot where I can dream: away from manic busybodies, puritans, dolts and foul-smelling men and women scrambling furiously to reach the top of the competitive shitpile. I've met them in every part of Canada and they all smell the same. In Halifax and St. John's no less than in Vancouver or Winnipeg. Is this what people mean when they talk about Canadian identity? I hope not. My country is wherever there are concrete objects to touch, taste, feel and enjoy; and it is where I can find another Miss Cook and her fat good-natured friend whose love was not something out of a leatherbound religious book but arose from a disposition as full of caress as a summer breeze. In actual unfolding truth it has been friends and enemies, wives and children, raspberry bushes, frogs and toads. It has been priests and nuns trailing their black habits over the snow-covered streets of Montreal; church bells delighting, affrighting me Sunday mornings. It has been Mr. Amos Saunders who read Tennyson's 'Ballad of the Revenge' and re-routed the life of a normal extroverted schoolboy from pugilism to poetry; and Mr. Dennison, the peculiar bank manager who loaned me three hundred dollars to bring out my first volume of poems, *Here and Now.*

My country has been an immense tree on the summit of a sunswept hill from which I plucked hundreds of poems or waited confidently under its boughs for them to fall like heavy fruit into my open lap. When I think of my life under that tree I am filled with an immeasurable thankfulness that extends beyond the coasts of this land to encircle the entire globe.

Normal human vileness, philistine materialism, racial prejudice, anti-Semitism, hypocrisy and the relentless pursuit of ass in parliaments, universities, Salvation Army hostels, editorial offices, courthouses, hospitals and morgues – out of this glorious fecund rubbish heap and out of occasional glimpses of beauty, goodness and mercy I have made my poems. I have dipped my broomstick into the life swirling around me and written it into the hearts and speech of men. Yahoos, sex-drained executives, pimps and poetasters, limping critics, graceless sluts and the few, the rare few, who gave me moments of insight or ecstasy: I am crazy enough to think I have given them immortality. They will, I hope, never die. Not, anyhow, for as long as style and passion are still valued; or the language which these have sometimes tinged with vitality and distinction.

Irving Layton

Toronto, Ontario
May 20, 1971

CONTENTS

THERE WERE NO SIGNS

By walking I found out
Where I was going.

By intensely hating, how to love.
By loving, whom and what to love.

By grieving, how to laugh from the belly.

Out of infirmity, I have built strength.
Out of untruth, truth.
From hypocrisy, I weaved directness.

Almost now I know who I am.
Almost I have the boldness to be that man.

Another step
And I shall be where I started from.

MRS. FORNHEIM, REFUGEE

Very merciful was the cancer
Which first blinding you altogether
Afterwards stopped up your hearing;
At the end when Death was nearing,
Black-gloved, to gather you in
You did not demur, or fear
One you could not see or hear.

I taught you Shakespeare's tongue, not knowing
The time and manner of your going;
Certainly if with ghosts to dwell,
German would have served as well.
Voyaging lady, I wish for you
An Englishwoman to talk to,
An unruffled listener,
And green words to say to her.

1

THE SWIMMER

The afternoon foreclosing, see
The swimmer plunges from his raft,
Opening the spray corollas by his act of war –
The snake heads strike
Quickly and are silent.

Emerging see how for a moment
A brown weed with marvellous bulbs,
He lies imminent upon the water
While light and sound come with a sharp passion
From the gonad sea around the Poles
And break in bright cockle-shells about his ears.

He dives, floats, goes under like a thief
Where his blood sings to the tiger shadows
In the scentless greenery that leads him home,
A male salmon down fretted stairways
Through underwater slums . . .

Stunned by the memory of lost gills
He frames gestures of self-absorption
Upon the skull-like beach;
Observes with instigated eyes
The sun that empties itself upon the water,
And the last wave romping in
To throw its boyhood on the marble sand.

GOTHIC LANDSCAPE

They stand like penitential Augustines
These trees; and in my Jewboy mind they are monks,
Brown-robed, fearful after their long sleep in dungeons;
When I was a child one of them nearly caught me,
But I escaped, tunnelling the snow to my mother's face;
Under her grey shawl I saw God's Assyrian beard,
And a page of *lameds* racing towards me like ostriches.

I've taken no vow not to forget
The torquemadas stirring in the frosty veins:
But the cloister bells deafen me with insults,
And sallowfaced acolytes inform
The snowdrifts what to whisper against me;
Autos-da-fé make red the immaculate sky;
Come soon, O bright Tudor sun!
I do not like this monastic whiteness of winter –
It is a Christ drained of all blood.

LADY ENFIELD

Lie down beside her, soldier,
And do but use her well,
And she can ease your passion
With cries and powder smell.

Be reckless in your loving,
Her grace makes no one poor
For only bullets issue
From such an iron whore.

HARUSPEX

As the afternoon wore on,
The wind rose like an American tariff;
I, more credulous than my parents,
Sat on my gardenstool, hoping for signs;
Something perhaps to fall out of the sky –
An eagle, like a piece of gunmetal,
Cracking the wall of air, flashing
The forbidden message from broken wings –
Perhaps a never-before-seen snake; or at the least,
A typewriter in the tall grass, its keys
Plucked by a legion of dry crickets;
But all I saw were great swathes of shadow
Moving across the fields like escaped jailbirds.

All afternoon
I watched the Mediterranean sky
Dotted with soft silver-ringed clouds
Like Greek city states,
Like white garlands for an Athenian holiday.
But look! In the north the Macedonian king
Has fastened his grey tunic
And moves slowly, slowly down the Thracian plains,
An armourer gathers the crimson daggerblades,
The heavens darken, and all about me
The rabblegrass, abject,
Whitens under the cruel skywind.

O helmeted goddess,
My little one, head nesting on arm,
I am afraid.

FOR DULLA WHO UNEXPECTEDLY CAME INTO SOME MONEY

He has what many men desire
What all labour for, few acquire.

He has this man's wit, that man's scope:
The Pauline virtues, Faith, Hope

And Charity he dispenses with.
We observe his words have more pith

Since the EVENT, and that he gives
Remembered friends and relatives

A large, accommodating ear
And on the affable stranger

Unloads advice like a bad stock.
There's an assurance in his look,

A quietness like September
Brooding over a blue flower.

Now finding wit unmoneyed flat
As autumn leaves that blur to death

In alleyways, he pities those
Who take to bed philosophies

As lean as themselves. So is born
A new Dulla, envy changed to scorn.

BIRDS AT DAYBREAK

In my back yard
There are birds
The birds sing
They hunt for worms and they sing
They hunt for worms to feed their young
And they sing
Soon the young will sing

In the morning the sun drops like a ball into my back yard
Zeus has hit another homer from some distant field away off
Zeus and Homer – that's pretty good, isn't it?
Almost every morning he bats a homer into my back yard
In summer his batting average is particularly good

When the birds see the ball coming into the yard
They get out of its way
They raise a big tumult of wings and whistles and cawings
And get out of its way
They fly to the trees to protect them
They fly in and out the trimmed hedge now beginning
    to smile its diurnal welcome to the sun
The birds fly in and out the hedge to show they are not
    afraid,
But they do not forget the worms
They keep their dry beady eyes fixed on the ground
Where the worms are,
They call to each other and to their young
About the good feast before them
The morning is filled with their delight

Is the sun a ball?
Has Zeus hit a homerun?
No, it's a gigantic bird – the aboriginal hawk
No, it's not that either
It is a huge primeval robin
It has eaten the worm of many colours: grey
And purplish and black: the dawn-worm!

The other little birds are ecstatic
At the ritual eating of the dawn-worm,
They dart, the hedge's shiver of sensual ecstasy,
                    along its bright margin;
The trees shake with their delight and excitement

It is a mild, beneficent summer morning
And all the birds crazily clap their dizzy wings
And whistle and sing, O
Rejoicing, they sing!

THE BLACK HUNTSMEN

Before ever I knew men were hunting me
I knew delight as water in a glass in a pool;
The childish heart then
Was ears nose eyes twiceten fingers,
And the torpid slum street, in summer,
A cut vein of the sun
That shed goldmotes by the million
Against a boy's bare toe foot ankle knee.

Then when the old year fell out of the window
To break into snowflakes on the cold stones of City Hall
I discovered Tennyson in a secondhand bookstore;
He put his bugle for me to his bearded mouth,
And down his Aquitaine nose a diminutive King Arthur
Rode out of our grocery shop bowing to left and to right,
Bearing my mother's *sheitel* with him;
And for a whole week after that
I called my cat Launcelot.

Now I look out for the evil retinue
Making their sortie out of a forest of gold;
Afterwards their dames shall weave my *tzitzith*
Into a tapestry,
Though for myself I had preferred
A death by water or sky.

7

ARCHETYPES

Although I had written
   of venery
(and of men's hates, too, my masters!)
and of the sun, the best thing in the cosmos,
for it warms my bones
now I am old and no woman
   will lie with me
     seeing how wrinkled
my hams are, and my bones decrepit;
and of the earth, mother of all loves,
mother of flowers and trees:

Some crying fool from the sticks
writes me petulantly
            to complain
I have used two choruses
in my great hymn to Pan
   when it's quite plain to him
and one other Greek scholar
that four
   would have been more felicitous.

ON MY WAY TO SCHOOL

On my way to school
I used to pass
A Baptist church
And fields of grass.

"Jesus Saves"
Above the gate
Would comfort me
If I were late.

The church is gone,
The street is paved,
The Home Bank thrives
Where Jesus Saved.

SOLEIL DE NOCES

I wait
for the good lines
to come.
At the right moment
the sun
will explode them
in my back yard.

Then I shall
pick them off
the lion-
coloured road
and this unfractured
greenery,
thistle
and speargrass,
like bits of clothing.

When the gods
begin
to batter me
I shall howl
like a taken
virgin.

EXCURSION

Their dufflebags sprawl like a murder
Between the seats: themselves are bored
Or boisterous. These are ignorant soldiers
Believing that when forever the violent die
The good receive their inexhaustible cow –
Grade seven and superman have arranged everything.
The other passengers are unimportant liars:
Salesmen, admen, the commercial trivia,
Blown between the lines of memoranda,
And across the aisle, disposed on thirty beds,
Two limp virgins eyes below the navel.

     Slowly the train curves around rich
Suburban Westmount that squats upon a slum,
Then like a hypodermic plunges past
Uniform fenceposts into open country;
There's glazed sunlight upon the hard serrated
Fields. Air is thin slightly neurasthenic
Over the distant indiscriminate trees
That posture on hillside gross and secretive
As women staling. Pins withdrawn suddenly
Barns collapse like real estate models. The senses
Run like swift hares along the fences.

These are the fire-lands and this a sealed train
Of cold excursionists, throats buttoned up
With yellow timetables.
                 On folded hands
The minutes drop like dandruff. The
Jetted column survives in a black foetus,
And the goats leap into their faces shrieking.

MORTUARY

Flesh has fallen away. Trees
And buildings are summer's skeleton;
Wind has loosened, disarrayed
The separate ribs, the evidence of bone.
Dead, deposited relics
Shored up clean against a stiffened sky,
Fixed by the mortician cold
Moving his fingers over them ceaselessly;
While the snow, decently to inter,
Drifts in between the spaces, everywhere.

DRILL SHED

The passive motion of sand
Is fluid geometry. Fir needles
Are the cool, select thoughts
Of madmen; and
Like a beggar the wind wheedles
Pine cones from the pines.
Inside there's no violence,
Only the silence
Of an empty church;
Drilled zygotes shift
From foot to foot or lurch
With half-closed eyes against the guns
While the ackeye shows
With delphic joy
The deeper things a dial-sight knows;
Curious now,
I marvel how
Lord Euclid's dream
Can stiffen a boy.

STOLEN WATCH

The gold shine wets his cheeks,
while the wheels tick it
into his ears;
the cool face is a fistful of snow
under a glass, and the hands
are black circus seals
lunging at classroom figures.
At play yesterday
he had known the intricate chain
as a trail of sun motes in the sand;
now the motes bubble
through the cracks of his fingers
as they curve heavier than a hammer
over this plural world of sand and snow . . .
behind the limp and legless coats
his heart races the seals.

DISUNITY

For one mystic
pure colour was rest of heart;
and ragged saints have seen God.

But how cold a thing
is lust, is malice. I've known
an old woman, an ache amongst hairs,

Hearing she would outlast her twin,
clack her gums; her mirth
confounded by decrepitude.

And I've known the lover's crooked
eloquence, and November's
snow, a death mask for the earth.

DE BULLION STREET

Below this broad street inverted bell-jars
Hanging from wooden crucifixes drop
Tiny moons upon the shaven asphalt;
Rouged whores lean lips to narrow slits: they stop
The young soldier with his bag of salt.

Under the night's carapace, the soft lanes
Are listening ears where sudden footfall
Starts a choir of echoes. A red light winks
Viciously; and the wind's occasional
Sigh lifts from the garbage pails their stinks.

Here private lust is public gain and shame;
Here the Oriental and the skipjack go;
Where those bleak outposts of the virtuous
The corner mission and the walled church grow
Like hæmorrhoids on the city's anus.

O reptilian street whose scaly limbs
Are crooked stairways and the grocery store,
Isolate, is your dreaming half-shut eye:
Each virgin at the barricaded door
Feels your tongue-kiss like a butterfly.

MONT ROLLAND

Pitiless towards men, I am filled with pity
For the impractical trees climbing the exhausted hillside;
Sparse, dull, with blue uneven spaces between them,
They're like the beard of an uncombed tolerant monk,
       Or a Tolstoyan disciple, circa 1890.

Below these, a straggler, a tree with such enormous boughs
It might have remembered Absalom, who dead,
Put by the aping of his father's majesty;
And one lone cedar, a sycophant, stunted,
       A buffoon with sick dreams.

While all around me, as for a favoured intruder,
There's an immense silence made for primeval birds
Or a thought to rise like a great cloud out of a crater,
A silence contained by valleys,
       Gardes Civiles in green capes.

Nevertheless the Lilliput train trivializes
The tolerant monk, the trees, and this whirlpool of silence,
Though it fling over its side like a capitalist's bequest
A memorial row
       Of blossoming cherry trees.

And the highway which seen from my window seems
A suture in the flesh of a venerable patrician,
In the distance falls like a lariat on the green necks
Of the untamed hills, that raise like wild horses
       Their dignified, astonished heads.

TO THE LAWYER HANDLING MY DIVORCE CASE

If at all, he thinks of me as a soiled fingernail,
Or the not-so-smart, or as simply unlucky;
Of course my humanness makes him uneasy;
He does not ask me for my private conception
Of him and his wife
And their intelligent dog;
I might never have heard of Nagasaki
Or debated the soul's immortality.
When he inserts his nail file into his vest pocket
And peers at me over his clean fingernails
In that instant I have plummeted the infinite distance
Between I and Me—
Me is always question-begging, diffident, undersized;
I am Me
When my lawyer addresses me.
We smell each other's absurdity
But for the time being mine
Has a name and a file number of more than six figures.

LOVE'S DIFFIDENCE

Love is so diffident a thing.
I scoop up my hands with air;
I do not find it there
Nor in my friend's pleasure
Nor when the birds sing.

I am confused, forsaken.
I have lost the way.
Love's not as some men say
In woman's eyes, blue or grey;
Nor in kisses given and taken.

Love, I call out, find me
Spinning round in error.
Display your dank, coarse hair,
Your bubs and bulbous shoulder.
Then strike, witless bitch, blind me.

15

ON THE DEATH OF A. VISHINSKY

Adults are children merely
with a larger vocabulary:
my fears are no different from
when I was a six-year son.

This I my wife abuses;
and others, my principal:
who lives by daily ruses
a desperate animal

Heard today how quietly
the fluent Vishinsky died:
if he could not out-talk Death
what chance have I, so tongue-tied?

SILVER LINING

There was a chap who, when
Wife and all six children
Burned, saw his affliction
Turn hearts to gold from stone
As one man sought him to sell
Cerements to his clientele,
Saying his experience
Outweighed dollars and cents.

I speak the sober truth:
The man of grief accepted
And by his tale became
The invincible salesman.
At last, his fortune made,
A chap whom all envied,
The trade requested him to pose
Attired in his own graveclothes.

16

ADMONITION AND REPLY

I have three acquaintances
A, B, and C;
"Why do you write of the wenches?"
They rail at me.

"Foh! For shame, man.
Christians, we disapprove
Your always singing
The pleasures of Love.

"They offend us,
Your songs bawdy and raucous;
Purify your soul, sing
The glory of suffering."

A's wife is algid.
B – a sick worm – prays for death;
C's wife has prurigo
And a vile breath.

NOT BLOWN AWAY

My wife's out of humour, and I barely live
So bewitched am I by creditors;
Yet here's a volume by a "sensitive" –
Thin, announcing the usual fevers.

He exhibits on each ricethin page
His "fine sensibility," a mind
Alien to contempt, contumacy, rage;
To all that's imprecise, undefined.

His aching poems, precious in Reviews,
Are overhauled by Southern exegetes:
Yet how often did Sigmund blow his nose
And Nietzsche, tickled by an Alpine wind, sneeze!

17

MAY DAY ORATORS

Having exalted
Social Justice,
Love, Comradeship, etc.

Windus is now racked
with envy
since Gusto speaking

To the same purpose
extorts a noisier applause
from the undiscriminating audience.

Indeed, its preference
for Comrade Gusto thus shown,
the noble Windus

Is quite cast down.

CANADIAN SKIERS

No, it is not *Die Welt als Wille*
Nor the *Phenomenologie* will account for them;
No, it is simply that these hills
Being white and silent grow them

They come out the enchanted slopes
Like children, around bends. It
Would seem as if ignorance of all perils . . .
Yes, ignorance is their greatest asset

Look at those banked deposits!
There is nothing . . . nothing they will not try;
I've heard them tell one another,
"If we cannot climb, we must soar and fly."

And the kindliness these hills grow
And the kindliness that these hills grow
As they come upon a lonely brother
Telling his Canadian troubles to the snow

GOLFERS

Like Sieur Montaigne's distinction
between virtue and innocence
what gets you is their unbewilderment

They come into the picture suddenly
like unfinished houses, gapes and planed wood,
dominating a landscape

And you see at a glance
among sportsmen they are the metaphysicians,
intent, untalkative, pursuing Unity

(What finally gets you is their chastity)

And that no theory of pessimism is complete
which altogether ignores them

AFTERNOON TEA

Five girls around a table.
One of them exhibits her fine teeth
Over a story. The Elohim made her.
Prepared this space and time for her.

And has the Elohim made a him for her?
Doubtless. The four others laugh.
Grow suddenly taut when they lift
Their cups mouthward: then spit out

Gobs of laughter as if the rims
Like fishhooks on a string
Had ripped the ha ha ohs
From their constricted throats.

PORTRAIT

Pay small attention to the chin
And the stiff Loyalist mouth
And the pallid complexion:
These are flesh or of flesh. Begin

Rather with the rimless glasses
Showing faintly, with restraint,
The wearer's openness
To the universal values

(Let there be no boundaries
Between the heart
And what the heart desires)

Then mark the dry abstracted brow
Above the austere glasses
Where others, equally joyless,
Have left an enduring shadow.

Crazed these many years dwells Right
In the tower above the high pink nose
Drawbridge to this remote schloss
Archaic in the level sunlight.

THE GREEKS HAD A WORD FOR IT

It's your fault
the summer moon
fell
from the sky
and rolled
down
     the asphalt
hill

But see!
I've caught it
between my legs

And if you
kiss me
here, on this convenient
   doorstep,
I will share it
with you.

BLOOD ON THE MOON

I saw the moon expire
Entangled in the barbed wire
Of the branches of a bare tree;
The stars looked on without pity
And moved across the dark pelvis
As crabs might, or tarantulas.

21

THE BULL CALF

The thing could barely stand. Yet taken
from his mother and the barn smells
he still impressed with his pride,
with the promise of sovereignty in the way
his head moved to take us in.
The fierce sunlight tugging the maize from the ground
licked at his shapely flanks.
He was too young for all that pride.
I thought of the deposed Richard II.

"No money in bull calves," Freeman had said.
 The visiting clergyman rubbed the nostrils
 now snuffing pathetically at the windless day.
"A pity," he sighed.
 My gaze slipped off his hat toward the empty sky
 that circled over the black knot of men,
 over us and the calf waiting for the first blow.

Struck,
 the bull calf drew in his thin forelegs
 as if gathering strength for a mad rush . . .
 tottered . . . raised his darkening eyes to us,
 and I saw we were at the far end
 of his frightened look, growing smaller and smaller
 till we were only the ponderous mallet
 that flicked his bleeding ear
 and pushed him over on his side, stiffly,
 like a block of wood.

Below the hill's crest
the river snuffled on the improvised beach.
We dug a deep pit and threw the dead calf into it.
It made a wet sound, a sepulchral gurgle,
as the warm sides bulged and flattened.
Settled, the bull calf lay as if asleep,
one foreleg over the other,
bereft of pride and so beautiful now,
without movement, perfectly still in the cool pit,
I turned away and wept.

CHOKECHERRIES

The sun's gift –

but the leaves a sickly green;
the more exposed curling, showing
a bleached white, many with ragged
holes;
Caterpillars have been
here
sliding their slow destructive bodies
over them.

I think of them, the leaves, as hoplites
or as anything ingloriously
useful,
suffering, dying . . .

But the chokecherries,
ah;
Still, the leaves' sacrifice
is acrid on the tongue.

AFTER THE CHINESE

1/ Since the writings of wise men
Are my chief study
I am not like you, Lu Du,
A close observer of the habits of birds.
On the other hand I am curious about people.
I find their inexplicable cruelties
A matter for sorrow and reflection.
   Nonetheless my lovers say
The birds chirping in their green coverlets
Gossip about my merry heart
And to please me further exclaim
They make nests from my smiles.
Why is it I have never once heard
Such reports about you
Who have studied the doings of birds all your life?

2/ To eat, drink, fornicate
And to rail at priests –
Was it for this
I was shaped nine months
In my mother's womb?

3/ When I was young I quarrelled with everyone. I put
Away my wife because she was fat and would not diet.
I took up soldiering since killing was agreeable
And the pay was good. When the victorious general
Disbanded his troops I found a soft berth
As his Keeper of Stores where my arrogant manner
Earned respect from the several factions. Age
And repeated sickness have at last brought me here.
I have learned humility and compassion.
Yet tell me, my sorrowful patient friend,
When I was acquiring such distinguished virtues
What were the long graveworms doing? Procreating.

4/ This man loves intrigue.
I have known him to upset a plan
Which he himself in great secrecy had set afoot.
In that way he maintains a good opinion of himself
And feels himself masterful.

5/ Having seen a drunkard stagger home,
And a philosopher pitched headlong onto the street
Because he could not pay the rent,
And a poet befouling himself in the ditch
I have shut myself away
From such disturbing occurrences.
All the motions of living are equally absurd
But one might as well have clean linen.

THOUGHTS IN THE WATER

Not of drowning. But of the female element
that swaddles my limbs thrashing.
I roll, a careless animal,
in the green ointment;
face down, my forehead bringing
intelligence into this featureless waste.

Confident as all hell, I am made one
with the waves' enterprise: they
bend over my bleached body
like submarine masseurs.
Then calm. The sun embroiders us –
a brilliant lotus on shantung.

Or she's an Asian goddess, the river;
who slides her fat cheeks over my elbows,
her green buttocks. I feel
her deep vibrations as if a seaplane
had plunged his ruinous shadow
like a sword through her coiling body.

25

I fall from her clasp, shuddering,
a senseless interloper, afraid;
    see I shall rise on the water
    drowned, and dismally rise;
remember the face of my child, Adrian on the hill
and all his hens that were laying like mad.

THE MOSQUITO

Meek now as any Franciscan monk,
his inflated sac
    a miniscule bomb, a dark capsule,
he was in the exact centre
of the white writing table – a bullseye!
A white butterfly circled overhead.

What stupid extravagance, I thought,
to show himself in this fashion:
that dark loot outlined, letting the sun
betray him.

I crashed my hand down,
startling the gay white butterfly
that sailed swiftly on, then
licked the circle of blood
    on my palm to a crooked star,
faint but one could decipher
it;

while the mosquito with a queer sort
of dignity clinging to its inert legs
trailed for both
        on the white circular table
a red flag of protest solemn
and useless.

FIRST WALK IN SPRING

I pass out of the door into the garden.
From my favourite tree one limb's broken.
An insect, egotist, strums his soliloquy
At my ear. I walk out under the open sky.

Theoretical man, my eyes have marked
Mounds of earth piled high and dark.
Earth, shovelsful – think of it –
In which to be born and buried.

Brown pads, brown leaves that lie
Beside quickening things, a kind of parody
On them and their increasing passion:
But that's a thought that's out-of-season

When everywhere beyond my hands I see
Green shoots, conferva near the railway;
And grasses, young ferns, that sprout into air
Wispy as a twelve-year-old's pudendal hair.

THE WELL-WROUGHT URN

"What would you do
  if I suddenly died?"

"Write a poem to you."

"Would you mourn for me?"

"Certainly," I sighed.

"For a long time?"

"That depends."

"On what?"

"The poem's excellence," I replied.

THE FERTILE MUCK

There are brightest apples on those trees
    but until I, fabulist, have spoken
they do not know their significance
or what other legends are hung like garlands
    on their black boughs twisting
like a rumour. The wind's noise is empty.

Nor are the winged insects better off
    though they wear my crafty eyes
wherever they alight. Stay here, my love;
you will see how delicately they deposit
    me on the leaves of elms
or fold me in the orient dust of summer.

And if in August joiners and bricklayers
    are thick as flies around us
building expensive bungalows for those
who do not need them, unless they release
    me roaring from their moth-proofed cupboards
their buyers will have no joy, no ease.

I could extend their rooms for them without cost
    and give them crazy sundials
to tell the time with, but I have noticed
how my irregular footprint horrifies them
    evenings and Sunday afternoons:
they spray for hours to erase its shadow.

How to dominate reality? Love is one way;
    imagination another. Sit here
beside me, sweet; take my hard hand in yours.
We'll mark the butterflies disappearing over the hedge
    with tiny wristwatches on their wings:
our fingers touching the earth, like two Buddhas.

BOYS BATHING

At a distance, dark;
each as the philosophers
would remind us
a compendium of history.

Not like the dead bass
I saw afloat,
its history
what my eye made for it.

One bounces like a porpoise,
the tallest ones
race for the boat:
squeals, unselfconsciousness.

But the youngest stops,
smiles at himself vaguely; at,
below the surface, the boulders
breathing like fish.

The sun is bleeding to death,
covering the lake
with its luxuriant blood:
the sun is dying on their shoulders.

SONG FOR A LATE HOUR

No one told me
to beware your bracelets,
the winds I could expect
from your small breasts.
No one told me
the tumult of your hair.
When a lock touched me
I knew the sensations
of shattering glass.

Your kissings put
blue waters around me.
I would look at you
with bold Cretan mirth:
I would forget
I am a cringing semite,
a spaniel suffering
about your tight skirts.

I slabber for your rippling
hips, your white shoulders.
I am sick
with love of you. Girl, o girl,
let our washed limbs make
a perverse Star of David
and cones of flesh,
Cythera all night
at my silvered back.

UNIVERSITY BUILDINGS

Like combs unhived
the pale yellow, geometric
buildings of the university
stand silent and useless
this peace of Sunday,
a pretension of glass
and brick
under the warm April sun;
and, vacuous, wear
the patient air of the blind.

Hand in hand,
mute or loud,
under the one cloud
the perfect couples ascend
the slopes of resurrected grass;
and I stricken
by slivers of light from cars
far below
lie like a meek Sebastian
and can neither move nor go.

A SPIDER DANCED A COSY JIG

A spider danced a cosy jig
Upon a frail trapeze;
And from a far-off clover field
An ant was heard to sneeze.

And kings that day were wise and just,
And stones began to bleed;
A dead man rose to tell a tale,
A bigot changed his creed.

The stableboy forgot his pride,
The queen confessed an itch;
And lo! more wonderful than all,
The poor man blessed the rich.

ON SEEING THE STATUETTES OF EZEKIEL AND JEREMIAH IN THE CHURCH OF NOTRE DAME

They have given you French names
        and made you captive, my rugged
troublesome compatriots;
        your splendid beards, here, are epicene,
plaster white
            and your angers
unclothed with Palestinian hills quite lost
in this immense and ugly edifice.

You are bored – I see it – sultry prophets
        with priests and nuns
(What coarse jokes must pass between you!)
        and with those morbidly religious
i.e. my prize brother-in-law
                    ex-Lawrencian
pawing his rosary, and his wife
sick with many guilts.

Believe me I would gladly take you
        from this spidery church
its bad melodrama, its musty smell of candle
        and set you both free again
in no make-believe world
                of sin and penitence
but the sunlit square opposite
alive at noon with arrogant men.

Yet cheer up Ezekiel and you Jeremiah
        who were once cast into a pit;
I shall not leave you here incensed, uneasy
        among alien Catholic saints
but shall bring you from time to time
                my hot Hebrew heart
as passionate as your own, and stand
with you here awhile in aching confraternity.

HALOS AT LAC MARIE LOUISE

Presently I heard a stir
    Of flying crows that came
And spread themselves against the sky
    Like a black plume.

One like a detached feather,
    Falling westward, stranded
On the topmost prong of a tree.
    The tree was dead.

It was a white skeleton
    Of a tree ominously gnarled;
And around the singular crow
    The stark crows whirled.

The heavens split, the dark rain
    Fell on the circling hills;
The thick gouts dropped beside the oars
    Like melting skulls.

The boat fell with the waves
    Into a still opening;
The halo of green hills became
    A black pronged ring.

FOR AVIVA, BECAUSE I LOVE HER

I saw a spider eating a huge bee.

First he ate my limbs;
and then he removed my head, feasting
   on the quivering jellies of my eyes
and on what passes among bees for ears.

And though dead,
I could feel, with each morsel he had,
that he enjoyed his repast
   and I was glad.

Afterwards he sliced me down the middle,
exposing my insides
   to the burning mid-day heat;
and slowly the voluptuous spider
feasted on my jewelled organs,
abolishing them one by one,
till I was all gone, all swallowed up,
   except for my love of you:

My radiant wings – these, ah, these
he did not touch
but left glinting in the sun.

JEWISH MAIN STREET

And first, the lamp-posts whose burning match-heads
Scatter the bog fires on the wet streets;
Then the lights from auto and store window
That flake cool and frothy in the mist
Like a beaten colloid.
In this ghetto's estuary
Women with offspring appraise
The solemn hypocrisies of fish
That gorp on trays of blue tin . . .
They enter the shops
And haggle for a dead cow's rump.

Old Jews with memories of pogroms
Shuffle across menacing doorways;
They go fearfully, quietly;
They do not wish to disturb
The knapsack of their sorrows.

O here each anonymous Jew
Clutches his ration book
For the minimum items of survival
Which honoured today – who knows? –
Tomorrow some angry potentate
Shall declare null and void.

LETTER TO LOUIS DUDEK

Lawyers lose cases and return
To wives, Havanas, cultivated talk;
Justice, they know, is after all
Perfunctory as a football
Plunging between upright posts.
  But I who run off fugues and overtures
For thirty twittering schoolboys
Feel my unsuccess—do not laugh—
More sore than a seminarist's prepuce
Inflamed with self-abuse.
  Unmoved by music, these
With peach-stone hearts
Will spread their father's lusts;
Haul kindling for poor Joan,
But glimpse no gods,
Nor mad with pity weep
For a crushed caterpillar.
  In this brown room,
With a beauty apparently no one wants,
With images in my head
Of proffered hemlock
And the broached blood of kinsmen,
I pray the trim spaceships
That seek a far-off Montezuman star
May fail and break like a laboratory bottle
While the ocean, a wheeling disk
Scored by the sun's electric needle,
Plays a passacaglia
For that curst event.

EPITAPHS

WIT
O you who read my epitaph,
Approve this final jest and laugh;
For if I stood where now stand you,
Believe me, friend, I would laugh too.

PHILOSOPHER
Space, I perceive, is what surrounds
My cancelled pinch of lime;
I have a whole eternity
In which to fathom Time.

POET KILLED IN ACTION
I said the moon looks like a lost gull,
Just as the shrapnel pierced my skull;
And as I stumbled I thought how blood
Equally can rhyme and mix with mud.

AN UGLY SERVITOR TO THREE QUEENS
Providing food and comment for a mole
Who nightly nibbles at my calluses,
Death altered not a whit my destined role:
I, who served three Queens in different palaces.

PROOF READER

I whose eyes are a transmission belt,
The words depositing like strips of steel,
Think Cyclops luckier in his wounded cave:
Death comes for brothers like Bela Lugosi,
My brothers dying in a Roman hedge;
Their ache is frozen into proper type
(For no blood dries along the metal's edge)
As marshals peering through binoculars
Drive their offensives through my hollow mind.

O my eyes are like extravagant bees
Hugging paper gardens where words are weeds.

For at my back daily the compositors—
Aproned morticians that with lacquered sticks
Lay out the columns like coffins—hammer
Upon the bones of heretics, martyrs,
Nepmen and the conquerors finally
The clockwork victims of insolvent guns;
As I, an egret in a mere of ink,
Idly surface the black frogs thick with speech
When History having eyes but no ears
Seeks out the winged serpent in the tree.

FOR ALEXANDER TROCCHI, NOVELIST

And you, Alexander Trocchi,
high on the high seas,
innocent Christ on the lam,
charged fugitive:
as the blue waves surged across the deck
did you believe them constabulary
flashing their sudden badges
to nab you before you could jab
the Father's peace into your veins?
And when the sky ejaculated stars
over its solitary pitching bed
did you hold the captains at bay?
At nervous needlepoint compel
the ship toward listless harbours
where tropical purple waves
lift forever their enchanting poppies?
Did you finally run
smack into the arm of the Almighty,
and was his arm scarred too?
I hope, Trocchi, before you die
the ancestral monkey on your back
will switch into the Most High;
give you his convulsed vein
to jab it full of heroin
and letting you lead his penitent hand
across your pocked and exiled face,
indite for each scared Jack of us
a truer version of Creation
– your first masterpiece.

NO WILD DOG

I tell my class
What man can do
No cobra can
And no wild dog

Or other kinds
Of vicious beast:
The prowling wolf
And the mongoose.

I'm told they hate
The smell of gas
And run from fires;
But that's not it

No, that's not it.
It takes reason
And spirit too
Which man alone

Evolved in time
So he can do
The amazing things
No cobra can

And no wild dog.

ANDROGYNE

Were Death a woman I should never die.
So jealous is my loving wife that I
Could look upon a passing hearse and sneer
At this dumb show of frail mortality.
For what from Death would I have then to fear

Who might not even by her darkest guile,
Her frowned commands, her most sensual smile,
Tear me from my Love? Tell me, who'd encroach
On her whose fingers stiffen to a file,
Seeing a woman from afar approach?

No, certainly I shall live forever;
For my dear wife will be immortal too
As one whom Death, androgynous lover,
Rages against my jealousy to woo.
Only by dread compact shall we be free
For waiting Death to ravish her and me.

THE PILLAR

Using the moist end
of a half-smoked cigar
and afterwards,
for apter demonstration,
a white pillar
in the crumbling graveyard,
I taught my darling
how to provoke love.

Now she cannot look
at a funeral wreath
or see a hearse
go past
without her pants
wetting.

41

THE CAGE

I turn away to hide my terror
Lest my unmanliness displease them
And maim for all a half-holiday
Begun so well, so auspiciously.
They are building the mythical cage
Whose slow rise allows janitors, whores,
And bank presidents to display love
To one another like a curious
Wound: the Elect to undertake feats
Of unusual virtue. Masons
Give stone and ironmongers, metal
As if these were forever useless
In a paradise of leaves and sun;
And a blacksmith, handsome and selfless,
Offers to blind me at once without
Charge. A quiet shiver of self-love,
Of self-approbation runs through each
At the discovery of so much
Altruism – unknown, hitherto,
Unsuspected – in their very midst.
The instance of the meek stonemasons,
The ironmongers and the selfless blacksmith
Seizes like a panic. Suddenly
Each one vies with his neighbor, avid
To seek out the more burdensome toil:
This one lugging spikes; that one, planks.
Affecting it is to watch their grace,
Their fine courtesies to each other
When they collide; or to imagine
Their tenderness in bed when they leave
The square littered with balloons and me
Blinded and raging in this huge cage.

THERAPY

When I was six
our cat littered behind the stove:
four kittens sound in mind and limb
and one lame.

The lame one
had all my love
– dragging its sick leg
in chase with the others,
all my agonized attention.

It was its playfulness
with a ball
broke my heart at last;
and I was glad
to see the kitten lying, one afternoon,
deadstill
when I returned from school.

Yesterday
for the first time in my life
I axed a young badger
rummaging in our garbage bin
for food.

And though he wobbled
a short distance
before he keeled over,
I am now strong enough for God and Man.

MASHED POTATOES

I walked into a packed restaurant.

I saw hundreds
of unimportant faces
working themselves into a fever of excitement.

Near the door
a repressed nine-to-five slave
green with matrimony
was adjusting his collar.

I asked him:
What about biography?
Has it a future?

He pointed to the cashier
who opened her mouth wide
and yawned: her lower jaw
was a stadium of culture-centres.

Over the remains of a calf's liver
a starry-eyed couple
was talking of love
and naming their prospective infant.

Skol! Abi gezunt!

I reached the bus terminal
at the stroke of seven.

Commuters pressed against me
as if my good looks were contagious,
and I had a sudden vision
of mashed potatoes.

But these had their coats on.

THE RITUAL CUT

At Paperman's Funeral Home,
noting my tremulous mouth,
the pious attendant
slit my tie
– a ritual cut.

Then for his service
held up his hand,
the dry palm towards me.

Truly ours is a creed
for the living,
not for the dead
in their pocketless shrouds.

And anyway it wasn't his mother
was going to be buried
that grey morning.

HISTORY AS A SLICE OF HAM

The Gks: they took stock of many gods.

The Hebes, out by only one,
suffered macerations and death,
being closest to the truth. Ah, Jesu,
jewboy worshipped in cloisters:
abhorring oysters and swinemeat,
they offended their gentle neighbours.

An odd people, greatly mad.
I, sprung from their loins,
and reverencing neither Dieu nor Gott,
only Eros in my body's temple
see my grandsire's bloodstained face
expiring in the slice of ham, ha! ha!
I daily relish and eat.

NO SHISH KEBAB

Mayakovsky had it.
Cafavy.
And Tuvim, the Jewish Pole.

Byron also: probably
the only English poet
who did, not forgetting
you know who.
(Form mistress, Miss Snell,
is nescient
of her hero's Greek bum boy
but knows the leaves
of his thirty-sixth year
were all brown and sere.)

Keats and Shelley didn't.
And not, definitely, Milton.
John Donne?
A smidgen, perhaps; no more.
And in his youth only.

Caught lifting it
from the decadent French,
Thomas Stearns Eliot
resolved to go straight
into the Anglican Church, and did;
nevertheless, the pew he sat in
was redolent
of spiced meats only.
Pray for him now
and at the cocktail hour.

And Maude Gonne
gave Willie Yeats
a smell of it;
and later, old age.
In between
he was a charlatan,
a flaneur
pretending to smell it
when of course
he didn't, not really.

Can it be
the nullibicity of its odour,
warm and corrupt,
is what makes
certain anal professors
of Englit.
stare all day at mirrors,
and their wives at inkblots
for the manifestations
of genius?

That must be it!
What else?

POLITICAL ECONOMY

My son, said the repellent old man,
make certain you never need do
the dirty work of civilization.

All political credos, all religions
are necessary persuasions
to get the poor beggars into the mines.

That a few be whole, many must be broken.
All reform rests on hypocrisy:
fringe benefits for slaves and menials.

Fixed and eternal is the law of gravity:
so, my son, are injustice and the class war.
Living is an affair for aristocrats.

THIS MACHINE AGE

For fifteen cents
the label read,
the Virgin's halo
would light up
for three minutes.
The man dropped
the pieces of money
into the machine's slot
and looked about
the vast, gloomy church
empty except
for him and me.
When his gaze came back
to the halo
it was still unlit
– a dark infuriating zero.

He gave the machine
a careful kick
to bring the lights
of the circle out.
It didn't.
"Damn it!" he shouted,
"Why doesn't it light up?"
He kicked again
and muttered something
I didn't hear.
But I could guess
from the way he looked
he thought divine sereneness
a poker-faced fraud
and himself taken in
by the Mother of God.

THE REAL VALUES

Rabbi, why do you move heaven and earth
to blow breath
into this lifeless body,
drowned under the surfeit
of Chinese food and pizzapie?

The good life destroyed him:
distilleries, supermarkets.
Long ago he packed away his soul
in the clothing industry.

Examine the hideous, putrefying face,
the fishy eyes
and gross mouth, open
as though to swallow
another cooked lentil.

Isaiah, hop to it, Moses –
bring on the condiments, the plum sauce –

Your noble gas
about Torah, Halachah
affords a passing tingle
to worshippers breathless with emulation,
especially to wives and daughters
musing on fabled hairdos.

Save your breath, rabbi.
No, save your money.

And learn from your bloated flock
bored by whisky and wifeswapping,
the burnt offerings on Sunday,
how to invest sensibly
in real estate values.

So that you can speak the truth
as I do.

TRUMPET DAFFODIL

At last I get up and go to where
Over the back of my wooden chair
The light hangs like a wet towel.
I scan the glass for my deathless smile.

I praise the hairs on my wrist
And an indestructible egotist
Resolve this day not to glance
At what I may not influence.

Then I thresh out whether the literati
With faces like garlic when I die
Will lay their opera hats on my coffin
And their voices soften.

To the devil with meditation
Which leads to nowhere and on;
I'd rather take a basket
Of opera hats to someone else's casket.

I look out of the window
At the people hurrying below;
These carry their disenchantment graveward
Like an identity card.

I think the sun
Has already begun
To burn their futility and need
And themselves to a brown weed.

PROVIDENCE

With careful fragments do we build lives
Not knowing when the wind moves nearer
How some Authority contrives
The show before a comic mirror.

In which atoms become skyscrapers
The fool's tower is flung to the skies;
There, even a miniscule capers
And the meanest pauper a prince dies.

But the silent wind matures, slow
Or swift, and loudly will the glass break:
That we may not hear before we go
The bitter comment that the stars make.

COMPLIMENTS OF THE SEASON

Returning with an annual passion
April winds suck buds, blow
Greenness into the palmate leaf and find
A passionate lady at dresser moulting.
Hair and cuticle stream with the season
Through her mirror.

Under the foraging sunlight
Humans rancid beside sweet-smelling trees
Sprawl between the thorns while Mount Royal
Slopes its green arms under their arses;
And the one-armed beggar
Brutal with red and yellow pencils
Dies with a windmill in his arms –
There were no shebas, not even jills.

At the base hospital behind the lines
Ideologies are carried out in bedpans;
And next april and the april after
The veterans of the two last wars
Will lay their crutches
Against the lighted cross
That shines steadfast upon the city
With the faith of its shareholders.

Against the curbstones like thick nostrils
The sunlight begins to dry
This snotflecked world.

NEWSBOY

Neither tribal nor trivial he shouts
From the city's centre where tramcars move
Like stained bacilli across the eyeballs,
Where people spore in composite buildings
From their protective gelatine of doubts,
Old ills, and incapacity to love
While he, a Joshua before their walls,
Sells newspapers to the gods and geldings.

Intrusive as a collision, he is
The Zeitgeist's too public interpreter,
A voice multiplex and democratic,
The people's voice or the monopolists';
Who with last-edition omniscience
Plays Clotho to each gaping customer
With halcyon colt, sex crime in an attic,
The story of a twice-jailed bigamist.

For him the mitred cardinals sweat in
Conclaves domed; the spy is shot. Empiric;
And obstreperous confidant of kings,
Rude despiser of the anonymous,
Danubes of blood wash up his bulletins
While he domesticates disaster like
A wheat in pampas of prescriptive things
With cries animal and ambiguous.

His dialectics will assault the brain,
Contrive men to voyages or murder,
Dip the periscope of their public lives
To the green levels of acidic caves;
Fever their health, or heal them with ruin,
Or with lies dangerous as a letter;
Finally enfold the season's cloves,
Cover a somnolent face on Sundays.

THE EXECUTION

Because the glowing morning
Dropped from the rooster's beak
 The frozen famous statue
Was too amazed to speak

But watched my mother go and come
Like a fish in an aquarium
 Sinister alone
And me upon my boycart throne.

Her cheeks were red with bargains
And she moved to the money cries
 Like an enchanted dancer
With wide enchanted eyes.

The yells, the cries were frenzying;
Her cheeks grew pale with bargains:
 I laid my boyhood head
Among the golden onions.

EX-NAZI

Playing blind man's buff
With scarred bushes
I come sharp at this unguessed-at pole
Spooky as an overturned ambulance;
Like a sick anti-semite
The morning struggles to reveal itself.

There's my neighbour coming toward us.
Where nations have decayed
My neighbour's veins are full of pus.
Brainsick, poor fellow,
He thinks one day he'll turn a snowman
And stream into a March landscape
That's ravaged like the face of Dostoievski.
At night the whitened streets
Lean into his dreams like a child's coffin.

But now at noon he meets himself
In the summer craze of the sun,
Boy eager, as springy as grass,
Innocenter than his bounding mastiff
Whose tail flicks from conscience
The yammering guilt.

The hot sun desiccates his guilt.
Between us the pale dust hangs
Like particles
Of sacrificial smoke.

GENIUS LOVE AND POETRY

Of a friend I observed
that he had genius
but wanted the talent
to give it expression,
and of a vigorous
woman of my acquaintance
who had married a spastic
I remarked that only
a woman with no heart
was capable of so great
a sacrifice;
and of a certain
proletarian poet that
his mind was like the grease-
covered bottom of a cold
unwashed fryingpan
and that he was prudent
to avoid all fires –
especially the Muse's!

REMBRANDT

I flung my bright eye into space
O wonder it became a sun
I hurled the other there
It grew an ochre moon.

Now the burghers that stare
At the moon and the sun
Call my face a ruin:
I have a hideous face.

Yet the boy's shelled head
And the hardiest flesh
Must go to grass
The virgin lie with her goldfish.

An Isaac of a sunbeam
Dances about in the wind
I bless
With blinded hands.

TO A VERY OLD WOMAN

Old woman, your face is a halo of praise
That excludes nothing, not even Death;
    I have looked upon your waxy and virginal torso
    And I see you now as a frail candle
Whose flame, the initial sputter of ignition over,
Burns gently and with composure.

So the first taste of death was bitter.
Now you burn with a composed glow
    Listening, half-amused like a superior person,
    To your bridegroom which is the Darkness
While each hour of your lovely embrace
Descends in ecstatic beads of silence.

56

Old woman,
What does he say, your bridegroom?

That his child, Death, grows in my womb.

What else, old woman?

That only my white and virginal skin
Seals off the darkness from the death within.

Old woman, with face ageless like snow,
What will you do now?

Flame serenely
Till like a warmed candle
I curve over
The arm of my hurrying bridegroom and lover.

Is that all, old woman?

Yes...
No. When Death and Darkness embrace
Over me
I shall have no face
I shall be utterly gone.
Use the blackened wick
For a headstone.

LAZARUS

He thinks because he once
tried to shoot himself
and failed
he now understands
everything about life.

Who will tell this Lazarus
in the pin-striped suit
that he smells of the grave
and that I've seen worms
stand up in his eyes and mouth?

PROLOGUE TO THE LONG PEA SHOOTER

A friend tells me I must not write
About the toilers and their sad plight,
That poetry like dress admits of fashion
And this is not the year for passion.
He thinks the times will change: tomorrow
The critic may approve of sorrow,
And anger be no blemish in a verse
Which today must neither taunt nor curse.
For now lampooners, themselves grown sick,
Prefer poets with a touch of colic
Who'll speak in soft, deflated tones
That menace no one's sleep or bones.
One may, he concedes, clear his throat
To flute a meek religious note
For it's the season now to cavil
At Original Sin and Evil,
And for the dull-eyed philistine
To be mistook for an Olympian
Since none in this country can tell
The one from the other very well.
For since our neighbours get their creed
From the latest comic strip they read
(Though kind, they're dumb – they come no dumber!)
You can spoof them winter, spring, and summer.
Let them but see a tale in print
They think at once the truth lies in't
And hotly with one voice they'll swear
They see hippogriffs coupling in the air;
That elephants fly, that gramophones swim –
There is no fable too gross for them!
The press on a rampage, hear them cry
With virtuous anger: "The knaves must die!"
The press grown quiet – why, the sods
Let their wrath expire, and virtue nods.

Consider therefore to what end you write
And whether vanity can survive this sight:
Your tomes piled ingloriously in a heap,
Your craft and wisdom sold absurdly cheap;
Assonance, sprung rhythm, internal rhyme,
The whole glittering shebang not worth a dime;
For of fourteen million odd citizens
No more than five have taste or sense
And these, alas, though not fools
Belong to different sects and schools
Fanatic in belief some rival
Mode of metaphor lacks wit and style;
Or fine poets themselves, they prefer
To see your thin volume gather
A coating of oblivious dust
Lest a sold edition and success rust
That friendship which the fates erect
Upon equal misfortune and neglect.

Resolve before ink you try
That your books may not remaindered lie;
Think only of kudos and a name
And failing greatness, acquire fame:
Assiduously learn the art to please
The pimps in the academies –
Their friendly syrop on the radio
May help to sell a book or so;
(I mean to give them no offence,
For these are pimps with a difference,
And allow this as their best excuse –
They pimp, it's true, but for some muse!)
Yes, be wise, plagiarize: above all,
Avoid ambiguous words like 'ball'
Or 'ass' or even harmless 'cans':
They give offence to puritans,
And robust males to whom a virgin
Is dearer far than any sturgeon.

And say nothing long, say nothing loud
To charm and please that motley crowd
Of cultured hags who like a poem
To waft them far from spouse and home
Or bring a fine synthetic gloom
Into their modernized living-room;
Refinement be your aim to melt the sort
Who take their verse as they take their port
Entirely by label and repute
And with no more sense than a new-born new
Seek out the poet that is most sought:
If it's Eliot – it's Eliot they've got!
But if you have the gifts of Reaney
You may help your verse by being zany,
Or write as bleakly in a pinch
As Livesay, Smith, and Robert Finch;
And be admired for a brand-new pot
If you're as empty as Marriott;
I'll say nothing about Dudek:
The rhyme's too easy – speck or wreck;
And be not right and be not left,
But mediocre like the C.C.F.

But the soundest, most successful plan
Is to compose like Douglas Le Pan:
Appear, though men and nations reeled,
A Lampman on a battlefield;
Express in words vacuous and quaint
The cultured Englishman's complaint
That decency is never sovereign,
That reason ought to, but doesn't govern –
That maids have holes, and men must find them
(Alas, that Nature WILL so blind them!)
In short, here's the sum of this advice:
Say nothing, but modulate the voice;
What though the lines lack heart and brain,
One can wrap the mess in cellophane;
The trick's to make quick and often
Neat chromium handles for a coffin
For critics with the nose of a setter
For verse that's dead – the deader the better!

These buzzards have no praise for him
Who cannot learn to tack and trim,
The honest bard who'll out and say
By how much profit exceeds the pay;
Or one who because his heart is pure
Will not affect to use 'manure'
Instead of that four-letter word
That is less often seen than heard,
But paints the world with sober brush
Though reviewers and Mazola Roche
Who type on their cash register
Declare such writing sinister.

Well, I tell my friend that I've written
About the parts where I've been bitten;
I write about where the shoe pinches;
I also write about the wenches;
Their lips, their hips, and other beauty
(Laying them is a man's first duty!)
Of all sad things the saddest sight
Are pubic hairs turned grey and white,
Or thinned by age, a spiritless down,
Ranged like a battered rusty crown
Or a harbour broken at the centre
Where no boat shall leave or enter.
Though of late, since I'm growing old,
And no longer wear my pants' fly rolled
I like to engage over a glass
Retired clergymen put out to grass;
Their craws well-stuffed with fish and fowl
They discourse sweetly upon the soul,
For I've noted often how the sight
Of a ravished duck will speed the flight
Of men's thoughts towards the ineffable,
The inane, and the indecipherable
Though it's difficult such times to tell
If they're moved to glory by taste or smell,
And whether it's their souls that yearn
Or what is speaking is some heartburn.
Strange that human blood can spiritualize

The breast of chicken or its thighs
And turn by wondrous transmutation
The creature's flesh into aspiration;
Strange, that pig en route towards the anus
Can disintegrate into loud hosannas!

So with such wit as I can muster
I surmise I've brought a lustre
To our national verse which before
Was lacking spirit and a bore,
Genteel, dull, and quite anæmic
To please a Bowell or Jasper Shittick;
And though the fat excitable fleas
Who breed well in our universities
Aver my stuff is unreadable,
Unedifying and unbeautiful
What fool will pay much or close
Attention to these same castratos,
What race will read what they have said
Who have my poems to read instead?

BISHOP BERKELEY GOES TO BED

God helping me
Esse is percipi:
So for an hour or so
From this bay window
I've looked
At a metaphysical tower of snow;
Now on returning to bed,
To warm my miserable Self
I slide my cold feet
Beneath this rational sheet
And cover myself
With the patch of white in my head.

TERRENE

The sun's a red-faced major
   That has no use
      For a prefatory memoir.

And this life a bourjui
   Who calls from his toilet seat:
      "Marya, I luff you; do you luff me, too, sweet?"

And power, everything.

I am exhausted
   Like a poem or a landscape
      Over which too many people have exclaimed.

Still, you flower in my mind
   Like a shopgirl
      Wooed by many dark maharajahs.

I shall knock out of your hand
   All your lottery tickets.
      You will be left with nothing but my love.

A VISION

From a wingless chariot I see
Immortally bleeding vines,
Guards, a hired soldiery,
Crowds of foredoomed Thebans;
I see the evil skulls of men,
Child-bearing women, and one
Who from this witless human freight
Breaks suddenly upon my eyes
To run on rodent feet
Across the blazing street
      Intent upon what malicious enterprise!

63

CRONE

When I plucked my moment of gold
Out of your hair,
Your hair became raven black.

When I plucked my moment of gold
Out of your eye,
Your eye became lifeless.

Black hair and lifeless eye,
Witch, when are you going to die?

THE POET AND THE STATUE

Bruno, my lord, we have been found out;
The envious brothers are always in the right.
We were incautious, eavesdroppers being about.

And I'm ashamed today to be the rich man's butt,
A literary fool. Wish me dear statue something other.
The dream about sheaves confused me. I was young.

O I was young and my father said fair
Who gave me princely garments to wear
But who never knew the sting of womanflesh
And laughed at my dream of moonsheaves then and there.

On this bald rock I'll sit then
At the city's outskirts
Till the confident evening whistle of birds
Signal me to rise, poplar tall, at peace—
A seedless Joseph, castrate, storing grain—
Knowing the universe is the home of us all
And that no man dies like an animal
Without grief.

GOOD-BYE BAHAI

he sniffs trends like a butcher
meat;
he's a punctilious critic and
what he does not comprehend
he has his wife read

and explain to him. She does that well.
on hot summer nights her green fingertips
budding innumerable little wineglasses
she has the appearance of a fallen dryad.

a monk with a novel refectory joke
he looks at you
out of the corner of his mouth;
he has trouble with molars.

good-bye Bahai.
I know an austerer religion,
having seen their etiolated faces
bent over
arcana canadiana.

FIRST SNOW : LAKE ACHIGAN

No noise of rowlocks, no ecstasy of hands,
No sound of crickets in the inextricable air:
But a Roman silence for a lone drummer's call.

Now noiseless as a transaction, a brown hare
Breaks from the cold fields, bounds ahead;
Now slowly slowly the season unwinters
On its spool of white thread.

Lonely and fleshed with hates, who here
Would be God's angry man, a thundering Paul,
When December, a toga'd Cato, slow to anger,
At last speaks the word that condemns us all?

THE PREDATOR

The little fox
was lying in a pool of blood,
having gnawed his way out to freedom.

Or the farmhand,
seeing his puny, unprofitable size
had slugged him after with a rifle butt

And he had crawled
to the country roadside
where I came upon him, his fur dust-covered.

Hard to believe
a fox is ever dead, that he isn't
just lying there pretending with eyes shut.

His fame's against
him; one suspects him of anything,
even when there's blood oozing from the shut eyes.

His evident
self-enjoyment is against him also:
no creature so wild and gleeful can ever be done for.

But this fox was;
there's no place in the world any more
for free and gallant predators like him.

Eagle, lion,
fox and falcon: their freedom is their death.
Man, animal tamed and tainted, wishes to forget.

He prefers bears
in cages: delights to see them pace
back and forth, swatting their bars despondently.

Yet hates himself,
knowing he's somehow contemptible:
with knives and libraries the dirtiest predator of all.

Ghost of small fox,
hear me, if you're hovering close
and watching this slow red trickle of your blood:

Man sets even
more terrible traps for his own kind.
Be at peace; your gnawed leg will be well-revenged.

MOSES TALKED TO JUPITER

Thick-wristed Moses talked to Jupiter
    But I to no one.
The pale trees unslaked
    circled the road
on which my bruised heels ran.

The dry frogs were gouts of blood
    at my feet;

And the wasted dermis
    of the white-hot day
    paring and rivelling
Made leaf and grass seem
    green miscarriages of summer.

Was it like this,
    thick-wristed one?

FOR MY FRIEND WHO TEACHES LITERATURE

I tell you, William,
there isn't a ghost
of a chance
people will be changed by poems.

Book Club editors
wish to believe otherwise,
Commencement Day orators
and commissars;
but we poets know the facts of the case.
People will remain stupid and deceitful,
their hearts will pump
malice and villainy
into their bloodstream forever.

All the noble lines of poets
did not make Hiroshima and Belsen
not to happen,
nor will they keep back the coming holocaust.

Why should you add
to the mischief,
the self-deception?
Leave that to the culture-peddlers.

Be truthful:
tell children who their forbears were,
the curse they bear.

Do not weaken
even a single one of them
with fine sentiments!

THE BISHOPRIC

Yes, and finding my small friar
sullen, cowled and scowling
in his beggar's posture:

Ha, my voice went sour
for the college girl squirming
under my length of form.
"I must reread my own poems,"
I said bitterly. "Or so it seems."

"Luckily for you," she breathed,
"no one will ever believe this
— not even your worst biographer."

I roared and that did it.
There was an instant election
as she brought her youthful face,
laughing,
into the sweet diocese of my body.

O.B.E.

How delicately
the Englishwoman
scratches her rectum

Firmly, yet gently,
and with what a regard
for the decencies

Centuries
of imperial rule
inform that touch

MAN GOING UP AND DOWN

Only he and I were in the lift.

"Do you like what you're doing?" I asked.

The lustreless stare he gave me was
One I've seen on coons crushed but intact
Lying inert on countryside roads;
But his voice burst like a tire: "I don't!"

"Then why not walk out with me – right now?"
We had reached my floor. "I'd desolate
This whole city, yes, massacre each
Man, woman, and child in it before
I'd let them put me into a cage
To run like a monkey up and down.
Come, leave behind you this accursed car.
Let it stand void for all eternity."

He now looked at me mistrustfully
As he opened the door. "Look, mister,"
He said, "You must be one of these men
I hear about with sharp ideas
For changing people's lives and the world.
I've been taught about the likes of you.
Well, no one is changing me, no sir.
I've my job and I'll stick to it, see?"

Not more proud looked young Alexander
In his tent among his Greek captains
The night he overwhelmed Darius,
Or blond Charles when he slew the Polacks,
Or Don Juan after his hundredth lay.

"You sad mutt," I said almost aloud
As he held up his head, offended.
I'd have thrown him a bone had I one.
"Civilization could not endure
A single hour without your trapped soul."
In the next instant he had changed back
Into the affable tool he was.

I strode out of the elevator.
A rush of stale air followed me out
And turning to find what had made it
I saw myself pursued by the shades
Of half-a-score indignant teachers,
Three pallid clergymen dressed in black,
And a vile woman, doubtless his wife
– Or the Medusa, if you prefer myths.

FIRECRACKERS

I saw a little Chinese boy
playing with firecrackers;
the face he turned to me
was so full of his fun-
loving disposition
that when afterwards I looked up
at the mountain Cross
wavering in the radiant noonday sun
it seemed like an enormous condor
with outstretched pinions ready to take flight.

The firecrackers went, pf-ff-t
and again, pf-ff-t.

The little flare was like a white bird.

71

THE APE AND THE PHARISEE

An ape, with a tail in his mouth,
A whitehot rivet in his mind,
Solemnly looked at the stars
And scratched his behind.

Chattering, he dropped on his hands,
The rivet went cold in his mind,
And the stars although beautiful,
Were now invisible:
He was left with his behind.

Which he rasped so much
That it fiercely bled—
Tourists seized their umbrellas and canes
And hastily fled.

When curvetting with proverbs
And prancing you came,
As graceful as a Percheron
With one leg lame.

And you said:
That's a silly thing to do
For a scholar
And a Jew.

The ape dropped the tail from his mouth,
He straightened up,
Proffered red wine
From a broken cup.

And he said: O Poet Mocker,
Get off your phylactery boxes
For how will you run
When you hear the foxes?

For wisdom is excellent
Far away from a rope;
The moon, if you look carefully,
Is a piece of soap.

Hillel was weary one day
Or he might have foreseen
The moon just over that chimney
And both supernaturally clean.

And stay here an hour,
You'll see an unusual sight:
The yard below the chimney
Will grow amazingly bright.

And outside that building,
As if made of schoolroom chalk
A thousand baby skeletons
Will bow gravely and walk.

They clasp tiny hands,
They go round and round,
The moon and chimney look on,
The wind makes scarcely a sound.

Ah, when it's always so dark,
Can I see you curvet and prance?
And when it grows bright, alas,
I can see only skeletons dance.

O Poet, Linguist, frantic Jew,
Get off your phylactery boxes,
For how, how will you run
When you hear the foxes?

73

LILITH

I would for beauty of face
Unpeople Persia and Greece;
Kiss any old murderer
Who'll quench my body's furor
Though his victims' bones should crawl
Up to my own gate and wall.
Let the balladeers complain
Until their runes split in twain;
And timid sages despair
That blood and lust fill the air,
And virtuous folk bewail
When I scratch them with my nail:
Yet what do I have life for –
Or must I hear burghers snore?
The great Masters alone knew
All a woman's mind could do
And gave her, to have her wish,
No more conscience than a fish.
Ah, men, before you were dead
I'd enjoy you all in bed;
Then, having tasted my thighs,
You'd die off like poisoned flies;
Or having touched my quick once,
Perish in flames like red ants.
Give me the hero who'll strike
Heads off to put on a pike;
A Samson with bone of ass
To kill the unfevered mass,
The clods and lumps who yet thrive
Like cold graveworms near a grave.
Where is my remorseless lord
With blood smoking on his sword
And his head like a ship's prow?
Come, my Sun God, come, come now!
Your loins melt me, I desire
You drill my body with fire
For I burn with love and feel
Myself flame from head to heel.

74

STREET FUNERAL

Tired of chewing
the flesh
of other animals;
Tired of subreption and conceit;
of the child's
bewildered conscience
fretting the sly man;
Tired of holding down
a job; of giving insults,
taking insults;
Of excited fornication,
failing heart valves,
septic kidneys . . .
This frosty morning,
the coffin wood bursting
into brilliant flowers,
Is he glad
that after all the lecheries,
betrayals, subserviency,
After all the lusts,
false starts, evasions
he can begin
the unobstructed change
into clean grass
Done forever
with the insult
of birth,
the long adultery
with illusion?

THE SPARKS FLY

1/ I go about making trouble for myself.
    The sparks fly.
    I gather each one
    and start a poem.

2/ On the waxed twine
    of her affection
    her mouth goes up & down
    like a yo-yo.

3/ Wives, womenfriends – something in me
    will not let them rest.
    What a queer universe this is
    when it takes three marriages
    to produce a seasoned poet.

4/ She was pregnant
    and spoke of air-currents
    in her chest.
    When I bent down to kiss her
    she made a rude noise
    and smiled.
    What would Tennyson make of this?
    Or that idiot, Eliot?

5/ The school where I teach
    is the bran pan
    of civilization;
    for kicks, I sometimes speak
    the lines of a poet
    to the caged astonished dimwits
    then wait for the gibbonous screech.

6/ The smell of a religious
    woman
    past her menopause:
    No star, I'm sure,
    ever smelled like this,
    No living flower.

7/ Why can't I let them die
in their swamps,
the sunless presbyterians of this country,
peacefully, peacefully
– not stir them up with my stick or pole?
Phew! What a stink arises.
What fetid, multi-coloured insects
strike my head.

8/ And the orgasmless women of Hampstead, why
must I always press them
to abandon their husbands and unsatisfactory
lovers,
or their deplorable tastes in literature?

9/ She thinks if she labels
the poison "love,"
it will not disorder my blood
or make my hair and teeth
fall out.
The bitch! whom does she think
she's kidding?

10/ Their everyday politics
is diseased sex;
had they a trifle more health
they'd vote for an early death.

11/ I heard three shit-birds
in council whistle and chirk,
while a castrato stood before them
shaped like a tuning fork.

12/ Ah, the dung-beetles that want my blood.
Age and possessions have turned me into stone.
There's no blood in a stone.
Bang!
Out of their crushed limbs
I also make poems.

WHOM I WRITE FOR

When reading me, I want you to feel
    as if I had ripped your skin off;
Or gouged out your eyes with my fingers;
Or scalped you, and afterwards burnt your hair
    in the staring sockets; having first filled them
with fluid from your son's lighter.
I want you to feel as if I had slammed
    your child's head against a spike;
And cut off your member and stuck it in your
    wife's mouth to smoke like a cigar.

For I do not write to improve your soul;
    or to make you feel better, or more humane;
Nor do I write to give you any new emotions;
Or to make you proud to be able to experience them
    or to recognize them in others.
I leave that to the fraternity of lying poets
    – no prophets, but toadies and trained seals!

How much evil there is in the best of them
    as their envy and impotence flower into poems
And their anality into love of man, into virtue:
Especially when they tell you, sensitively,
    what it feels like to be a potato.

I write for the young man, demented,
    who dropped the bomb on Hiroshima;
I write for Nasser and Ben Gurion;
For Krushchev and President Kennedy;
    for the Defence Secretary
voted forty-six billions for the extirpation
    of humans everywhere.
I write for the Polish officers machine-gunned
    in the Katyn forest;
I write for the gassed, burnt, tortured,
    and humiliated everywhere;
I write for Castro and tse-Tung, the only poets
    I ever learned anything from;

I write for Adolph Eichmann, compliant clerk
  to that madman, the human race;
For his devoted wife and loyal son.

Give me words fierce and jagged enough
  to tear your skin like shrapnel;
Hot and searing enough to fuse
  the flesh off your blackened skeleton;
Words with the sound of crunching bones or bursting
      eyeballs;
  or a nose being smashed with a gun butt;
Words with the soft plash of intestines
  falling out of your belly;
Or cruel and sad as the thought which tells you
      "This is the end"
And you feel Time oozing out of your veins
  and yourself becoming one with the weightless dark.

JUNE WEATHER

In summer it is easier:
the sun puts emblems
in the gaunt sides of trees
and my summertime heart
forgives the bright blind
eye of the sun,
the green vegetation
multiplying like cancer
and the flukes that live
in the manyplies
of the imagination

79

THE PERVERSE GULLS

Nothing's more absurd
Than a Latin verb,
Said clod-poll Dirk
With a pretty smirk.

So I've gone for a walk
With a stick of chalk
And I shan't be back
Till the stars crack.

Who made the first star?
It wasn't my mother,
Nor was it my sister:
It was someone other.

Tell me but why, Sir,
I promise I'll drink
A penful of ink
And turn a blue geyser;

O I'll rise higher and higher
Like a spout of fire
And I won't be done
Till I put out the sun

And on ocean and all
Spread a blue pall
Till the gulls come flying,
Flapping their wings and crying,
"We're dying, dying!"

Then over my ruff
I'll shout, "Enough!
Seven camels must drink
To make me shrink
To a mere bubble of ink.

Seven leopards must tear
A lion in his lair
And leave him a forepaw
To wave in the air."

The seven camels drank:
Down—down—I sank!
The sun came out
With a joyful shout.

The brave leopards came
With tongues of flame;
They kindled the fire
Of mortal desire

And the perverse gulls
Abandoned their hulls
And fished for prawn
In the watery sun.

OVERHEARD IN A BARBERSHOP

"Nature is blind,
  and Man
  a shaggy pitiless ape
  without Justice,"
  the razored
  old gentleman said,
  his acidulous breath
  fogging the barber's
  round mirror.
As he talked
I remarked
  the naevi, black
  and dark purple,
  on his crumbling face:
Death's
  little victory flags.

81

COMMUNITY

In a boarding house
There is nothing mysterious,
Even when an old man drinks
Becomes delirious
And dies.
The several stinks
Acquaint you with the other roomers
Though cooking is strictly forbidden;
For no one humours
In these high-cost-of-living days
The fat proprietress and her saving ways.
Fortunately she's bedridden.

Where your neighbour is an alarm clock
Minding your own damn business
Becomes a virtue.
Alright let the pastor talk,
The poet moan
Of little acts of kindness,
Of tenderness,
Of sweetness:
You
Are three short for the telephone;
The mechanic next door,
Four.

Beauty is truth, truth beauty
That is all you need to know
Where community
Resides in a Yale key.

LOVE THE CONQUEROR WORM

Mid-August the frenzied cicadas
Apprise the scene-shifters
Where each prop goes:
    Where the dark empery of bush,
And where the spacious blossomers.

Now lofty for the spinning year,
For the stripling I see pass
Dragging the summer by the ear;
    The flooding sun,
And the green fires in the grass

I pardon Nature her insanities,
The perversity in flesh and fern;
I forget her lecheries,
    Her paragram:
Love The Conqueror Worm

And praise these oaks which bare,
Straining, the hoar
Frost on them, stand each winter there
    Like courtly masochists
Whimpering "Encore! Encore!"

T.S. ELIOT

Harvard and English mist;
the sick Christian;
the American tourist
with an interest in monasteries
rather than castles:
in shrines for aging knees;
a zeal for poetry without zest,
without marrow juices;
at best, a single hair
from the beard of Dostoievsky.

83

VEXATA QUAESTIO

I fixing my eyes upon a tree
Maccabean among the dwarfed
    Stalks of summer
Listened for ship's sound and birdsong
And felt the bites of insects
    Expiring in my arms' hairs.

And there among the green prayerful birds
Among the corn I heard
    The chaffering blades:
"You are no flydung on cherry blossoms,
Among two-legged lice
    You have the gift of praise.

Give your stripped body to the sun
Your sex to any skilled
    And pretty damsel;
From the bonfire
Of your guilts make
    A blazing Greek sun."

Then the wind which all day
Had run regattas through the fields
    Grew chill, became
A tree-dismantling wind;

The sun went down
    And called my brown skin in.

CEMETERY IN AUGUST

In August, white butterflies
Engage twig and rock;
Love-sheaths bloom in convenient fissures
On a desiccated stalk;
The generation of Time brings
Rind, shell, delicate wings

And mourners. Amidst this
Summer's babble of small noises
They weep, or interject
Their resentful human voices;
At timely intervals
I am aware of funerals.

And these iambic stones
Honouring who-knows-what bones
Seem in the amber sunlight
Patient and confounded,
Like men enduring an epoch
Or one bemused by proofs of God.

RED CHOKECHERRIES

In the sun
The chokecherries are a deep red.
They are like clusters of red jewels.

They are like small rubies
For a young queen who is small and graceful.
When the leaves turn, I see her white shoulder.

They are too regal to eat
And reduce to moist yellow pits.
I will let the air masticate them

And the bold maggot-making sun.
So I shall hardly notice
How perfection of form is overthrown.

IN MEMORY OF FRED SMITH

Alive, he daily spun
Schemes for the active bone
And went about arranging
The unchanging.

He fluttered his kite
Like any hopeful trotskyite;
Knew (Machine Age sciolist)
Sex and politics

And sampled the flawed
Ridottos o' the world
Like the melancholy cakes
Consumed at wakes.

For unreason occupies
A man until he dies;
Then healed but dumb
He learns a new equilibrium.

But I was known to him
Who loved my single aim:
His term accomplished
By that much am I diminished.

LESTER

A cold potato from chin to crown,
he speaks with an obstruction in his throat
his bowtie holds and won't let down.

And he's too well-bred to touch his mouth
though the hand he waggles with such a frown
itches to yank the damn thing out!

86

DEATH OF MOISHE LAZAROVITCH

My father's coffin pointed me to this:
O arrogant with new life his black beard
Fierce and stiff and partner to the dark wood
Sent me the way to what I most had feared

Became at the last a ring of bright light,
A well whose wall of mourning faces turned
My sighs to silence to a deep wound
Which stained the outstretched figure as it burned.

I swear it burned! If not, why the bright light
Like a tall post that had caught the sun's ray?
White the figure was and bright O so bright,
I have not seen its equal since that day.

I do not know how they lifted him up
Or held the vessel near their mourning silk,
But their going was like a roar of flames
And Matter sang in my ears like poured milk.

WHAT ULYSSES SAID TO CIRCE ON THE BEACH OF AEAEA

You are beautiful
As a remembered song from one's homeland,
  Snake-eyed enchantress,
And desirable beyond compare;
  Not even Penelope
In the first marriage blaze of passion
Could heat the red juice in my veins
As you do.
  Yet even you, all-puissant goddess,
And your bewitched minions
Must scrape the oozy mud of the seafloor
  For squids and periwinkles
To nourish me thereon
Should you want, O lovely and divine Circe,
   Another erection.

TO THE GIRLS OF MY GRADUATING CLASS

Wanting for their young limbs praise,
Their thighs, hips, and saintly breasts,
They grow from awkwardness to delight,
Their mouths made perfect with the air
About them and the sweet rage in the blood,
The delicate trouble in their veins.

Intolerant as happiness, suddenly
They'll dart like bewildered birds;
For there's no mercy in that bugler Time
That excites against their virginity
The massed infantry of days, nor in the tendrils
Greening on their enchanted battlements.

Golda, Fruma, Dinnie, Elinor,
My saintly wantons, passionate nuns;
O light-footed daughters, your unopened
Brittle beauty troubles an aging man
Who hobbles after you a little way
Fierce and ridiculous.

KARL MARX

They most dear, the sad-eyed astronomers,
The unprevailing princes who broke and fled;
Or Calvin, his golden beard full of the virtues,
And Luther who in a panic maimed a devil
Later repented caught and flogged a peasant –
The Moor has tidied their bones with a newspaper.

Now the winds are lashed howling to the Poles
And these bones charged with lightning
While his secular horse,
The shadow removed like a halter,
Moves magisterially into the sun;
And O you black ugly beast O my beauty
Churn up these white fields of leprosy!

PHILOSOPHY 34

When I was at McGill (O
World O
Time) I ran upstairs
two stares at, I was
in such, I was in such a
BANG into my seat I slid

and there were a lot
of defunct birds
lying about,
a blue discoloration
on their stripped bodies

as well as a professor
luculently explaining
how admirable their wings were
for mounting, when alive.

In the ambrosian air
we formed a half-circle
on fire to probe
the darkening alar flesh

when an Apollonian roared
from the back side of the room:
What shameful rites are these?
What desecration?

In the perturbation
the professor was ditched by mistake
but I of course stayed on
for I saw a bronzed goddess
whose profile enchanted me
all the way down.

EROS

With the best side of my tongue:
   "I am no maker of hockeysticks and pigstys;
     No shepherd am I, no goatherd, no swineherd;
I am no barbarus come from a fisherman's village
         lost in the mists;
   My grandsires were not rustici
      were rabbins."

"Rabbins?
     That's quaint," she said.

I pardoned her because she moved her head
    for the sun to put a white flower in her hair;
   Because inevitably her bared throat would become
     a mouth organ for my lips' kisses;
   Because she had lank firm thighs.

"Thinkers   artists matter,"
                   I resumed;
  "The rest don't matter,
     useful perhaps as guano
  but not to be looked upon . . ."

  Her head dropped.
    The chrysanthemum in her hair
              crumbled.

"Bullfrogs! Murrain! Pismire!"

She moaned,
    "Be quiet. Let me sing for you."

   So she sang.

When she ended her slim thighs
    were knives in my temples.

I said,
   "We must see to it, Love,
      there are more
               of the one
     and fewer of the other . . .
   Let us reproduce ourselves."

So I gathered her
  flower and all.

HOW POEMS GET WRITTEN

Like
a memory
torn
at the shoulders,
my darling
wears
the chemise
I gave her –
a wedding gift.

At night
I tap out
my poems
on her hip bone.

When
she can't
sleep
either
we write
the poem
together.

ODYSSEUS IN LIMBO

It was a neat trick
The glass of beer floating through the air
And coming to rest on my round table –
I spit on your one good eye Polyphemus –
Then the foam fell away from the rocks
To the sound of the drinkers' voices
Like the noise from the throats
Of a thousand flushed lavatories singing together
I could see their fishhook eyes menacing me
Sly at the bottom of the cool gloom of the tavern
But I wanted to write something on the waves
Carried towards the shore on the backs of a million snails
For I knew that arrived there
They would go begging like a long poem.

To the movement then of dark and light
A Byzantine angel slid down from the smoky wall
Hovering over me with his wings outstretched –
But I saw the shape where the flat tiles were not –
Before I could make a salt out of my astonishment
There was a meadow of surf in the bay of my elbow
And while the hungry robins picked at the air
White blossoms fell on their sad faces
Held in a frame of grass and ground for sentimental poets
Who weep when they are told of such things.

I do not remember when I first noticed
The human smell below the eyes
But the ghost of an unhappy sailor
That sometimes uses my body for a night's lodging
Blew a fistful of spray into the corridor
An eye started to twinkle like a crazy lighthouse
Rocked by a giant and the waves to bob
All around me like lopped heads
Their hair as they came to the surface combed down
Like Russian peasants tolled to a green Sunday church
I think someone called me brother
And pressed my hand clammy with many misfortunes

He must have seen the smoke curling
From my ears and from my mouth too
For he or someone who resembles him closely
Suddenly began to shout fire to the lavatories.

Heaven bless the three angels who lifted me up
Though my body turned into a picnic table
With six boyhood legs on St. Helen's Island
I heard their wings brushing the foam off the rocks
But they or the boys who had drowned that summer
Made too much noise
For the robins left off picking the air
And the blossoms decomposed at my feet into a bad odour.

RELEASE

I shall rejoice when you are cold, dead clay;
Nor shall my hate be cheated by the dust
That fills your eyeless bones or cools your lust
With passionate embrace of quick decay.
At last no perfect art of yours can stay
The spoiling hand of unenchanted death
Or attitude of love restore the breath
To tease the flame from one impatient day.

Then will my soul aspire beyond the flesh
To tread bold ways to a remembered peace
And find life's blasting fever ebb and cease
In spacious realms where light is born afresh;
And no more marvel how our sullen mirth
Provokes the ancient anger of the earth.

PINE AVENUE ANALYST

His face a priest's: wise, round, contemptuous:
One hears the faint rustling of his surplus.

93

RECONCILIATION

Betwixt the harbour
and the great Crucifix
the snow falls
white and astringent.

I can not cancel
this wind
nor the wild cries
of the pitiful men
that fling themselves
against the Cross

hang there a moment
lighted Christs
and fall like tears
down the mountain's sides.

You are like my city
full of perverse appetites,
devout, beautiful:
cobras coiled in the snow,
white foxes, priests' surplices;

and in the tinfoil air
I doubly marvel
that after estrangement
should come
such fine unhoped-for
delirium.

BEAUTY

Omah who keeps house
for us says when she
was a girl in Russia
they didn't have toi-
lets but had to go
out and pee over
a rail with bare bot-
toms in the dead of
winter.

       So at night
she and her three
sisters would go for
a last one before
turning in and sit
on the freezing rail
inside a sort of
roofed shed but open
it was

             and listen
to the shepherds play
their sad pipes.

Hoh chee, Mrs. Layton,
It was so beautiful!

THEOLOGY

I believe, though not in God, in Original Sin
And believe in Hell, but see nowhere Heaven;
And Man, no God's creation, no, I see desire
Goodness and Light – yet Evil ever blows up that fire.

95

BACCHANAL

You there, and you, and you
Come, I want to embrace you
With beer on your breath and halitosis
Come with your Venus-rotted noses

Here is man's true temple, cool
Gloom, sincere worshippers –
Before them the tapers of beer
Like lights lit on many altars

Come, pleasure's my god and yours
Too, to go by your charming noises
Let's hiccup our happiness
And belch our ecstasies to Bacchus

He hears us and sends the room
Spinning. May his touch be always upon us.
May we, as he spins us in the cool gloom,
Be forever in his keeping.

ÉLAN

He phoned, the eldest brother,
To ask about his agèd mother.
"O she does well," I said,
"Though just now her stern is red
with a large ulcer."
"And doesn't that disturb her?"
"No," I quickly replied,
"It's on the opposite side
to one she had a month ago;
This comforts her so.
She says, 'If ulcers can get around,
So can she,' – and stays above the ground."

96

MAXIE

Son, braggart, and thrasher,
is the cock's querulous strut
in air, an aggression.

At sight of him as at the sound
of "raw" my mind half-creates
tableaus, seas, immensities.

Mornings, I've seen his good looks
drop into the spider's mitre
pinned up between stem and stem.

All summer the months grovel
and bound at his heels like spaniels.
All seasons are occult toys to him,

a thing he takes out of the cupboard
certain there are no more
than two, at the most four.

I suppose, spouse, what I wanted
was to hold the enduring folds
of your dress. Now there's this.

This energetic skin-and-bones. You'll see,
he'll pummel the two of us to death,
laughing at our wrinkled amazement.

Yes, though his upthrust into air
is more certain
than delight or unreason,

and his active pellmell feet
scatter promises, elations
of breast and womb;

yet his growing up so neighbourly
to grass, us, and qualifying cobwebs
has given me a turn for sculptured stone.

IN THE MIDST OF MY FEVER

In the midst of my fever, large
    as Europe's pain,
The birds hopping on the blackened wires
    were instantly electrocuted;
Bullfrogs were slaughtered in large numbers
    to the sound of their own innocent thrummings;
The beautiful whores of the king
    found lovers and disappeared;
The metaphysician sniffed the thought before him
    like a wrinkled fruit;
And the envoys meeting on the sunny quay
    for once said the truth about the weather.
In the midst of this rich confusion, a
               miracle happened: someone
    quietly performed a good deed;
And the grey imperial lions, growling, carried
    the news in their jaws.
I heard them. So did Androcles.

O from the height of my fever, the sweat
    ran down my hairless limbs
Like the blood from the condemned patron
    of specially unlucky slaves. Then, O then
Great Caesar's legions halted before my troubled ear,
    Jacobean in Time's double exposure.
My brassy limbs stiffened
    like a trumpet blast; surely
The minutes now covered with gold-dust
    will in time
Drop birdlime upon the handsomest
    standard-bearer,
Caesar himself discover the exhaustible flesh,
    my lips
White with prophecy aver before him.
But the conqueror's lips are like pearls,
    and he hurls his javelin at the target sky.

In the depth of my gay fever, I saw my limbs
    like Hebrew letters
Twisted with too much learning. I was
Seer, sensualist, or fake ambassador; the tyrant
    who never lied
And cried like an infant after he'd had to
    to succour his people.
Then I disengaging my arm to bless,
In an eyeblink became the benediction
    dropped from the Roman's fingers;
Nudes, nodes, nodules, became all one,
    existence seamless and I
Crawling solitary upon the globe of marble
    waited for the footfall which never came.
And I thought of Time's wretches and of some
    dear ones not yet dead
And of Coleridge taking laudanum.

MISUNDERSTANDING

I placed
my hand
upon
her thigh.

By the way
she moved
away
I could see
her devotion
to literature
was not
perfect.

IT'S ALL IN THE MANNER

It's all in the manner

> How a bold fly circles the greenleafed
> stalk: or the dog yawns and stretches
> in the sun: or my neighbour,
> his wife, like quiet monks, kneel
> before the chickpeas
> to weed, clean, again and again,
> the earth sockets
>   and their blazing cotyledons

And it's how
I dance my shanks, here, in the fields, reply
to a question, tell some one off, piss
open-legged, wake
The dead with a yawp, B—,
make love (One hand
tied behind my back

It's all in the manner of the done

> Manner redeemeth everything:
>   redeemeth
> man, sets him up among,
> over, the other worms, puts
> a crown on him, yes, size of a
>   mountain lake,
> dazzling   more dazzling!
> than a slice of sun

WHEN I SEE A GIANT

When I see a giant seven feet tall
married to a donna frail and small
    I marvel most at Nature's wit
who when they're bedded hot and bare
perfectly pairs them so they fit
    hair to hair.

100

THE SWINGING FLESH

"Affirm life," I said, "affirm
The triumphant grass that covers the worm;
And the flesh, the swinging flesh
That burns on its stick of bone."

ICE FOLLIES

You always were one they said
To stand tiptoe while peeing . . .
I know better.
You were seeing over the frozen canadian urinals,
The white discs for the expert skaters.
And if all your friends have grown compliant
(Happiness is if you ask them as round,
World as shapely as their wives' buttocks)
Their ecstasy is as you say only an effluvia.

That woman there, an excellent bourgeois wife,
The piecrust falling over her fat fingers—
Did you say she looks like a whore
That has been slept in all night?
Did you say in canada
You can not say shit too often?
I'm happy, brother, happy to find you unchanged:
A single heirloom in your pocket
For a cup of coffee at Horn's
And a store of political wisdom in your head.

This is March nineteen fortyseven.
I swear to you
A decade from now or perhaps two
And these bastards here or their grandchildren
Will be glad and made whole . . .
Self-discovered because you farted here.

MILDRED

"Beneath this huge oak
Your passion, my dear, seems trivial
And your vexation
Not important, not important at all."

This is what I might have said
In words like these. But there was
A shadow in her face
Annealed like porcelain or glass

That held my tongue:
Oaks have a way of concealing
By a sudden tumult of leaves
What it is they are feeling –

With humans it's otherwise.
The darkening of lip or eye
The painedged voice
Are treacheries.

So I bid Mildred speak.
But she was silent
That windless day
As the unstirring oak.

"You'll not always remember
His hands, his eyes: things pass.
See how the sun's white body
Now lies rotting; there, in the deep grass."

Two spots glowed in her cheeks.
Then she smiled, derisively;
And because she had much to say
Said nothing, turning her face away.

When my carefree three-years daughter
Came rushing upon a moth;
Crying and stumbling, she drove it toward us.
The child was out of breath.

She chased it on – on – into the fields
With wild imploring cries,
Pursued by my brute laughter
And Mildred's still derisive eyes.

FOR PRISCILLA

Sitting by this idiot
radio
on a windy night
I recall you
tight and impervious
as a pebble
and prototype
of your unmagnanimous sex,
a female hyena
of the spirit
who sniffed the delicious foetor
from my rotting psyche;
and I think whether
the neat dot
of your posterior
incrassating
like a gourd
into the steamy vegetation
of your middle years
will traitorously swallow up
the wedge-shaped virgule
of your back, once,
ah, firm as a ballet-dancer's.

LACHINE, QUE.

Here, the skies
crimson with sunset
disappear
into blast furnaces;
emerge
rows of red-bricked
houses
whose guardians,
their bellies
full of apples and lard,
wave shirtsleeves at the summer.
And all day long
the trains
coming and going
expel soot
upon this workmen's suburbia
which lies glistening
at the foot
of the highway
like a safe
used by an idiot.

MONTGO

The young doncella
strides ahead of me
on long graceful legs,
her green velveteen slacks
giving the curve of her swaying ass.

Over a ruff of cloud
the grey stone-faced mountain
appears solemn
and so old, so old.
It does not sway.
How many evenings, I wonder,
have washed over and against its face
to burst into unquiet star-foam?

THE MADONNA OF THE MAGNIFICAT

I shall wander all night and not see
    as much happiness as this infant gives
to his plain sisters who are adoring him
and his mother cradling and covering
    him with her love.

She has borrowed the white moon from the sky
    to pillow his golden curls
and at her magical cry the dark roofs
the length of the street lie down
    like quiet animals.

The night will wear out and disappear
    like soiled water through the city's drains
but now it is full of noise and blessed neighbours
and all the tenement windows fly open
    like birds.

DUDELUS, POETASTER

If you or I
should thoughtlessly
commend the verse
of another poet
his speech falters
— his cheek goes
red and white by turns.

It is however
this flux & reflux
of colour
    which fans
the small emication
of his talent.

105

PORTRAIT OF AILEEN

Unlike others, near cousins to fatuity,
you walked carelessly into my thoughts of you;
and with a tired movement of your eyelids
defined yourself to me
under your absurd hair.

To begin with, I had never seen
so much sadness on a woman's mouth.
There were no answers for your grief.
My curiosity like a trained domestic
left everything as before, as if untouched.

Though an incredible wound in the air
the bowl of apples on the garden table
sustained itself with simply being.
It is the architecture of sanity, I thought.
But you wove the air with charred fingers.

"The centrality of the fly," you said,
"It's impassive, a black demi-god. The
flowers choke the weeds. No matter."
The look on your face appalled at being there
has taught me severity, exactness of speech.

THE DARK PLEBIAN MIND

When I finished my poem he said,
"Eros, man, Eros is not dead;
In all, in men hateful, yet dwells
Love – Love, concrete and fabulous!"

Curse, curse my dark plebeian mind.
For as I heard my clement friend
I queried was it wholly Love
Which hastened him to this reproof
Or – O perversity of heart! –
Unease at my surpassing art.

AGAINST THIS DEATH

I have seen respectable
death
served up like bread and wine
in stores and offices,
in club and hostel,
and from the streetcorner
church
that faces
two-ways;
I have seen death
served up
like ice.

Against this death,
slow, certain:
the body,
this burly sun,
the exhalations
of your breath,
your cheeks
rose and lovely,
and the secret
life
of the imagination
scheming freedom
from labour
and stone.

GATHERING OF POETS

Repression is here, and so much failure.
And so much suffering. Each one accompanying death
    With mincing steps, with horrible gestures.
And their poems? The pepperminting of bad breath.

EARLY MORNING IN CÔTE ST. LUC

So I awake and see the white
table under the willow tree,
a fragment of edge, a smile
of paint.

      The sun has wiped the dark off it.

Also off the grey steam shovel,
an immense praying mantis,
poised
for thrust.

Soon in action
it will fling itself
against the gravelled road
with the violence
of a sex pervert.

      Cunilinctus. Infertility.

Frantically it lanes the earth for sewers.
It prepares an accommodation
and an easy way out
for excrement.

In the neighbourhood
a professor
glances at his collection
of tomes, slowly yellowing
into favour.

A plumber, heir of the Fr. Revolution
true egalitarian,
installs a porcelain
toilet bowl.

      Some housewife
      cooks her lavish poisons
      for the household

And the children in their warm soft beds
dream of white butterflies
with unplucked wings.

How to make room
in my mind for these
and the black bitter men –
my kin –
the inconsolable, the far-seeing?

PAYSAGE

When I slumped down on the cut grass
in the rich man's fancy golf course
I must have deranged a detail
of slumbering noonday mosquitoes
for they came at me with the distemper
                of outraged innocence;
storming my brown wrists and ankles
exposed like a Mexican bandit's
surrendering to the forces of law & order
– you've seen them, barefooted,
hands outstretched, holding their useless carbines.

Since they were stupid and greedy
it was no great matter to kill them;
but not before they had devised
thick welts that rose red on the soft flesh;
though in the outcry I thought
how like three shapely nuns
sharing a ball or a secret between them
the silky devouring ravens
                in the distance
walked away from the young poplar
– an arrow lodged in the bright turf,
its green feathers still quivering.

SEVEN O'CLOCK LECTURE

Filling their ears
With the immortal claptrap of poetry,
These singular lies with the power
    to get themselves believed,
The permanent bloom on all time-infected things;
Indicating the will to falsehood in the hearts of men,
The music in a pismire's walk, the necessary glory of dung,
    immortal coal of the universe,
Leibniz's mirroring monads, daybeams of consciousness

I see their heads sway at the seven o'clock lecture;
I imagine they forget the hungers, the desperate fears
    in the hollow parts of their bodies,
The physiological smells, the sardine cans, the flitch of bacon,
The chicken bones gathered neatly
        to one side of the plate;
Life is horrifying, said Cézanne,
                but this is not
    what he meant who picked flowers blooming
    in the slaughterhouse; he meant the slit throats,
The bear traps smeared with blood, the iron goads,
   the frightened
    servant-girl's Caesarian,
And this planet dancing about Apollo,
    the blood drying and shining in the sun,
Turning to Titians, beauty, the Arts . . .

My heart is parted like the Red Sea.
It cracks!
And where the cleft is formed
The BARBARI carrying their chromium gods
    on their sunburnt arms and shoulders
Ride on my nightmares, a hot desert wind
    pushing them swiftly toward these faces
    washed clean of Death and Agony;

God! God! Shall I jiggle my gored haunches
       to make these faces laugh?
Shall the blood rain down on these paper masks?
Flammonde, Light of the World, in this well-lit
       fluorescent age you are a failure, lacking savvy;
Gregor Metamorphosis, fantastic bogeylouse,
       you are without meaning to those who nightly
       bed down on well-aired sheets;
In the fifth row someone pulls out a laundered emotion
       and wipes his long, false nose.

At last the bell goes, Lear lamenting Cordelia, the wall's
       piercing cry . . .

       You may grieve now, gentlemen.

HOW TO LOOK AT AN ABSTRACT

When I got the hang of it
I saw a continent of railway tracks
coiling about the sad Modigliani necks
like disused tickertape, the streets
exploding in the air
with disaffected subway cars.

So help me, when I got the hang
of it I said (the nylon stockings filled
with liverwurst; an honest word
for rage weeping by broken pylons)
middle-class America is pooped, played out,
she's had it.

Cut up the hash, chef,
and take out the chromium cinders.

MR. THER-APIS

I saw no friend blooming
In the ugly middle-class parlour
But only chromium knick-knacks
And ugly middle-class furniture.

On his wife's face the hard lines
Of pride like lesions;
A middle-class harpy, she
Sat beside her glass of gin.

And they both said: "We like
Chinese food immensely." He:
"Look at my income tax returns."
I could see they were not happy.

After a life of success
He was haggardly thin;
His wife long ago had ceased
To interest him.

While she seemed waiting, waiting,
For someone at the stroke of twelve;
But when Mr. Ther-Apis came
He did not announce himself.

I was aghast to discover
He had the face of a bull.
All evening, not once did he frown,
Nor did he smile;

But sat there like some fleshly god
On their gleaming sofa:
I thought, then, of the epigraph
To Kuprin's Yama.

When finally he arose
On his sturdy legs
And reached for the plateful
Of Egyptian figs.

That was the signal
Between my friend and his wife;
She rolled away the cushion
And uncovered the knife.

My friend's face grew pale
But she was past alarm;
"Mr. Ther-Apis," she said,
"You'll come to harm."

And there before my horrorstruck eyes
They snipped off his balls
And plated them with chromium
Into a pair of handrails.

Now when they go up and down
They feel his touch, and kiss,
And love the world with the tested vigour
Of Mr. Ther-Apis.

FOR GOVERNOR STEVENSON

Excellent and virtuous governor
your speech more beautiful
than troubadour song
has set free
like tears from stinging eyes
the chilled mid-
century prisoners
Hope and Valour

If for a brief hour
the loudmouth caleers
above the vespers of the meek
noble governor
you discern the white and pointed stars
turn for the ragged
their petitions being stored
like thunderous drops of mist.

Among broken statues
and the rubble of once great faiths
you move
a nimbus of light and affection
your name rinsing
every square and city lane.

Sir, when I heard
your great speech of acceptance
I was stirred
as a dead poplar
by a wind.

PARACLETE

I have studied history, he said.
I expect nothing from man
Save hecatombs.
C'est son métier. And ferity.

No longer perhaps to his own kind
But to the sulphur-coloured butterfly
And young seals, white, without defence –
To whatever crawls, flies, swims.

It is life itself offends this queer beast
And fills him with mysterious unease;
Consequently only half-movements
Delight him – writhings, tortured spasms

Or whatever can stir his derision
By defect or ungainliness
Or, maimed, flutters from weakness like a bird:
Say, a noble falcon, with splintered wing.

It is as if, killing, he looked for answers
To his discontent among severed veins
And in the hot blood of the slain
Sought to inundate forever his self-horror

Or like a sodden idiot who plucks
A thrush from a willow, grief in her green hair,
Throttles it to uncover the root of its song.

Let the gods who made him, pity him.

PERSONAE

Clibus, The Poetaster
God knows I find no happiness
In drinking whisky to excess;
But stretched out on a privy floor
With every belch my spirits soar.
The plaudits of the noisy bowl
So flattering are to my poor soul
They are at last persuading me
I am the poet I am said to be.

Amaduce, The Critic
Inspiration
Is heat and candleflame;
Amaduce, the critic, able
To gumble the wax on the table,
Opines that melted wax and flame
Are one and the same.

Chloris
Had I the talent
Of Ovid or Horace
I'd write for Chloris
An extravagant sonnet
Who lives for her belly
And another on it.

Casca, or Suum Cuique
Casca was right to do as he did:
Stab the great Caesar and make him bleed –
The gods are just and the same gods made
Caesar's greatness and his own sharp blade.

Thersites
Let your mind go like a greyhound
Past all bolted doors –
In this north country, Thersites,
Your spit
Makes ice for brilliant skaters.

Corypheus
When I was at school
Corypheus said I was useless
And that I would come to a bad end.
Now after many summers have passed
    I frequently meet him
On the Main Street that leads to the Mountain.
Disappointed ambitions
Have made his skin yellow
And he is bent double with age;
But I have a beautiful wife
And friends who when I am angry or boastful
Remember my affectionate nature.

Elpinor
Elpinor,
The suave and talkative foreigner,
Disliked me for I thought him dull;
He got up and like a true Christian, sir,
With a single blow split wide my skull.

ARACHNID

Sun-purpled, the clover
bussing the outermost strand
was pure camouflage, as were
the innumerable grasses,
dogrose, timothy, vetch.

Nature's geometry, the exact design.
With what grace so ominous
a contraption held the beauty
of the dying day, the fly
dying with faint and futile buzz.

117

METZINGER: GIRL WITH A BIRD

Your eyes, heavy-lidded,
half-closed, make of sadness
itself a caprice, or seem to.
I have the feeling, miss,
you dream too much
of flight – on winter evenings!
Yet the mist
of those nerveless evenings
lives in your clouded eyes.

Your face
tilts toward the gay edifice
through whose casements
birds might go in and out;
and your elbow is,
to be sure,
a gesture that makes known
your will – yet hardly more;
the flexures of your breast and skirt
turn like an appetite also there.

Too small
for a swan, a raping Zeus:
the still bird, symbol
of decession and freedom,
that you fold between your full
breasts
pins you by a paradox
against the air.
There is no happiness here;

Only the desire
of the impotent, the weak
who, if they wish to speak,
must first grow indignant;
It taxes my brain,
miss, to guess at the monster
or tyrant
who inhabits the shuttered building
the lines of your head and breasts
turn away from with such disdain.

THE HUMAN CONDITION

And not ten years ago
my neighbour wept
at the fashionable horrors
of the crematoria.

The desiccated matchsticks
ready for burning,
the tortured heads . . . grey skin;
under flashlight, at night,
building his modest cottage
brick by brick
he wept for the human condition.

Now, a trough in a green wave,
the mounting synagogue
finds him apprehensive
for the price of real estate.

This is the first House
of Worship, he says,
savouring his own disgust
—is it a church?
a mosque?

Why do Israelites
push so hard
to get in first?

WESTMOUNT DOLL

For saying this
curse me to see seven Canadian winters
        but your emptied stare
is the death of all poets. You, depthless,
and your face a school, a discipline,
        magic away the martyrdoms, dissipate
the tragic pneumas in my brain-box
to as little meaning as
        disturbed flox on wet sand.

Or hex me to see
the great black-bearded Agamemnon
        slain by a danceband leader
:bonged on the head on the polished floor:
yet wreathing your brittle fingers you make
        a sweatless funnel through which fall,
insubstantial, love, and mysterious
as the contempt for the harmless
        the desire to strike and dishonour.

Certainly, what fazes me
        even more than the satisfaction
you take in your throat and white shoulders
is that all dark verse,
        Hebrew or Sophoclean,
in your cascading neighbourhood seems
aberrant, out-of-keeping,
a lout or playboy
                if you know what I mean
discussing the schizoid features
of the Absolute.

THE BIRTH OF TRAGEDY

And me happiest when I compose poems.
        Love, power, the huzza of battle
        are something, are much;
yet a poem includes them like a pool
        water and reflection.
In me, nature's divided things —
        tree, mould on tree —
        have their fruition;
I am their core. Let them swap,
bandy, like a flame swerve
I am their mouth; as a mouth I serve.

And I observe how the sensual moths
        big with odour and sunshine
        dart into the perilous shrubbery;
or drop their visiting shadows
        upon the garden I one year made
of flowering stone to be a footstool
        for the perfect gods:
        who, friends to the ascending orders,
sustain all passionate meditations
and call down pardons
for the insurgent blood.

A quiet madman, never far from tears,
        I lie like a slain thing
        under the green air the trees
inhabit, or rest upon a chair
        towards which the inflammable air
tumbles on many robins' wings;
        noting how seasonably
        leaf and blossom uncurl
and living things arrange their death,
while someone from afar off
blows birthday candles for the world.

COMPOSITION IN LATE SPRING

When Love ensnares my mind unbidden
      I am lost in the usual way
On a crowded street or avenue
Where I am lord of all the marquees,
And the traffic cop moving his lips
      Like a poet composing
Whistles a discovery of sparrows
About my head.

My mind, full of goats and pirates
      And simpler than a boy's,
I walk through a forest of white arms
That embrace me like window-shoppers;
Friends praise me like a Turkish delight
      Or a new kind of suspender
And children love me
Like a story.

Conscience more flat than cardboard
      Over the gap in a sole,
I avoid the fanatic whose subway
Collapsed in his brain;
There's a sinking, but the madonna
      Who clings to my hairlock
Is saved: on shore the damned ones
Applaud with the vigour of bees.

The sparrows' golden plummeting
      From fearful rooftop
Shows the flesh dying into sunshine.
Fled to the green suburbs, Death
Lies scared to death under a heap of bones.
      Beauty buds from mire
And I, a singer in season, observe
Death is a name for beauty not in use.

No one is more happy, none can do more tricks.
                    The sun melts like butter
Over my sweetcorn thoughts;
And, at last, both famous and good
I'm a Doge, a dog
                    At the end of a terrace
Where poems like angels like flakes of powder
Quaver above my prickling skin.

MOTET

Lord, let me love

>   them: the pious
>   dropping on their careful dress
>   crumbs of God on Sundays
>
>   the sinisterly unwell
>   poet-and-intellectual
>   freezing in his paper hell

the women on their married feet

And lord, let me love

>   the beaten, the starved, the dumb
>   for whom Charity's diseased heart
>   beats like a public drum
>
>   Alas, poor thought for a winter
>   to find on growing older
>   I am more capable of murder

THE LONGEST JOURNEY

In want of an author's omniscience
They strove with shadows in the fast-dying light;
But the shadows were themselves, things of time,
Which they cast without courtesy at each other's feet.

I saw them in the rain, near other debris,
The rusted cans the drops ping'd accurately and often;
There behind the house outlasting architects
The weather and the angry voices flayed them.

Now the children were spies to be out-smarted;
Neighbours grew suddenly in the air
Or in the trees, where the scrupulous robins
Kept signalling to them that they were there.

The leaves twitched to the words like wolves' ears
And gulped them down in heavy swallows,
Till they were open to every passer-by
And naked and humble as the grass.

Then they were quiet: quarrelling dogs,
I thought, silenced at the approach of men;
After a moment to catch furious breath
They will go at it hound-and-bitch again.

But I was wrong. In the end seeing
That they were finite as the rusting canisters
They solved the monstrous riddle of time and self
And forgave the hour and the changed weather.

For the point of view, they saw, was everything,
Though necessarily final. Yet the good life holds:
Like great art, is unsensational; and there time
Does not rush upon us but unfolds.

SANCTA SIMPLICITAS

Write me a poem, said Reb Magid,
simple and uncomplicated
as a little spaniel;
show me –
a humble, hungering man –
God's careful mercy
in the fell
and the four warm paws
placed on His field of glory.

And staring at the pupils
of his guiltless eyes
I could see
they were of the same
elemental order
as a bird,
as bread or a tree,
and it was clear
that I and the angels knew
what the good man meant.

But a breath later, catching
behind his curved
complacent back
my face's pale reflection
in the windowpane,
I became confused
and to his elation
bitterly silent.

THE ANTS

I watched them
wriggling out
      of the
electroluxed dirt,

jots of life
whirled out of a vacuum –
a Time Machine –
on dead plateaus
on craters,

iotas of energy
black specks of determination
——irresistible!

they lifted
concealed lids
and tossed them aside

they opened
mystified doors
in the slopes of mountains

they poised themselves
on withered rocks
as if waiting
for Time to begin:

retrieving their intuitions
in the hard grains of sand
they adjusted
their tiny grey helmets

then took soundings
and came down
guardedly, lacking
their usual assurance;

shook the carpet lint
from their polished bodies
contemptuously
as if to hear better,
            skeltering now
like African warriors;

at the edge
of the newspaper
their polished bodies
            gleamed
like tiny limousines

——magnetized filings,
they waited
for signals.

LATRIA

Give me, Dark One, these
A woman's white knees
A woman's fine eyes
Her hot, lathered thighs

The nuptial embrace
The first look of love
A bird, sparrow or dove,
The unscheming face

Any bloom, a rose,
Creation's frenzy
The thrill of pity
– The rest is prose.

BRIEF ENCOUNTER

The damage
was not much
either way.
Running red-faced
towards me
he turned out to be
an old schoolfellow.
He gave me his hand
as if he were selling it
over the bruised
grill and bumper
and said, Fancy
bumping into you like
this, or some such
wisecrack. Saul, Saul,
I said, you haven't
changed much.
Should I? he grunted.
My reply
was lost in the blare
of angry horns
which he didn't hear.
Pull over, he said,
and let the local yokel
pass. Yah,
I mean you, mister, he
shouted at the sinister
motorist in black garb
just behind us.
Then putting his lobsterlike
arm over my shoulder: I've
no time
for reminiscing, chum.
Ring me up some time,
or better still
write me a poem,
I gotta make
a Fireworks Convention
in Godsden, Ill . . .

Take note of our encounter,
ministers of religion,
and you, artists of the beautiful word.

TWO POETS IN TORONTO

Entering the city
at a quarter of eight
they brought up the rear
of a Christmas parade

and thought the hosannas,
the plaudits of the crowd
were intended for them:
the poets bowed.

But the acclaiming thunders
were all for a clown
who clambered like a fly
on a rented van

and tugged
at his loose comedian collar
at so many paidfor
tugs to the dollar.

The poets acknowledged
the welcoming noise
and wiped the tears
from their sensitive eyes

only staying their dulia
to fry with a curse
the clown in front:
so inglorious

'ly stealing
with the frisk of a limb
the civic ovation
planned for them.

ON FIRST LOOKING INTO STALIN'S COFFIN

When I was
a burning idealist
I wanted very much
for Comrade Joe
to live forever

he was so good
for the unborn children
and for the grave cows
that gave
extra yields of milk
whenever he riffled
their tails
with a *pieteletka*

Jubilating
like a bleeding
bride
I even wrote a poem
which began
"Comrade Trotsky
is dead . . ."
after one of the boys
had polished him off
with an icepick

That shattering minute
was it remorse
went suddenly
like steel
to the Vohzd's head
Or was he
brainstruck
thinking how feasible
to recreate with him
and Comrade Death
an old triumvirate

Kaput
in his coffin
lies the world's
benefactor
giving off odours
but no answers

VETERAN

As he crawled past
the service station,
his wrecked torso
bobbing upanddown
crazily
like a bust spanner,
the attendant
when they were nearly
abreast
hailed him
from the pumps:
"How goes the war, Tim?"

The cripple
turned his green face,
grinned,
and for rejoinder
lengthened one foot
behind
the other.

NOW THAT I'M OLDER

Now that I'm older
When I see a man laughing
I ask myself: who
Got it? Whom did he do in?

And when he cannot constrain himself,
But the tears run down his cheeks
And he slaps his thigh
Repeatedly,
I become worried and ask:
How many? A whole city?

And when I see
A woman smiling, showing
Her well-cared-for teeth,
I think: boredom
And lust – and note
The gathering imbecility
On her face.

I suppose one day
The sun will black out
And these creatures
With their ingenious contraptions
For perfuming and surfeiting their bodies
Will die.

In the meantime they multiply.

And that other event
Is more than a billion years away.

MARIE

Believes men want one thing only
        And she's got it
High or low, learned or ignorant,
– To pluck the dark rose below her navel

She thinks also
That I'm a poor lover: I
Am too romantick
        She herself is not so

She uses sentiment like a perfume:
To stimulate action
        She is always ready

She says when she closes her eyes
She can see men's hands waving plantlike
Under the table, undulating towards her dress:
Her thighs: her IT
        their lips moving
As if they were playing harmonicas
In a harmonica band
Lips: teeth, lips: teeth, words, words, words
        But she never attends to the words

She likes to feel that their pale hands
Are out there seeking her panties
And when I ask her what she's thinking of
She invariably answers:
        O, certain childhood memories

Tell that to Tennyson and to Ezra
Of the troubadours

LOOK, THE LAMBS ARE ALL AROUND US!

Your figure, love,
curves itself
into a man's memory;
or to put it the way
a junior prof
at Mount Allison might,
Helen with her thick
absconding limbs
about the waist
of Paris
did no better.

Hell, my back's sunburnt
from so much love-making
in the open air.
The Primate (somebody
made a monkey of him)
and the Sanhedrin
(long on the beard, short
on the brain)
send envoys to say
they don't approve.
You never see them, love.
You toss me in the air
with such abandon,
they take to their heels and run.
I tell you
each kiss of yours
is like a blow on the head!

What luck, what luck to be loved
by the one girl
in this Presbyterian
country
who knows how to give
a man pleasure.

THE RAVENS

Where's the poem, my companion said,
Which yesternight made me cry out
Like a sick bride or child, naked
Before you and that moneyed lout
Who smiled into his broad palm to see
A man might be touched by poetry.

And at that, two sick ravens flew
From my companion's eyes, curtsied
As only ravens can, then grew
Small, smaller than a pepper seed;
Crooked fowls that have flown from hell
I saw their trace on his black lapel

And knew that he'd lived with his shame
A day. Man, I cried, here's the poem
Which if now read without the flame
You will curse for a shapeless stone;
From mixed emotions I made that song,
Like yourself weak where I would be strong.

But my companion laughed out loud:
I am disgraced in my own eyes
To have dropped tears worth a cloud
For versicle as weak as this,
And brushed the pepperplumes angrily.
Nor has he spoken to me from that day.

RAIN AT LA MINERVE

All day the heavens have opened up
and it has rained rained rained
rained
with the maliciousness of a minor poet.

It's not my element; I cannot live with it.
Perhaps because my forbears were thrifty merchants
it dispirits me to know
so much excellent water
        is going to waste, is going under bridges
to serve an outworn metaphor, expending
so much effort to so little effect.

Snow I can take, if I have to:
if only because of the satisfaction I have
in supposing that snow
is what someone has done to rain,
his contempt for it published in a million white bulletins.

It has rained for three days and three nights
and the vegetation is lush and very green.
They say Ireland is like that, the green rolling hillsides
a brogue in your eye and a lilt in both ears.
But I have never wanted to go to Ireland
now that her great sons are dead
(real Irish giants – Shaw and Joyce and Yeats
– not mythical ones)
and each little green blade, a rosary around it,
saying a paternoster to the wind.

Ireland? More like Africa.
I'm afraid to peer under my armpits, I might find
        tropical ferns growing sideways; and my limbs
    have begun to feel thick and rubberish and tubular.
I have the feeling if I step on the floor
                        of my room,
water will splash out of my ankles
as from an old water boot or water bag.

The rain makes numerous thunders in my head,
　　but it could be the tom-toms
　　announcing the white man's love for the blacks.

Help me, someone.

I imagine my body is the whole steaming
　　　　　continent of Africa,
and millions of animals are squishing
through the torrential jungle rains inside me
but one lion in particular
　　　　I see him, the fierce proud beast –
roars, and roars again:
roars roars roars roars

VIGIL

Evening . . . the feathery grass . . . boughs
That coldly lift a silent offering;
The shadowy swaying of trees
Like graceful nuns in a forbidden dance;
The yearning stillness of an ended night,
And clouds the colour of oyster shells
Clustered about a comfortless moon.

Dawn. A crayon held in a master's fingers
Pencilling in soft outlines the earth.
The hills. Humps that tell laconically
The labouring age of earth;
And suns that turn the wayside streams
To moving panes of light.

137

STILL LIFE

We were speaking of modern art.

"The human's no longer interesting,"
  said the stranger.
"God, nature, man,
  we've exhausted them each in turn."

It was a warm August afternoon,
  and the linnet kept wiping its beak
  on the fallen leaves and grass,
  joyfully ignoring both of us.

As if he had done this
  many times before,
  the stranger dislodged the flat stone
  near his hand
  and let it crash down heavily
  on the hopping bird.

Only the fluttering wing was visible,
  and it looked
  as if the ridiculous stone
  was attempting to fly.

Then stillness: stone on wing: both partially
  in shadow.
There was a sweet smell of earth.

"That makes an exciting composition,"
  observed the stranger.

THE IMPROVED BINOCULARS

Below me the city was in flames:
the firemen were the first to save
themselves. I saw steeples fall on their knees.

I saw an agent kick the charred bodies
from an orphanage to one side, marking
the site carefully for a future speculation.

Lovers stopped short of the final spasm
and went off angrily in opposite directions,
their elbows held by giant escorts of fire.

Then the dignitaries rode across the bridges
under an auricle of light which delighted them,
noting for later punishment those that went before.

And the rest of the populace, their mouths
distorted by an unusual gladness, bawled thanks
to this comely and ravaging ally, asking

Only for more light with which to see
their neighbour's destruction.

All this I saw through my improved binoculars.

THE POET ENTERTAINS SEVERAL LADIES

The solid hunchback, the poet said
(boarding the summer at Les Solitudes)
throws a bigger shadow on the ground
than any of us; moreover
the children enclose it like a corolla.

> My dog licks his fur,
> paws his torn ear

And the driftwood I perceive
in the spray and lifting mist, twisting tongues
licking the shore, only momently
blackens an antique lamp; rots
and settles back into the Heraclitean fire.

> My dog licks his fur,
> paws his torn ear

Fishermen, the original village
on their brows, small and dark with the hour,
row towards the urgent sun. There
all human cares dissolved they burn
like sheet metal in the burning lake

> My dog licks his fur,
> paws his torn ear

My glands that sweat pity, sweat
for oars greying in the sun, for old men
and clouds and in the cloud-filled lake
the ripple that breaks from its round sleep
like a child crying out from weariness.

> My dog licks his fur,
> paws his torn ear

Hourly such images flood the mind;
touch memory, detritus of appetite,
into fire; though destiny who plays it safe
uses always and only the same rigged wheel,
I gain incongruous poems and bells for buoys.

My dog licks his bruised fur,
paws his torn ear

THE YARD

No one prospers outside my door:
I sit like the first criminal with an old woman,
Her hair timesoaped her hands folded
Like a hymnal. Here everyone is dying out a pain.
I spy from my restricted gallery, a turret.

Outside my door everything is prepared:
From wooden scarps the clotheslines arch like scimitars,
The windingsheets swell under a bolshevik moon;
This evening the yard is full of fatal actors
Waiting with their garbage pails for the blue corpses.

Outside my door no one prospers:
The crumbling shards multiplying like flowers,
Tomorrow the casual stroke of a dirty urchin leg
Will prod the fire from them, a marathon blaze;
Later the cold-eyed men will infect the weather.

A column of whispers rises from the summermoist yard:
I think it is the neanderthal
Tree of Eden lifting its immense branches
Over my banisters for manslayer and saint;
And I am neither I am neuter I am you.

141

SUMMER IDYLL

At home, lying on my back,
Lying with perfect stillness I saw
The scene dispose itself differently
Like a backdrop held by an enormous claw:
On either side the even expensive
Sod; the bungalow with the red border
Of roses; the woman past her middle years
In gaberdine shorts, and her hard fists
That held in place over her suntanned knee
A book, half-shut, in spectacular covers.

And building up the summer afternoon
Music that came thudding upon the air
Music that came it seemed from nowhere
But came in fact from the vacant bedroom
And came from a persistent gramophone tune

Did I contrive this, or did I inerrantly see
The line of hair on her lip?
Surmise her frown? Her talipes?
Did the enchanted hour suddenly darken?
And did the roses
Really uncurl and stretch upon their stems
And order their ignorant centres
Toward the chill anonymous tune,
Then abruptly with the afternoon
Erupt into thick ash against the window frames?

142

GOD, WHEN YOU SPEAK

God, when you speak, out of your mouth
drop the great hungry cities
whose firetrucks menace my dreams;
where Love, abandoned woman, hatless and void,
snares me with her thousand pities;
ambulances pick up my limbs.

When you speak, you put phantoms
before me, unloyal friends who smile and envy;
great clouds crushed between my opulent arms
have not washed out deceit
or the barbed recollections of guilt, but
have wet me through for my ambition.

When you speak, I turn monument
to all my years misspent and good;
lovers have scratched their names
upon my base, birds have come and gone;
stationed at Place d'Armes or
the civic square I have sweat the same.

Curse all statues that rigid
whether as flesh or angel's wings
stand their weight of stone upon the moment:
speak, yet now let all be unpinned again
to flow like colours from an exposed frame
into the earliest pools of morning.

143

WOMAN IN THE SQUARE

The benches stain and blister in the sun.
The many ignorant pigeons all day long
compliment the stone-deaf poet, wheel for crumbs;
and the matter-of-fact horses wait
for their load of usual gawks,
drag at the gutter to no purpose.

Across this important street
she pauses under the awning to examine
her white glove.
It is hard to believe she ever ate green things:
celery, lettuce, or the stems of young onions;
it is hard to believe flowers grow for her
in the same innocent way they do for others.
Her perfume is wasted on the incurious tramps
and on the stone-deaf poet
who once wrote a beautiful poem to a louse.
There's authority in the clean body,
in the white creamjar face;
her bladelike arm
dispatching the bellhop
has the secret of power in it;
frowning, however, she seems
suddenly in the sun's hot pallor
a female chimpanzee on whom bracelets glitter
like the lascivious eyes of young boys.

She has made the day trivial.
The painted evening in mauve and pink
slides, a furtive homosexual,
around the enormous thighs
of the tall puritanical trees.

THE DANCERS

Through envy
Of the propulsive movement
        Of your hips
You have swept
All other dancers
From the centre
        Of the naked ballroom;
The glass-fluted table
In the feline shadows
        And the white leopards
Applaud you under the pagan chandeliers;
Moreover you have made
A pie-eyed poet weep
        From a loss of balance.

What more do you want or need,
My tuxedo'd Alpha,
My flaring red-dressed Omega,
Perfect, gifted with gracefulness,
Your genitals moist with dancing?

ME, THE P.M., AND THE STARS

I was walking with the frost
    and winter flakes in my face
when I stopped near a cottage marbling white
in one of the better suburbs of Montreal.

The windowpanes yellow with warmth and light
    made a perfect target
for a piece of coal embedded
in the white and innocent snow.

It flew from my hand like a crow.
    A pane splintered in the night,
making a noise that set the stars ringing
like Munch's picture of hysteria.

One head, then another appeared.
    A man and his frightened wife.
Hu-hu-who is that? the face with the least hair
on top of it asked in a faraway voice

although I was only a coal's throw
    away from him. This, I replied calmly,
holding up my left hand. Then feeling
the irresponsibility of the wind

and the white stars flaring
    up there above me
I changed my story and held up
the other, the right.

Alright, I said, go on, go on
    call the Prime Minister;
tell him what I've done.
He was beside me, the P.M.,

at the last recorded syllable. The couple
had gone off to the delights
of copulation, having first boarded up the abyss
against the white and anxious faces of the stars.

Now what's this I hear of you,
enquired the P.M. in a soft, stroking voice
— breaking into other people's windows
at the stillest hour of the night?

I met a sage, I said, I met a sage
lying on his face
under a despoiled berry tree who said
God was slowly decomposing

decomposing year by year, leaking away.
Little remains of him now
except a faint odour that might be found
in the better churches of the city.

He also said pity was loss of power.
Someone had to tell the people
what was happening; it's indecent to let
the death of the last god go by unnoticed.

When I finished the P.M. began
searching for a frightened hare
at the bottom of his portfolio; finding none
he buttoned up his overcoat, but left

three unattached buttonholes for the
horrendous stars to peep through.
As for myself, I mark time
from that eventful night.

THE BUFFALOES

Autumn: the leaves? Of course they fall.
The wind? The same dirge as last year.
In broad daylight the mist surrounds
Grips you like a friend's displeasure.

Certainly, look up, there are clouds;
And look down, poor flamboyant leaves.
Careless, you commence to moralize:
If a dog barks, you say it grieves.

The leaves. Ah yes, they bleed to death.
There's not a hand can stanch that flow.
The winds like sad sensualists
Disgusted by excess wail, blow

Them from their pride; for good measure
Roll them, sick queans, in their own blood.
I raise my atheistic eyes –
So much vivacity, now mud.

Even that most ambitious cup
That held the dying sun awhile,
Cut down, prepares itself to lie
In winter's white infirmary.

And yet in all this business this,
This stabs me: my two buffaloes,
Their heads bowing in the light breeze.
That now unleaved cannot kiss and close.

BOYS IN OCTOBER

Like Barbarossa's beard bright with oil
The maples glisten with the season's rain;
The day's porous, as October days are,
And objects have more space about them.

All field things seem weightless, abstract,
As if they'd taken one step back
To see themselves as they literally are
After the dementia of summer.

Now hale and sinewy my son, his friend
(The construction sand making a kind
Of festival under their feet while leaves
Fall and heave about them, drift and curl)

In their absorbed arm-on-shoulder stance
Look I think for all the world
Like some antique couple in a wood
Whom unexpected sibyls have made rich

– Something perhaps tricked out by Ovid!
On one condition, alas: they'll not use
The gold but hold it as a memorial
To Chance and their own abstinence.

METAPHYSICAL

Aware, love, on waking
How the hours can bring
The effectuation of only
One paradigm of things

Or to put it all
As sages do, metaphysically,
And talk of the potential
Becoming actuality

I must beg mercy, love,
When you offer me your eyes
Your lips for kissing
That I so surlily refuse

For this loss, this sacrifice
Is my commemorating stone
To all that might be
Yet this day will not be done.

INTERSECTIONS

The small swelling of the empty cokebottle
just showing above the nicked grass:
the one curving presumably forever,
the other yellowing with the season.

The bulge is like a piece of coloured glass.
Ochre. Ochre and wan. With it the knoll
fixes a vacant stare on eternity. Uncovered,
the bottle lies like a short runway for the sun.

The impatient golfer looking for a lost ball
is not looking for that. Still it is more than
beautiful; as is the brilliant spray which the girl
watering the impermanent border of a lawn
holds out to him like a painted fan.

SCHOOLTEACHER IN LATE NOVEMBER

The scriptural weight of snow
has pressed everything dark to the surface;
the houses stiffen; and the snowflakes fall
on fretted gates like a well-turned epithet.
As comic relief perhaps
the brush-tailed trees in the schoolyard,
weather-mocked, stand striped like skunks.

Trees, houses, gates back away as from a corpse,
and winter begins like a murder story.

Inside is a region of chalk-dust; and no ragged track
to lead you from face to face. The instructor
bends scythelike over the crafty heads –
harsh burdocks on the frozen ground –
and as the season festers on the windowpane,
looks up and stares (mockery of schoolboys in his ears)
at rocky slates, the taint of winter there.

ANGLO-CANADIAN

A native of Kingston, Ont.
– two grandparents Canadian
and still living

His complexion florid
as a maple leaf in late autumn,
for three years he attended
Oxford

Now his accent
makes even Englishmen
wince, and feel
unspeakably colonial.

151

ORPHEUS

Poets of a distant time
Mix madness with your rhyme
And with my dust I'll weave
     Dark rhymes for your reprieve

God was not Love nor Law,
God was the blood I saw,
The ever-flowing blood
     Staining water and sod

Woman I loved. Enough
She made me dream of love
And in that sexual dream
     Forget the whitethroat's scream

Saw men could finer sing
For someone's suffering
Laugh with you and after
     Envy you for your laughter

O these talented beasts
Might on your dead eyes feast,
Or pluck them from your head
     Plant jonquils in their stead

And with your dying spasm
Sing loose their gates of prison
Yet this transforming song
     Engender bitter wrong

Saw they could demolish·
With love love's foliage
And that the poet's heart
     Has nowhere counterpart

Which can celebrate
Love equally with Death
Yet by its pulsing bring
     A music into everything

DEATH OF A CONSTRUCTION WORKER

Over the shoulder
of the sun
throw, March wind,
a ragged coat of cloud.

Gather
at the temples, blood,
and fall dropwise
on the frozen ground,
splintering the windows
in their mourning shadows.

Flap your booted feet
on mud and stone
like a fat penguin,
priest.

And shine, officer,
your bright badge
on the cooling corpse.

Like a long, black nail
the morgue's polished
limousine
holds this day together.

LINES ON MYSELF

Here rots Irving Layton
Claimed by no kith or kin;
Friends I had none, for who
Could love an ironic Jew?

Being a misanthrope
I gave manunkind rope,
But woman I loved well
And still want them in hell.

Next I loved poetry,
Though knew the poets lie;
I sometimes loved the sun,
Clouds and thoughtless children

All mercurial things:
Streams, air, bright-coloured wings.
I hated cruelty.
The world's well rid of me.

POET AND DANCER

If in some different sphere we two had met
we'd have played our parts like other liars;
you the bright dancer and I the poet
each on the lookout for his admirers.

You would, dear girl, have feigned an interest
in my verse though ignorant of half-a-line
and I praising you with my lips and eyes
had thought you empty and too much a pagan.

But here, our knees touching, was Spanish wine
and at your right side (one brute leaving us)
an unamusing bacchanalian
who mocked all verse and versifiers.

This made you kind; and kind, most bewitching:
you took my hand – the touch of you lingers,
then as the sot belched, you smiled and counted
each stagnant belch upon my fingers.

So the fates wove their net most carefully
and took account of all save you and me,
for you the dancer danced away from it
and I the poet plucked it for my wit.

155

THE POETIC PROCESS

Faces I too have seen in clouds
And on the walls of an outhouse;
And this morning I saw a frog
Deadstill, showing its moist, grey
Belly to some twigs and dry straw;
And a young terrified grass-snake
That threw off M's and bright S's
At the exact ferns as it streaked
Across my black boot into sedge.

To begin with there are the mysteries;
Though Klee recommends character
And Maritain has one lattice
That gives upon a monastery.
They write well: moreover, Klee paints.
To make a distinction, I think
Then that the poet transfigures
Reality, but the traffic cop
Transcribes it into his notebook.

In any case I'm adjusting
My organs to the future. Lies?
No: Language. The great days of Liz
Are mere Marlovian bombast:
The truth is dung, bubonic plagues
And London a stinking midden;
The maids unwashed and credulous,
The men coarse, or refined and corrupt
Reading their folios.

Sure I've come upon calyxes
And calicos, and melonrinds,
And fruitstones that reminded me
Of the bleeding heads of soldiers;
I've sworn then by the blood and gall
Of Christ and shouted eurekas
Till seven beavers watered me,
Putting out the fires. I've prayed,
Prayed and wept like a lunatic.

So I come back to the white clouds
And the outhouse wall. One may see
Faces anywhere if one's not proud.
The big words? I'd rather find lips
Shaping themselves in the rough wood;
Or connect my manshape's shadow
Floating like a fish under me
With – fish! Or think the day closes
Like the sad, red eyes of your English cocker.

FOR THE MORE DEVOTIONAL

A man in clothes
is dangerous;
naked, arse in the wind & all,
he's a tolerable animal.

If they had photographed
Hitler's ballocks,
plastered the picture
in the German Wallachs

Or advertised his rod
like any dog's stiff & red,
there'd be fewer
rotting for the Fuhrer.

And Stalin's posterior
enlarged, in technicolour,
would disillusion
the fellow-traveller

Though the more devotional
could be shown of course
the Leader's inquination
vacating its source.

SARATOGA BEACH

Knowing that the blade dies
Makes our kind unkind or wise
And writhe in the white fear
Of the death-knowing terror,
Of the flukes that tunnel in
The human imagination.

There is no escape from this.
Each out of his nothingness
Like bankrupt with creditor
Conspires with Death for power;
Ekes from the day's cruelty
His small immortality.

The insubstantial armies
The high wind today raises,
Grey manshapes of sand
Dissolving: this too's our end.
We hate, are insignificant.
But you, dear boys, are innocent.

Innocent as the flower-
Mauling bee of this hour,
As the self-indulgent waves
And the worm-eating sparrows;
And pleased as a naturalist
Whom randy lions have kissed.

For you this wind and water
Do not impugn all laughter.
They tell no tales. Clean of limb,
You play ball on the beach, swim,
Laugh at anything, are gay
At the sand column's disarray.

This, then, is my goodbye wish:
Calm not harsh through bitterness
Of gross finitude grow. Be
Fresh and changing as the sea.
Clear-eyed. Truthful. Go, children,
Improve your conversation.

THE COMIC ELEMENT

As our terrorized bodies sought the floor
And we lay prone near the pilasters
We saw the handsome chivalrous Nick
Who was that much younger and vainer

Than the rest of us
Rise up to confront the bearded outlaw;
A gun barked in the obscure element
And the bullet spurted towards him

Like a red spaniel maddened by pain,
And when we looked up we saw
Our brave and silly friend, Nicholas,
Execute a kind of piaffer

On the waxed belly of the dancefloor;
Only it was air he was holding
Languidly, distractedly in his arms
And when he fell we knew that he was dead.

159

THE EXECUTIONER

At last I was alone with the executioner

Outside the cell the factories were humming furiously
producing artificial lime for the affacement of grass and trees

My visitor, springy and massive, was confident
with an absence of theories. It was evident
that he liked and even valued me and this,
absurd creatures that we are,
moistened both my eyes with pleasure

Perceiving that we had read the same authors;
and my wife, his own, had known
each other in the identical small town
where a decade ago a moratorium
had been declared on all death poems,
we laughed; he, with more restraint
as befitted his position. We agreed without
fuss that the conditions of our lives
made mandatory the murder of others';
also, it was merely good sense
my death should go unreported
in the nation's press: could only provoke
unneeded comment and by disturbing
one or two over-intense persons
snarl up the traffic

Then pulling on gloves of white cotton
he urged me to the door
excusing himself for inevitable brusqueness
(he was well-bred) in phrases taken
from the same books that both had read

The last object that my eyes saw —
a single roach on the polished inside
of a wineglass, moving up the curved surface —
fell into the lees and was drowned in the tide

160

It was noised abroad afterwards
the bullet was made in the place
where Mabel works; but this invention
of human malice should astonish no one.

I WOULD FOR YOUR SAKE BE GENTLE

I would for your sake be gentle
Be, believe me, other than I am:
What, what madness is it that hurls me
Sundays against your Sunday claim?

True, there's enough gall in my ducts
To cover an area, and more:
But why you – free from evil, poor bird?
Why you – my heart and saviour?

I swear I'm damned to so hate and rage.
But your fair innocence is my guilt;
And the stream that you make clear
I must, to fog my image, fill with silt.

Bear with me, bear with me –
Your goodness, gift so little understood
Even by the angels I suppose
And by us here somewhat undervalued

Is what I hold to when madness comes.
It is the soft night against which I flare
Rocketwise, and when I fall
See my way back by my own embers.

WINTER FANTASY

At the explosion of Peel & St. Catherine
O under the green neon signs I saw
        the ruined corpses of corpulent singers
arise from their tight mounds, sigh and
stumble upon each other dragging
their tattered shadows in their arms

They moved their bony mouths like the
fatalistic bulbs going on & off; teeth
        fell from their jaws, fell with such roars
it stirred the carpenters on the sleeping hills
who straightaway thought of the failure of nails
and the rubigo of all boards

What made the whiteflakes change
direction above my head? A flock
        of ravens shriek under the tramcar
and a lock turn in the air? Madness,
ah, a newsvendor, melting the snowflakes
came towards me & my distaste for winter

Or was it my spouse among the frenzied shoppers
looking at the white columns of lost & found
        for the eyes with which I first beheld her?
This night who . . . what bankrupt
will sell her small diamonds to fill
my unresisting sockets when I am dead?

I draw near some woman shawled & shivering
and flakes of sorrow in her empty palms:
        "Ah, come home, come home, love," I mutter.
"Here in my arms, mouth to mouth, we'll make
the splendidest tree that ever was
for this or any other Christmas."

And raising my hand above the teeth
that rolled like cigarette butts in the wind
        I made, lo! the Cross which inflames our city
plunge hideously through the electric air
and turn into windowlights which glowed only
through the recollection of a former brightness

All night, all night the autos whizzed past me
into heaven, till I met men going there
        with golden nails and ravens whose wings
brushed the night up the tall sides of buildings
and behind them in the morninglight the windows shone
like saints pleased with the genius that had painted them.

POPLARS

What did they do, these poplars,
To grow so straight and tall,
And cradle the sky between them
Without any effort at all?

FOR LOUISE, AGE 17

She came to us recommended
By the golden minutes and by nothing else;
Her skin glowed, sang with the compliments
Which these same minutes paid her.

Her hair burned like a yellow fire
To celebrate the strange beauty of her face;
Herself, she walked unconscious
Of the need she started in us to praise, admire

The elegance we found in us
Like a vein of rare silver when we saw her;
But all our thoughts were caught in the compass
Of her royal arms and we sank down

Into the dark where the blood sings after dark,
Into the light because it was the light,
Into the clear valley where her body was made,
Her beauty had lain, now resurrected

Raised by the minutes which start, slay,
Their ivory hafts fiery with sun-motes
Which, crying, we seized to make an immortal ring
For beauty which is its own excuse and never dies.

DIALOGUE WITH A YOUNG AND PRETTY WIFE

"While looking at me still gives you wet pants
  You love me; but will you when I am old,
  When the member is limp and my crown bald:
  Or when I totter will you think I dance?"

"I'll still love you; I will," said the fair cheat,
"And bring you strawberries when you're a-bed."
  I smiled and drew her towards me and sighed,
  "Which lover will you send to fetch them, Sweet?"

164

WHEN IT CAME TO SANTAYANA'S TURN

When it came to Santayana's turn he,
His stomach cancer-riddled, turning sod
Upon the Sisters' white linen, canvassed God,
The Essences and Immortality,

Unriddling to the last. Brave philosopher,
As you piped your wisdom to friends your breath
Doubtless was heavy with puke, taint of death.
But I mean you no discourtesy, Sir.

Socrates did no better with a jest
About a cock; though artful Plato
And seminars've made that damned bird crow
For every longhead pegging out. My guest,

The world's, fare well in Limbo. You dead,
I shall want that bright eye, that huge bald head.

ORIGINAL SIN

Because he was not made
into a detergent or blue lampshade
proud, proud
he represses a faint smile
– his wreath for those who died.

And because
he watched the vile impalement
of his father, this one
a veined light has in his eyes,
interesting to himself and others.

In the trembling brake
such an odd smile
have serpents in profile;
such a veined light
have their knitted coats.

THE SATYR

My Lovely, my impossible Love,
In a lane in Kishinev
Three hundred years ago
Silent in a quiet place
An old Greek with light green eyes
And wrinkled face
Sits and stares and sees nothing at all.

The years fall before him like a decayed wall.

And resurrected in the rooms
Of gambling houses
The violins scrape
And the Magyar women are beautiful
And the Magyar women have kissable napes
Perfumed and beautiful their blouses.

Quadrilles, mazurkas play everywhere
Play with a bold, intoxicating air
I could put on a caftan
A red fez, a turban
And sweep you into my arms
Across the roofs and churches of St. Catherine.

Ah, what bands! what crowds!

I tell you, my inviolate Love,
Till you and I embrace,
This Greek, trouserless and undignified,
Too old himself to sing or dance
His quiet gaze lost in the distance
Must like some ill-used god
Smoke his infernal pipe
And turn his green insensate eyes on us.

And you and I smoulder and burn.

METAMORPHOSES¹

I looked up expecting fire
    To find instead
Red flowers and inert stalks
And through the grasses
Snapped from too much heat
Irregular shadows in the trees
    Of leaf on leaf.

New butterflies went round my chair
    And stitched me there;
I could not move but sat as one
Hypnotized by the sun;
Then as my limbs grew mould,
Grew stems and grass
    I saw a thrush.

And with that attention
    Envy lends
I steered its sunward flight
Till, dispossessed, I caught
The motion of the bird
And heard within my blood
    Its singing pleasure.

ENEMIES

The young carpenter
        who works on his house
has no definition for me.

I am for him
        a book. A face in a book.
Finally a face.

The sunlight
        on the white paper
The sunlight on the easy

Summer chair
        is the same sunlight
which glints rosily

From his hammer.
        He is aware suddenly
of connections: I

Am embroiled
        in the echoing sound
of his implement

As it slides nails
        into the resistant wood
from which later, later

Coffins will emerge
        as if by some monstrous
parturition. Is it any wonder

He so mislikes me
        seeing his handiwork
robed in black?

Seeing I shatter
        his artifact of space
with that which is

Forever dislodging
  the framework for
its own apprehension?

Over the wall
  of sound I see
his brutal grin of victory

Made incomplete
  by the white sunlit
paper I hold on my knee.

He has no metal
  gauge to take in
a man with a book

And yet his
  awkward shadow
falls on each page.

We are implicated,
  in each other's presence
by the sun, the third party

(Itself unimplicated)
  and only for a moment
reconciled to each other's

Necessary existence
  by the sight
of our neighbour's

Excited boy
  whom some God, I conjecture,
bounces for His joy.

THE COLD GREEN ELEMENT

At the end of the garden walk
the wind and its satellite wait for me;
their meaning I will not know
              until I go there,
but the black-hatted undertaker

who, passing, saw my heart beating in the grass,
is also going there. Hi, I tell him,
a great squall in the Pacific blew a dead poet
              out of the water,
who now hangs from the city's gates.

Crowds depart daily to see it, and return
with grimaces and incomprehension;
if its limbs twitched in the air
              they would sit at its feet
peeling their oranges.

And turning over I embrace like a lover
the trunk of a tree, one of those
for whom the lightning was too much
              and grew a brilliant
hunchback with a crown of leaves.

The ailments escaped from the labels
of medicine bottles are all fled to the wind;
I've seen myself lately in the eyes
              of old women,
spent streams mourning my manhood,

in whose old pupils the sun became
a bloodsmear on broad catalpa leaves
and hanging from ancient twigs,
              my murdered selves
sparked the air like the muted collisions

of fruit. A black dog howls down my blood,
a black dog with yellow eyes;
he too by someone's inadvertence
            saw the bloodsmear
on the broad catalpa leaves.

But the furies clear a path for me to the worm
who sang for an hour in the throat of a robin,
and misled by the cries of young boys
            I am again
a breathless swimmer in that cold green element.

PROCESSED

The work of an epileptic
and of one
who was
probably impotent

The Pauline religion
of love
made man
ashamed of his instincts.

More kind, anglosaxon
commercialism
has left him
with no instincts to be ashamed of.

LETTER FROM A STRAW MAN

I loved you, Bobbo, even when you knuckled me
And pulled the straw out of my breast,
Pretending to weep yet secretly glad to note
How yellow and summer-dry the stuff was.

You will surely recall how amazed
We both were the straw was endless;
At the time I did not know it was your fingers
Made the straw grow there and blaze

Yellow in the fierce sunlight. . . . How when
I once caught your cold blue eye
It first burned like sulphur, but affected
Let down a tear like a drop of dirty sea-water

Into my prized open chest; though after
That encounter of our eyes, your own –
The pitiful one – grew into a porcelain saucer
White and blind. That I could understand.

But why did you give great handfuls
To the visiting firemen? And when the mayor
Asked for some to decorate his fireplace,
Why did you not refuse? No, rather,

Plunging your green delicate fingers
Into my gaping breast you drew
Out for him the longest stalk
Which he snatched with a cough and a compelling eye.

I have left you for another,
Who wears black panties and is as crazy as the birds;
But when the straw comes away in her hands
She is careful to burn it immediately afterwards.

MAURER : TWIN HEADS

The one is reticent, carries himself well;
Is free in manner, yet unapproachable;
     He makes us think certain temperate days
Can put a chill between the shoulderblades.
He uses courtesy like a knife.

Listen: for all his careful fuss,
Will this cold one ever deceive us?
     Self-hating, he rivets a glittering wall;
Impairs it by a single pebble
And loves himself for that concession.

The other, seemingly his opposite, grabs friend
Or cousin with an elastic hand;
     Is, if anything, ridiculous
In his intemperance to please:
Yet is to sovereign eyes his brother's brother.

For by unloading favours on
Friend and unsuspecting cousin
     He subverts each with guilt and crawls
Happily at last among equals.
He loves himself for the moist confession.

The cold one coming slowly down;
His brother, on knees, the easier to climb,
     Meet upon a safe and velvet stair:
All footfalls deadened, here's
No father's tread, and no terror.

173

HARLEQUIN AND VIRGIN

Behind me, the natter of young girls.
I turn round, praying that you are there
that I might catch the smiling emptiness
of your unique uncapturable stare.

False, and false. Time had thinned my hairs
when you, innocent, were half my age.
Bleat or bellow, I am mad – mad to rage
about your skirts, rage, and not smash the glass

Which tells me to my skin I'm fatuous:
un saltimbanque. Let it go at that!
No girl has yet loved excellence for what
it is, or what's ripe more than promises.

Dear girl, do I cast these shapes I fear,
believe or not as the blood runs hot
or cold? . . . O warm O superficial earth
over which I bend like some grassy spear

You yet flow under and away from me
in whorls of light I cannot keep or see.

FOR ADLAI STEVENSON

I, when I heard
your wise and witty words,
prayed for the lonely great:
thinking that mandarin right
who says
there is no art of government
can upraise
what fleering storms have rent,
nor any civic power
to prosper Beauty by a single hour.

174

FOR MY DETRACTORS

You are astonished
when I open my mouth
to speak of poetry

Who is this butcher, you ask,
with his nose
broken and twisted
like a boxer's?

Look, you exclaim,
at the mat of hair
that covers his neck
and his heavy gait
like that of a startled bruin's

The curious among you
and the more impudent
approach quietly
to scrutinize my ears

By the slow looks
you throw one another
I see you conclude
degeneracy or worse

Ah, my detractors,
this is a rough profession
I have chosen

I need all my strength

And if my face scares,
so much the better;
I have that more space
for myself, and for quiet,
and for the poems
that I gather
with a tenderness
you could never
imagine or intuit.

KEEWAYDIN POETRY FESTIVAL

As a beginning, the small bird
And the small twig will do; the green
Smudge across the windowpanes
And the gathering dark; the insects
Outside, hungry, harried, hopeful,
Clamouring. As a beginning,
The bottles of amber ale, or the vexed
Stillness in the pioneer room
When no one spoke.

Then say, these were the gifted
Actors whose egotism, not green
Nor lovely as that of towering trees,
Broke the silences in the forest
Like a bulldozer. Smith, a mild
Eighteenth century man, warm
And wanting praise, therefore not dead.
Frank Scott, proffering us the hard
Miracle of complexity
And humaneness, his face serpent
Benevolent.

And my proud friend,
Dudek, put out because the blades
Did not sufficiently applaud him
And the long-tailed thrashers ignored
His singing altogether.
A sad man. Rouault: Le Clown Blessé.
And Currie, drained of sex, a blight.
And other, littler firtrees giving
Their gay needles to the breeze.

All of them coughing like minor
Poets; all of them building
To themselves tall monuments
Of remaindered verse; all of them
Apprehending more of goodness
And wisdom than they could practise;
All of them, in word and act,
Timesputtering, foaming white
Like sodium chloride on water.

And then add this: though not trees
Green and egotistical making
Somehow a forest of peace,
Nor a lake dropped like a stone
Into the stillness which thereafter
Reproves the intruder in liquid
Accents; though no unsullen harebells
But a congregation of sick egotists,
We shall endure, and they with us;
Our names told quietly across
These waters, having fixed this moment
In a phrase which these – trees, flowers, birds –
For all their self-assertion cannot do.

LA MINERVE

And if I say my dog's vivid tongue
Clapped the frogs under their green fables,
Or the rock's coolness under my hand
Told me clearly which way the sun passed

And if I say in a clean forest
I heard myself proclaimed a traitor
By the excellent cones for I thought
Where the good go, green as an apple

And if like our French grocer, Mailloux,
I lay these things on your white table
With a hot involuntary look,
And add a word about the first gods

I take satisfaction from your smile
And the inclination of your shoulder
Before the birds leave off their singing
And slowly the dark fills up my eyes

But when you stand at night before me
Like the genius of this place, naked,
All my ribs most unpaganlike ache
With foolstruck Adam in his first wonder.

SONG FOR NAOMI

Who is that in the tall grasses singing
By herself, near the water?
I can not see her
But can it be her
Than whom the grasses so tall
Are taller,
My daughter,
My lovely daughter?

Who is that in the tall grasses running
Beside her, near the water?
She can not see there
Time that pursued her
In the deep grasses so fast
And faster
And caught her,
My foolish daughter.

What is the wind in the fair grass saying
Like a verse, near the water?
Saviours that over
All things have power
Make Time himself grow kind
And kinder
That sought her,
My little daughter.

Who is that at the close of the summer
Near the deep lake? Who wrought her
Comely and slender?
Time but attends and befriends her
Than whom the grasses though tall
Are not taller,
My daughter,
My gentle daughter.

MOUNT ROYAL

Whether in high key or low
no litanies of sorrow, please
      – no apprehensions;
the poets with their sadness
      and their cultivated anxieties
can, for once, go hang.
Here, sing, choristers, of the Mozartian snow
   and the fast-moving skis

No pus. Or, if you must pustulate
do so decently, at a distance
      away from the gay playmates,
the happy many . . .

For this afternoon
   settling itself in between the trees
any tree bending with the light wind
can take your measure;
they've seen, a few times, your likes
   here before
      sour with affectation;
You put them in mind with your sick theories
(gone the skis and skiers)
of these same hills
     poxy with early april

Then delight, see?
Sing, spring, fling yourself on the slopes
     of these unattempted hills,
      these iron brides or burgomeisters

For, fool, poor fool, cry;
     what does it matter?
They will tear your cry, the loudest,
   to tatters.
Listen to the shouts, their ring
     (Delight only remains)
     more beautiful
   than absent birdcalls

Approach, fill your pockets
    with so much free affection;
praise this mood
    more fragile than a poet's oath.

DANCE WITH A WATERMELON

Cool; moist and fresh; belly of my beloved.

Wild music from a tightskin drum
(Hear the obscene fife!)
And my forsaken neighbours not in, gathering
Fallen stars washed-out moons and withered leaves.

Before I split open the green melon
I shall do the dance of the erect phallus
I shall do a Simchas Torah dance, naked
I shall do a Temple dance, making my summer buttocks
    quiver like chocolate jelly.

Dancing, I shall put green signs all over paradise:
    NO LEVITES ALLOWED HERE
I've no means for carting off dandruff & dry hairs.

I hold aloft the melon like a sheathed Torah.

Now split the melon: smile of a Negro having an orgasm
    and sighing sighing.

180

ROSE LEMAY

Her face and teeth yellow from the christs
she embraces idiotically in her sleep;
her arms long and thin like wax tapers;
her eyes red, their sockets preternaturally deep.

Her lips cracked, from churning prayers;
the spittle – like pus in an infection –
manifesting how the soul has agents
to surround and grapple with each heavy sin.

On her untidy dresser pills by the dozen;
medicaments, loose hairs, syrups "pour la rhume";
encompassing me, a sour body odour
vindicating empirical Hume.

Poor ignorant lass whom evil priests
like incubi from a foetid ditch
have sucked dry and left your very nipples
mis-shaped, and black as the hat of a witch.

SAGEBRUSH CLASSIC

And letting fall, "All life's a gamble,"
I assailed the desert's lush casinos
With craps, blackjack, and even keno.
Swift slung it: civilization is faecal.
So take a flyer. Which I did. Fickle
Or foolish one's luck; though I'd poems to show,
Was tanned-handsome, my movement deft and slow,
Some bunko artist raked my dimes and nickels.
All's shit. Luther protesting from a can,
Down-to-earth dealer dealing twenty-one,
Who clued me into a richer idiom;
Result? I can curse better. Caliban,
Roll those bones. At the end comes fuckface death
– Shows a pair of goose eyes on a green cloth.

181

THE WAY OF THE WORLD

It has taken me long, Lygdamus,
    to learn that humans, barring
a few saints, are degenerate
    or senseless.
The senseless ones are never by design
    evil; but get in your way
like the ugly stumps of trees; order
    bad taste or out of boredom
start long wars
        where one's counted on
to dredge up manliness, fortitude, and valour
    for their stupefactions.

But wicked are the clever ones.
    Cultured and adept
they will seduce a friend's dear one
with praises of her husband on their lips.

As for the wife
    a little alcohol parts her thighs.
Do not blame her: her husband's name
on the seducer's lips
    makes her the eagerer to satisfy,
teaches her she lies with her very spouse.
And that way is best: no pricks of inwit,
    but the novelty's stab of pleasure is there.

Therefore give me only lovers.
    Come, my latest one, sloe-eyed,
your firm breasts whirling like astonished globes
    before my eyes cross-eyed with lust;
though my legs are bandy
        the heart's stout
and this provocative member smooth and unwrinkled.
Till the morning parts us, I'll lie beside you
    your nipple at my tired mouth
and one hand of mine
        on your black curling fleece.

UNDINE

Your body to hold, your perfect breasts.
Your lips; your hips under my pregnant hands
　　That when they move, why, they're snakes
Sliding, and hiding near your golden buttocks.

Then as your great engines of love begin
Intestinal, furious, submarine
　　They spark into small bites
Whose hot spittle inundates all my deserts.

And I'm like water in a scoop of stone
Kissed into absence by a drying sun;
　　Or I'm dried Sahara sand
Wanting your wetness over me without end.

So possessed, so broken's my entire self
No rosy whipcord, love, can bind my halves
　　When queen you squat: you moisten
My parched nipples into a blazing garden.

And I your paramour-Paracelsus
Fish a soul for you from between my loins;
　　You shudder in my embrace
And all your wetness takes the form of tears.

183

SUTHERLAND : PORTRAIT OF A.C.

Move, mademoiselle, with the wind,
move with the rivers: under
the clean sun the two keep fresh forever
and you pitching like a gull's wide wing
rise white and fathomless. Do not sit, pray,
    ever, as you do now, rigid, head
shoved forward and hands to one side
in a clasp of prayer: so, they
cannot unclose to feel the sudden gusts of wind
    or glide their eight good arches
of bone and blood for the rushing tides.

    Here like two lilies in a day grown
dry, which yet not wholly dead no
Cyprian will shy at a trash heap
but keeps in a useless place your arms,
weightless, lean on the foetid air.

    Aloof, the begging hands stir
each other to a bliss the face being sad
declines, the lips opening
for a sigh, an O! as remarkable
    as the simple food.
they say the ghost of Jesus had.

    Sick defiant heathen and faithless, the
Faith put by for chaos whose sequel
is not a dancing star but green toxins;
the antinomies for a moment balanced
and all excesses cancelled out
    you sit queerly stable, intent
on the inner brawl and the single
familiar peal that holds you sane
as it comes reprieving each time creaking round;
    as one knocked silly by a blow
may fool the assaulter by looking quite serene.

SPIKES

The night being without moon or stars
the poplars
have become black streaks of air.
Intense points of light flicker, outstare
each other to extinction.
The suburban windows gleam like tombstones.

I've advanced upon you, City, from different stations:
poverty, the humiliation of sex, my first marriage;
one day in winter
I vaulted over my father's grave
to detain his retreating shadow – somebody
plucked the jacinths from my stiff fingers!

Now your catholic gaze
blinded by too many lights,
or like a magnifico averting his face
from the bent petitioner
you've showered me, City, with lore sagacity
divers ingenious friends. Even my darling
hangs from my neck, estranged, without understanding me.

And my son, fronting the calendar
with the level glance of a gardener
plucks days unwrinkling on his open palm.
Is it, O City,
sullen and arbitrary,
because I, his forerunner, was bruised by spikes,
the spikes of flowers;
or that so often with white face I have wept
in your great empty pall-black squares?

185

FIAT LUX

Do not, son,
the Sabbath dishonouring,
switch on the lights, the black beard said,
for with a quiver from His bag of cloud
God kills in a revenging wrath.

Alone in the dark shall the boy sing?
Shall he pray? No, let his father pray.
His father's lips are red, red and full,
and the beard black. Bald and skinny the boy
stared at the switch, a nipple marooned in the wall,
and could not keep his trembling hand from it,
no more than Achan from an emerald.

The dull metallic click he heard
was like a small bone that had snapped
perhaps in his skull
or somewhere below his perspiring neck;
and though the room,
reeling with vertigo, filled
with a salt light that all but blinded him,
God has yet not struck or killed.

ABEL CAIN

If it's a woman she dreams of
Chinese lovers with perfect manners;
Their hands open for her like wide doors.
But his dreams are all of criminals.

Down the rattling fire escapes
He stalks them with poison and gun;
Is killed; reading his own epitaph
Learns his sister dubbed him Abel Cain.

And *there's* your decent citizen.
He shows interest in how machines work;
He likes to pat an infant's head; he
Owns the common fears of height and dark.

Liquor makes him tearful or glad.
So does sex. He hates people, himself
Most of all; and is much perplexed by
His voluntary shifts from lamb to wolf.

The old men at a village store: –
Broad smiles like the shadow of my hat,
And in their skulls a secret trap-door
For one another, and a greased rope.

I come back to dreams. Who caught up
In this stale melodrama of guilt
Will weep forgiveness for the goats and
For oneself so symmetrically built?

THE MODERN POET

Since Eliot set the fashion,
Our poets grow tame;
They are quite without passion,
They live without blame
Like a respectable dame.

Bountiful Lady, good Sir,
In search of a pet?
Would you therefore consider
A modern poet?
He's for purchase or to let.

His pedigree? Uncertain.
But come now agree
He's the one to entertain
Your guests after tea.
A wit and scholar is he.

Poets are shocking, you say?
Villon, Baudelaire –
Ho! They come gentler today;
Their language most fair . . .
Ah-ha, you'll order a pair?

POST-CREMATORIA

Gray-haired, soft-spoken, and her blue eye bright,
No, she's not your graceless anti-semite;
For while decrying them does she not use
That nice word *Israelites* instead of *Jews*?

HUMAN BEING

When my wife
was in the hospital
and near dying

the emergency
housekeeper, a
woman with merry
Russian eyes
and a real liking
for my two children,
seeing
my great distraction

asked me
the next day
to double her salary.

Now she's dead,
with a mound
to mark which way
she took back to hell.

Except death,
there's no end
to the vileness
of people.

LESBIA

Lust without love, and for this we strain
    And in agreement twitch, bellow
    To ringmaster Satan and his whip
Of lies: call it a sweet harmony; so
My tongue speaks and your false grey eyes.

The perversion of mind and for this
    We maunder, puff; and cheeks aglow,
    Praise our false good looks; or woodlice
Dropped on a trivet, our nimbleness; so
My tongue speaks and your false grey eyes.

The cold dismemberment of the heart.
    Our proud virtues uncoifed, brought low
    By lust we're poplars in late autumn,
A ruin of greatness, bald queens; but so
No tongue speaks and no false grey eyes.

A STRANGE TURN

A moment ago, in my embrace
She rode me like a Joan of Arc;
Then seeing my fifty-year-old face
Where Time's acids had burned deep their mark,
My head of hair coloured gray and rust,
And my old eyes wise with genial lust
She stiffened and held herself in check.

I felt her limbs slacken at my side
As sweetly she kissed my wrinkled neck;
Desire unspent had all but fled
Leaving behind its wraith, mere sentiment,
That poised her astride me motionless.
Ah, if my flesh were but firm, not loose,
And I were young, how she'd ride and ride!

FROM COLONY TO NATION

A dull people,
but the rivers of this country
are wide and beautiful

A dull people
enamoured of childish games,
but food is easily come by
and plentiful

Some with a priest's voice
in their cage of ribs: but
on high mountain-tops and in thunderstorms
the chirping is not heard

Deferring to beadle and censor;
not ashamed for this,
but given over to horseplay,
the making of money

A dull people, without charm
or ideas,
settling into the clean empty look
of a Mountie or dairy farmer
as into a legacy

One can ignore them
(the silences, the vast distances help)
and suppose them at the bottom
of one of the meaner lakes,
their bones not even picked for souvenirs.

BOARDWALK AT VERDUN

Birds
    fly far out
        over the water; and return.
They forget (O Immortals)
    where they have been.
        They perch on discoloured rails.

That sun-bronzed diver:
    Impersonal, free; what gay laughter!
        I think of the Nietzschean Uebermensch.
He raises his arms – like a god! – slowly;
    becomes an exotic water flower
        then plunges knifelike to sever his roots.

Sullenly
    the hot citizens
        seat themselves in the ferry.
Faithless
    they invent new grimaces
        for the water's stretch there and back.

But a gull too
    gives form and arrangement,
        curving solitary in the grey distance;
Its arcs,
    unstable parentheses,
        holding a waste of air.

Myriads of insects
    suddenly appear –
        some transitory July creature –
A white swarm, a milk of wings.
    World, you are a brilliant madman
        and these your fevered notions.

ONE VIEW OF DEAD FISH

Had it been a drowned child
it should have owned some proof
of birth, and sagacious forbears
    for this neutral water;
    someone to mourn, a name.

But being a rotting fish
its fins, a red streak in the crumpled
water, mattered to no one
    nor the white
    of its decomposing beauty.

Ludicrous its solemnity
on the throbbing water.

SACRAMENT BY THE WATER

How shall I sing the accomplished waters
Whose teeming cells make green my hopes
How shall the Sun at daybreak marry us
Twirling these waters like a hoop.

Gift of the waters that sing
Their eternal passion for the sky,
Your cunning beauty in a wave of tumult
Drops an Eden about your thighs.

Green is the singing singing water
And green is every joyous leaf
White myrtle's in your hand and in the other
The hairy apple bringing life.

EARTH GODDESS

I adore you, Marilyn.
You teach sex is no sin
Nor that anguishing fire
To which the saints aspire;
You make absurd for us
All love that's chivalrous:
There is more wisdom
In your shapely bum.
Real pleasure and goodness
Are in your rippling breasts,
Animal health and pride
In your magnificent stride.
Wench, you teach the race to know
Forms forbidden Plato,
A music of the stars
Locked from Pythagoras.

For those denying sex
Or lost in politics
For the intellectual
Writing on the Fall
Or stilted volumes on
Sarah Hutchison;
For the smelly puritan
Or the sulky christian;
The arrogant, the fool
Disparaging his tool;
For the inhibited
Twisted by a simple need;
For all those who hate
Man's natural estate
Or lined with inner guilt
Trail, as some bugs do, filth:

O cinema goddess
More lovely than Venus,
More explosive than
Deirdre or Helen;
O beauteous wench, embrace
Me in an hour of grace,
Bounce me like the ocean
On each surprising limb;
Then let your kisses fall
Like summer rain on all;
Teach us the happiness,
The carnal blessedness,
The warmth, love, sanity
Of your redeeming energy:
Blest of women, earth goddess,
Teach us to delight and praise.

THANATOS AND EROS

One night beside her spouse suddenly
Her heart was ambushed and her naked
Buttocks quivered with death's agony;
Her shoulders twitched, she gave a low cry.
Love's frolic the weak churl thought and shed
Hot seed against her indifferent thigh.

THE DARK NEST

Once and once only
With clear eyes I saw
Mine your false heart was,
Mine your insolent brow.

Your tongue lolled between
My teeth, a red root;
Caressing mine it
Folded up my queer breath.

Your bright member twined
Once about my mind,
Became in that dark nest
A dark bisected post.

Whose pliant furlongs
Far reached down to where
Impurity's duff
For strength, guilts engender.

Raving you plucked it
From my face, revealed
Shiny on its nib
Hell's puerperal bead.

VICTORIA SQUARE

Ha,
in stony silence
her back is turned to the urinal.
                              Her cold eyes
do not see the men unbuttoning their flies.

A municipal
charade.
Tableau of an era.

196

TWO LADIES AT TRAYMORE'S

Ladies, your unlived faces
innocent and old
are caught up with footfalls
dying in the turquoise air.

Ladies, making a ceremony
over the hot scones and tea,
God hoofless beyond roofs
pipes reservoir music
for your imaginary appetites.

Ladies, why do the refractory
mirrors reject you; and why,
the eccentric stranger
meditating on suicides
and the conception of bats,

Am I suddenly made sad
with an illusion of two heads
framed by coffins,
the coifed ringlets still moist
going dry on dry
impeccable skins?

FOR PHYLLIS WHO SNATCHED
HER POEM IN ANGER

What, Phyllis, what, what —
You show me the Muse and her naked twat.
Shall I become excited
Show I'm delighted
Caper and go silly
Before the handsome young filly —
What, Phyllis, what, what?

Shall my tongue hang out
Shall I stifle a shout
Shall my eyes blear
Shall I bite off my ear
Shall I stammer and sweat —
What, Phyllis, what, what?

Why, the muff that lies
In the nicest thighs
Stuns no gaffer
Dickering year round in fur,
Or wimpling strip of leather
The sandal-maker —
What, Phyllis, what, what?

Expect rather one
To excite a Solomon
Amaze him to a handspring
Before that too-familiar thing
Than I, wedded to the Muse
And long adulterous
Should stand awed and quiet
Admiring it.

For here's the reason
For loving maids to think on
And here's the lesson:
A much-married man
Must whenever he can
Appraise and treasure –
Turning habit into pleasure.
That's what, Phyllis, that's what.

ON BEING BITTEN BY A DOG

A doctor for mere lucre
performed an unnecessary operation
making my nose nearly
as crooked as himself

Another for a similar reason
almost blinded me

A poet famous
for his lyrics of love
and renunciation
toils at the seduction of my wife

And the humans who would like to kill me
are legion

Only once have I been bitten by a dog.

THE DWARF

Today the butterflies weaving in and out
between the sunlight and the weeds
would teach me the language of ambiguity
though a dwarf was brutally killed
and baked in his own blood. Is my
wisdom so much greater than theirs
as they dive into the dark of the hedges
or kiss in flight? The dwarf in any case
was ugly and she who loved him,
mistress to a neurotic manufacturer
of sardine cans, herself had ordered his death
for although she had favoured him
with her best pair of smoke-eyes, he
would not grow tall to her whisper.

The rails I followed
were not laid out by butterflies
weaving in and out between the sunlight
and the weeds: they were straight,
curving only when engineers spoke, and the two
white butterflies imprisoned in the steel
were specially trained to resist the smell
of pinetrees. I had no trouble
following them to the decayed shack
for as long as I kept my eyes on them
they were there. At the broken hill
I saw them prepare for the journey back.

Inside the principals were all assembled.
No one denied the crime. The blonde,
her globes of sex moving a continent
of men when she walked, rose abruptly
to kiss me to cinders unless I exploded
my gun – outside. The jealous manufacturer
puffed his cigar making the smoke come out
his burning mouth the shape of sardine cans;
and the gunman, a velvet kerchief around his neck,
at last looking like his favourite movie hero,
held up the religious text:

I espied an abstracted citizen but he
turned away from me to a corner and was sick.

The blonde swore she had loved the murdered
dwarf; often had let him rest his small head
on her soft vulva, a favour she had denied
the manufacturer till he had bought her
a golden can-opener. The manufacturer excused
himself, saying he had loved her, that he was
not a sentimental philistine but a poet: he
had provided the money.

He was that fond
Of his fucking blonde
He had cashed a bond

Poet turned manufacturer. The times breed them.
The real killers.
The gunman shyly held up the religious text.
"You see, he would not grow up to my whisper,"
the blonde said, dabbing her attractive nose.

"Yah, he was too small," concurred the others.

PLAZA DE TOROS

I stand on a hill;
my mind reels in terraces
and I'm sucked into a whirlpool
of earth.
An evening wind rattles the almond trees.

In the hushed arena of the sky
the bloodied bull sinks down
with infinite majesty:
the stanchless blood fills the sea.

Triumphant matador, night
flings his black cape across the sky.

201

MACDONALD COLLEGE 1905-1955

At the semi-centenary
of my college,
a poet flew from the clouds
and flicked his wings among the crowds.

– I'm the only poet, he shouted,
these ivied walls have bred.
And as this is a true fable
he began putting his books on a table.

– Hear, O hear everyone:
I come from Apollo, the great creative sun.
Come rushing, friends, to buy
the plumes of immortality.

– See, chicken-raisers, my excitement,
my authentic fever.
The books leaped from the table.
There was a clap of thunder.

Three old pigwidgeons asked him
was he selling the new Cook Books
and one, alumnus of '27,
where they were showing the famished ox.

The rest, over two thousand,
here a motley and there a blend,
went on chewing their barbecued birds
as if nothing had happened.

MY EYES ARE WIDE OPEN

With his voice husky, with teeth that shine,
Lovable and bright, my rising son
Measures his fist daily against mine.

His grows, mine as certainly declines.
And what is affection, trust, or praise
But offense turned pure, turned crystalline?

And should you wed a girl of nineteen,
Your body aging, what shall hold her
If neither virtue nor attention?

Estranged my wife, my daughter estranged;
Like a rare thought, like love, they are gone.
But my lipless smile, that has not changed.

Can you not see it beneath the skin?
A thousand years from now from the grass,
From the dust I'll flash you the same grin.

For the sun and moon, for maids and men;
For those who labour and those who stare;
For the death in each resurrection.

Let ghosts riot in a wicked brain
When lust shrivels like a cut foreskin;
I laugh, and my eyes are wide open.

IN PRAISE OF BENEFACTORS

Because of a dead multimillionaire
whom I did not know
I, in my forty-seventh year,
witnessed a spasm of sunrise
in immense and hairy folds of cloud.

Flew through thick canyons of cloud
and stared down at measureless Siberias.
I knew at last the meaning of power.

Heartfelt thanks, my dead millionaire.

Yet, this side of your grave
(thick, bone-chilling mausoleum?)
I am your better self,
your ambassadorial eyes;
with every curvet of this strange machine
transmute your gold, your pelf,
into the truer metal of amazement and love.

MODERN LOVE

Saying your enterprise cannot fail:
You have no drab inhibitions
And your lovers no intelligence

Saying you are fantastical bawdy shameless
Exquisite false amorous
Your lips breasts and thighs in perfect control

Saying you know how to delight each of us
For I you swear am your true love
And the other you have promised marriage

I impaled you on your rumpled bed.

204

DIONYSUS

When Eubolus the Greek learned
that his wife had taken
         a lover
he cried a little
         with the smart of it
and then
         to her marvelling delight –
his appetite increased by vanity –
         tupped her eight times
         before the sun roused up:
a phallus hung in the whitening sky
bringing peace to their humid limbs.

IN RATTLESNAKE COUNTRY

I'm not afraid
of that rattler.

What's its poor venom
compared to that of a human?

BY ECSTASIES PERPLEXED

By that, by this, by sharp ecstasies perplexed,
illumined, a saint streaked with foibles,
    I wore at the heart a hairshirt of fire,
wrapped my thighs in a loincloth of bees.

Honour foreswore and talent, and with these
burnished those bluedyed baubles which hang
    amorously from sad and arid bantam trees
in one-room apartments cheaply furnished.

Yet now with lust and indignation spent
and even remorse and other troubles
    I ask whether by deliberate will I went
or frenzy at a woman's beauty.

And cannot answer. But recall
a flaxen-haired boy five years old
    who one bad night put fire to his gown
and watched the flames about him rise blue and gold.

THE CONVERTIBLE

Her breath already smelled of whiskey.
She lit a cigarette
And pointed to a flask in the glove compartment.
Then our mouths met.

She placed her hand on my groin;
She hadn't bothered to remove her wedding ring.
Her eyes closed with a sigh.
I was ready for the gathering.

You, Dulla, may prefer maidenheads;
But give me the bored young wives of Hampstead
Whose husbands provide them with smart convertibles
And who are reasonably well-read.

206

CAFÉ POLITICS IN SPRING

I read some famous Montenegrin duke
has intuitions about a peace. Hurrah.
But when May comes I close my eyes to walk
    over the bodies of lovers
    slim and languorous
whose naked skins soft to the soles of my feet
make the toes curl in at the rose nipples.

The waitress who genuflects like a nun
rubs the dado clean from customers' grease
till the wood glows with her own devotion;
    and a scent imprisoned
    between her breasts
leaps over the wall of her collar
to flee along the galleries of my nose.

Behind her back gleam the Silex cups:
helmets of a defunct Wilhelm;
and on the firm aluminum prop
    the coffee orbs,
    the liquid pouring in,
slowly acquire a religious look
black and reproving as her own.

WOMAN

Vain and not to trust
unstable as wind,
as the wind ignorant;
shallow, her laugh
jarring my mended teeth.
I spit out
the loose silver
from my aching mouth.

With candid gaze
she meets my jealous
look, and is false.
Yet I am lost, lost.
Beauty and pleasure,
fatal gifts,
she brings in her thighs,
in her small amorous body.

O not remembering
her derision of me,
I plunge like a corkscrew
into her softness,
her small wicked body
and there, beyond reproach,
I roar like a sick lion
between her breasts.

SUZANNE

I look up
from the book I'm only
half-reading, drowsily,
in the sun.

When the wind stirs
I feel myself one
with the apples
reddening there on the black boughs.

I think of Suzanne
(absurd name for a girl
half-Jewish, half-Russian)
who journeyed back to Moscow

And before doing so
loved me for the bedraggled
Icarus I was, gave me
Ibsen and Shaw.

I owe to her
beside simple thanks
my notion of poetry
as visceral sanity.

Her cheeks were red as those apples.

HOLIDAY

"Quebec roads are damned tricky," he shouted
  To his wife out on the lake rowing;
"Adrien's girl will travel a-ways with me,
  But I do not know why or where she's going."

He saw his stolid wife drop from the boat
And stand, the water around her flowing;
And he saw the bent father near the shore
Where the farm tumbled into weed, mowing.

The sensual sun was mounted on a hill.
His passion too was mounting, O growing
With each quick step in unison they took;
And where the road dipped, he felt like crowing.

Black horsedung, stones, and yellow butterflies;
A young bull and his herd of cows lowing;
The white cock fastened on top the roadside cross
That could not tell which way the wind was blowing.

NAUSICÄA

"I'm the sort of girl
      you must first tell you love."
"I love you," I said.
  She gave herself to me then
      and I enjoyed her on her perfumed bed.

By the gods, the pleasure in her small
      wriggling body was so great,
  I had spoken no lecherous falsehood.
Now not I nor my beloved,
      such is our heat,
can wait for either words or scented sheet
but on her or my raincoat go roughly to it.

THE PUMA'S TOOTH

Man's a crazed ape
A balled-up parasite
Whose first thought's to kill you
If his health is right.

Kill you or enslave you.
Or if his heart swells
With love of purity
To crush your genitals.

Go armed with a club
Advised a sage when you run
To woman for delight
Or intoxication.

O most subtle
Most skilled psychologist who knew
The hatred of joy
That lives in the common stew.

The club was not advised
For the lady's bones
But for the savage townsmen
And decayed crones.

To lace their dull brains
On a rosebush where
Wrapped in sweet smells
They'll sweetness engender.

Joyous ones, grow tusks.
And your poems grind with truth
As fierce and as beautiful
As a puma's tooth.

PROJECT

See, ah, how stricken, the branches
Of a catalpa drop their shadows
On the ground – a torero's cape.
The sun licks the funereal blobs of shade,
The relentless sun has done the grass dirt.

Near a mound the derelict garden hose
Is coiled cobra-like, digesting the heat.

But the multiple tappings will go on
Till past six. Round me, my hedges,
And this febrile bush some medium
Rears a ghost town of bungalow-duplex.
Clean christians will be here, one synagogue.

There will be a police depot
For vagrant revellers, alien drunks.

I have come face to face with the owners
At evening watering their drives;
I am a most ignorant man,
But is this not new for our days: these wish
Neither to be loved not written about

And they will endure history
But will neither celebrate nor praise.

DIVERSION

Whenever I'm angry with her
and hold up my hand to slap or hit,
my darling recites some lines I've writ.

The crafty puss! She thinks that she
diverts my anger by vanity,
when it's her heaving breasts that does it.

212

JOSEPH K—

The blade pushing to one side the sod
Explains its ecstasy to no one
Not to other shoots nor even to the sun
Least of all to State or a God.

But this deformity this cripple
Mad and from the womb made answerable,
With his crutch and out of air shapes
Trial judge and advocates.

And at the last real accusers:
A mother-earth laundress
And her evil parody, the whore; a landscape
Running with his own escape.

Then let him rise like a hawk.
Fiercely. A blazing chorus
Be, or like a painting by Picasso
Drawing energy from its own contours.

BARGAIN

In fourteen years
        of married bliss
not once have I been disloyal
to my wife;
and you, I am told, are still
a virgin.

If you are set
        to barter your maidenhead
for my unheard-of fidelity,
call me between three and five tomorrow
and it is done.

213

HIEROPHANTS

In this cold realm where nothing important,
Nothing great can ever happen, one sees
Archiaters on calloused hands and knees
Assume the postures of the hierophant.

Here craterlike the vacant poet gapes
And belches calumet smoke; which pleases him!
And fervent geldings praise when most he seems
The dismal floundered penis on a corpse.

In this philistia of the wealthy dunce,
The evangelical hick, the boor, what
Marvel the Muses and their critics rave
Through page after page of pretentious crut?

It's the felt lack, the wanting to be filled,
The despair and fury at emptiness;
Hierophants? Ah, dummies in a white field
That toss in the wind their frozen tatters.

GENTS FURNISHINGS

After the casual fret of tramcars,
The flowing of time against the traffic lights,
The engine's re-assertive snort,
And people vindictive, elate,
Spawning by contact ambition
Of affluence and the magic arc of influence:
I, rooted to carpet, note
The fabulous street of St. Catherine
Carve through the boulders of buildings
Like a river's bed a furious sun
Dried gradually in heats:

And am re-assuring, friendly, know all the answers,

But the dire question dropped from dying mouths
Rolls down the Caucasus, through disputed lanes
Of water, the passage people make
For their escorted hero, deposits
As a sick vapour on my showcase:
Does truth unite or divide?
History walks in like a customer,
And I sell systems and suspenders
As panels open on Australian farms,
On blackskinned men transpierced
On diamond pin,
A sapper falling suddenly
As if the air had fouled him.

Punching the register
I murder laissez-faire;
And though change here seems circular and illusory,
Beginning in some Bulgarian street,
The creative winds blow equally
Through pyjama sleeves;
And surely today or tomorrow
A stranger will tell me the news,
The morning greet me like a handshake.

DANS LE JARDIN

Dearest girl, my hands are too fond of flesh
For me to speak to you; and you are too tall
For me to think you beautiful, though beautiful
You are. You are some other's fortunate wish

Though alone and your idle limbs inviting.
If I should call to you, give you this verse
And later caress your thighs with these fingers
You would rise like a wraith, like some wan Viking

Come from the North, mists upon her shoulders.
Your eyes are too grave and too luminous
And pledge but one cold nocturnal kiss,
Their gaze putting out the fires that it stirs

Till I hear bells, a slowly dying sound,
Where no bells are; how then should I suppose
You passionately flinging off skirt and blouse
And letting my squat body pin you to the ground?

So as you move your blanket and thin buttocks
To catch the failing sunlight on your face,
I watch you from my stationary place,
My limbs as immovable as these planted rocks

And think of Fate and of your immoderate height
And of your spoiling gauntness; and of what blind
Excuse to make the ceremonious stars who'll find
Our bodies uncoupled by the coming night.

THE CAGED BIRD

There lies the ship, the *Wolfgang Russ.*
After the Trojan War, Odysseus
With his young and fast brother on deck
Impelled her out of flaming Lubeck.
All's changed. The Krauts are blond and phallic;
The day bland as a Dutchman. I look
Indifferently at the trim boatswain,
His scrubbed elliptical head too clean
For a man; and at the officer
Haunched hermaphroditic before
The caged bird carolling; smile, again
Take in the ship's Heraclitean name.
In the sunlight brilliant are the floes
Shuttling past in their icy furrows
Like white ducks in a shoot gallery.
The Kraut officer, rising, sights me;
Salutes across the forbidding rail.
With an old confounding ritual
We turn out our pockets full of change
And loose tears. I stare at the wide range.
And freely the river seems to run –
O endless madcap exultation!
So the sky and its reddening bergs
Moving eastward, moving more slowly.
Beyond abodes that rot, the glory
The bridal lock of water and sky
Where chime the friendly oppositions
That shred us like knives, smiling; in plains
Leaving white nests of untroubled skulls
Spoiling under the sun where chance flung,
Their joy like that of the wheeling gulls
Mindless: how fiercely the caged bird sings!

THE FICTIVE EYE

I wear a fictive eye
in my head —
bright centre of the world!
And white hairs
adorn my temples
like Greek stars.
At forty-nine whom should I fear?
Neither do I brag or lie
like an unripe youth
nor pursue ambition and injustice
regelated
in the snow of my fortieth year.
Ah, like that Roman emperor
who dying
turned into a god,
I also am turning
into grave sage and hero.
Remove, Venus,
your urgent hand from my thigh
and let me rise:
let me go
to caress my exalted destiny.

KEINE LAZAROVITCH
1870-1959

When I saw my mother's head on the cold pillow,
Her white waterfalling hair in the cheeks' hollows,
I thought, quietly circling my grief, of how
She had loved God but cursed extravagantly his creatures.

For her final mouth was not water but a curse,
A small black hole, a black rent in the universe,
Which damned the green earth, stars and trees in its stillness
And the inescapable lousiness of growing old.

And I record she was comfortless, vituperative,
Ignorant, glad, and much else besides; I believe
She endlessly praised her black eyebrows, their thick weave,
Till plagiarizing Death leaned down and took them for his
    mould.

And spoiled a dignity I shall not again find,
And the fury of her stubborn limited mind;
Now none will shake her amber beads and call God blind,
Or wear them upon a breast so radiantly.

O fierce she was, mean and unaccommodating;
But I think now of the toss of her gold earrings,
Their proud carnal assertion, and her youngest sings
While all the rivers of her red veins move into the sea.

I KNOW THE DARK AND HOVERING MOTH

For vilest emissary of death
I know the dark and hovering moth
Whose furred wings overwhelm the sun;
And the blind minnows that cannot swim.

Oh, a fat black moth was my first wife.
She sat her weight on my greenest leaf.
Another moth was so fair a prize,
Melted my manhood into her eyes.

William Blake spied the vanishing heel,
Made all the white stars in heaven reel.
I heard his wild, dismayèd shout.
Rib by rib Urizen lugged me out.

Now at early dawn, my heart with joy,
Like any carefree holiday boy
I look at the minnows in the pond
And catch and kill them: they make no sound.

Lovely Aviva, shall we crush moths?
Geldings stone till we're out of breath?
Wipe the minnows from the goat-god's brow?
He hears their screams; he rejoices now.

For sun throbs with sexual energy;
The meadows bathe in it, each tall tree.
The sweet dark graves give up their dead.
Love buries the stale fish in their stead.

From crows we'll brew a cunning leaven;
From harsh nettles: lock them in a poem.
The virtuous reading it at once
Will change into rimed and sapless stumps.

My proud Love we'll water them, embrace
Over their unleaving wretchedness:
Till snakes cavort in gardens and sing
Melic praises for each mortal thing;

And from Lethean pond beneath a scarp
There rush the vigorous hunting carp
At whose gorping jaws and obscene mouth
Flit the vulnerable black-winged moths;

Poets, each the resurrected Christ,
Move like red butterflies through the mist
To where the shafts, the sloping shafts of Hell,
The globed sun enclose like a genital.

STOCKTAKING ON THE DAY OF ATONEMENT

I swear restaurants
are stomachs;
at Ruby Foo's
I watch wave after wave
of Yom Kippur Jews
fill up the dark, elemental cave.

A discreet rumble
of chairs, of tables,
while the hard brilliants
of the women
flash signals: *Côte St Luc,
Hampstead, Town of Mount Royal.*

In unison
the peeled brats,
the wives and husbands
gnaw at the assorted meat jellies;
the maître, smiling,
makes his tolerant rounds.

Then with filled bellies
they push out
in small knots of family,
leaving the restaurant
evacuated.

WITH THE MONEY I SPEND

With the money I spend on you
I could buy ice cream for Korean kings.
I could adopt a beggar
  and clothe him in scarlet and gold.
I could leave a legacy of dolls and roses
    to my grandchildren.
Why must you order expensive Turkish cigarettes?
And why do you drink only the most costly champagne?
The Leninists are marching on us.
Their eyes are inflamed with social justice.
Their mouths are contorted with the brotherhood of man.
Their fists are heavy with universal love.
They have not read a line of Mayakovsky's poems
    for twelve whole months.
The deprivation has made them desperate.
With staring eyeballs they hold off
    waiting for the ash from your cigarette to fall.
That is the signal.
When the ash crumbles, the man with the smallest forehead
    will smash a cracked hourglass, the sound
      amplified into a thousand manifestos.
Can you not see them? Can you not hear them?
Already they are closing in on us.
Your fragrant body means nothing to them.
Under your very eyes, velvet and remarkable,
    they intone that Beauty is not absolute.

They shout for an unobstructed view of your shoulders,
    your proud and beautiful head gone.
They will break your arms and slender legs
    into firewood.
The golden delicate hairs I have kissed
    into fire a thousand times
      will blaze more brightly;
But who will bend down to gather the flames
    into their mouth?
Who will follow their white light into eternity?

222

Because I love you better
　　than artichokes and candles in the dark,
I shall speak to them.
Perhaps they will overlook your grace for my sake,
　　ignore the offending perfection of your lips.
Perhaps, after all, you and I will start
　　a mass conversion into elegance.
I will tell them my father made cheese
　　and was humble and poor all his life,
And that his father before him turned ill
　　at the mere sight of money;
And that a certain remote ancestor of mine
　　never saw money at all,
　　　　having been born blind.
On my mother's side, they were all failures.
Calliopes will sound for my undistinguished lineage
And the aroused Leninists will at once guess
　　I am a fool in love, a simpleton,
　　　　an ensnared and deranged proletarian
With no prospects but the wind which exposes
　　my terrible hungers to them,
My counter-revolutionary appetite to be lost
　　from all useful labour
　　　　in your arms hair thighs navel;
And parting the clouds, one solitary star
　　to show them where I am slain
Counting the gold coins
　　for your Turkish cigarettes and costly champagne.

BEUTEL'S NAME IS INSCRIBED FOR ETERNAL LIFE

As the angry hawk flies towards the sun,
Taking some small creature into the skies,
So shall your fame be taloned fast to mine
And like the clawed rodent rise as I rise.

223

WHY I DON'T MAKE LOVE
TO THE FIRST LADY

Of course I could have her!

In a flash, with a snap of my fingers.

An arrogant magician,
I'd put words under her perfect feet
and make her fly to me.
She'd land in my arms
reciting one of my poems.
She'd remember nothing of the White House
except what I told her.
To draw from her one of her exultant smiles
I'd persuade her my lips
were official Washington.

Pah, I'm a degenerate poet
with a sense of honour!

I shall not take her.

Not while serene contractors
build kindergartens
for robots and goons,
and skinny Caribs
with beards sprouting from machine-guns
clamour
for blood, education, and cheaper roulette;
or the Chinese have a leader
who writes flawless verse.

President Kennedy does not write verse.

Not while Africa
explodes in the corridors of the U.N.

Lumumba, Kasavubu: a
D'Oyly Carte of exotic names;
but the drums,
East & West,

thwack unearthly rhythms,
and the opera-loving Congolese
lie much too still
on their dead faces.

A President
must stay up night after night
deliberating such matters:

My lovely, unlucky Jacqueline!

Still, when a husband
is so harassed,
shall I add to his burdens
by running off with his attractive wife?

Not I, not Irving Layton.

I'll wait until
the international situation has cleared.
After that it's every poet for himself.

HOSTIA

This one deceives her husband with her eyes,
And this one with a thousand proper lies;
Hostia, such is her regard for me,
Deceives me not at all but lets me see
The queer bites on her voluptuous thighs.

THE WOODEN SPOON

If the sky is an inverted bowl,
Let us turn it over;
Before you have done counting my locks,
It will be filled with nectar.

Here is a wooden spoon, my Sweet.
If your thoughts are subtle
And innocent as your breasts
It will reach the sky.

My first pet
Shaved my favourite knoll
And covered it with a bourgeois smirk;

She ordered me to walk
Always ten paces ahead of my shadow
And carried the spoon's image on the sand
To measure the distance.

Using the wrong end of a parable
She began to erase the crescents
Of my fingernails.
I made her swallow them
And soon after she died in an asylum,
Asking the full moon to draw closer
Asking the sun
Why it wanted to go on living forever.

Another darling begged the wooden spoon
For stirring her own broths;
At last she digested a splinter.
It came out of her ear
A twig of jellied moths;
The sinister purity of their colour
Blinded her for seven whole days.
Then I made my getaway.

Petite Calan said the spoon
Was a sexual talisman
And kept it wrapped in a bloodstained brassière,
Praising its hermaphrodite economy.

At Victoria Bridge I broke it carefully
Over her yellow hair.
The pleasure-hating tugboats
Saw the body fall into the loose water
And screamed.

My other wives, reared by Carmelite nuns,
Had never seen a wooden spoon.

Nevertheless, child, do not be frightened.
I am no Bluebeard.
Murdered poems are what you will find
Behind that locked door, my dear.

MORAL WITH A STORY

Her mother used to tell her
only bad women
had well-developed busts.

When her young breasts
began to grow
she was certain Herr Satan
had marked her for his own
and would grab her from below.

They grew & grew,
and their very size
has made Gretchen bold:
one fine swing of them, she says,
would knock the devil out cold.

SILENCE

The word betrays the act;
The act alone is pure.
The rest is literature:
Fishbait for fools and pedants.

Look at that mountain back,
Knife-edge poised against the sky.
A single bird flies over it
And disappears.

At that height nothing dies;
All is unyielding, eternal.
And I imagine the cries
Of the unsacrificed birds.

I imagine the only music
I hear – soundless, unchangeable.
I am in love with silence,
With the hardness of silence.

I shall become
Like that stone
Through whose single cleft
Flows the stillest water.

THE IMBECILE

By mistake I came to White Mountain Lodge,
Thinking it was an inn. I asked for beer,
And the thin man who opened the door grinned:
"It happens almost each day; people think
This damned place an enchanting public-house
But it isn't . . ." He peered to make certain
No one would overhear him. "It's for boys
Who . . ." and made a sign I took in at once.

And, appearing moved, I said: "Cretins, eh?
The feeble-minded? Or perhaps the sins
Of the too rich?" I could see my bluntness
Displeased, and he believed me God-knows-what.
"Yes, that's what they are," he nodded.
                                    "They work?"
I then asked. Behind me were small hillocks
And untouched fields that could be put to use.
"Why don't they raise onions, leeks, flowers?"
The man now smiled. "These boys are fortunate;
They don't have to, having sires with wealth."
I saw his careful frown as I flung back:
"But what of those who chose penniless sires?
Or would no one here be such an idiot?"

And, laughing, went off warmed by my own wit
To run straight into a small slackjawed boy
With eyes that were vacant. A net of froth
Hung from his thickened lips. "Hi, chief," he called
As a slouching dog – pure mongrel – approached
From behind to bark and worry my boots,
Though with an undertone of fear, I thought.
The idiot boy shushed him into silence.
"Chucky's like that since a bad old truck
Knocked him down . . . an' . . . an' he almost died . . .
His skin was all torn up n' everything . . ."
He bent down and held the dog. "Poor doggie . . ."
O inextinguishable spark of love!
I marvelled at the imbecile's pity
Welling up through the slime that hid his lips
And the blank eyes that held the world's dumb grief
Like panes made clean for a single image.
And my own were wet for him, this cockeyed world
That makes disasters for the human heart,
And myself shamed by this cretinous boy.

229

ELEGY FOR MARILYN MONROE

Last summer, it was "Papa" Hemingway
This summer it's Marilyn Monroe
Next summer, who? – Who will it be?
But Orville Faubus gets re-elected
Two hundred million X-Laxed Americans
    go on defecating as before
and Congress acts as if nothing has happened.

How come I asked of Lyndon Johnson
    there's no Committee
to investigate
the high rate of suicide
among those with a tragic overplus
of sensitivity and consciousness;
and received a postcard
    showing a Texan oil field.

Gentlemen, take it for what it's worth
but I suspect something more terrible
    than radioactive fallout
or the unmentionable gases of Belsen
has penetrated our human atmosphere.
The PTA's haven't heard of it yet
or the Board of Directors of Bell Tel
or President Kennedy;
moreover if I manoeuvred to let them know
    what it is
there'd be a Congressional committee
to investigate me!
They'd get cracking at once. O yes.

You ask, what is it
that goes straight for its victims like radar?
I name it the Zed-factor,
lethal only to the passionate, the imaginative,
    and to whatever is rare and delightful
in this brute universe.

Invisible as halitosis or body odour
it makes no warning of its presence;
therefore no TV outfit
will sing commercials to it
with chuckling hooligans
    poking fingers through plugged drains,
and anyhow since only an infinitesimal part
of the nation
is susceptible to attack
why bother? See, why bother?

Good-bye Marilyn
It's raining in Magog
    a town you probably never heard of
where I sit in a tavern writing this;
nor did you ever hear of me
though I once composed a whole poem to you
and called you "Earth Goddess."
The janitors to whom you said hello,
the cabbies who spotted you by your stride
    and magnificent blonde hair
and whistled and honked their horns
to let you know their good luck,
the men all around the world
who touched your limbs in irreverent sleep
will miss your wiggle and crazy laugh,
but no one more than I
dazed this afternoon by grief and drink;
for I loved you from the first
who know what they do not know,
seeing in your death a tragic portent
for all of us who crawl and die
under the wheeling, disappearing stars;
and who must now live with the self-complacent,
    the enduring dull,
without your sustaining radiance,
your rarity.

From here on in
they have it, the pygmies have it,
it's all theirs!

Good-bye Marilyn
Sleep, sleep peacefully tonight
One poet at least will remember
    your brightness,
the unique fever in your form and face
(O insuperable filament, now black, now ash!)
and love you always.

BUTTERFLY ON ROCK

The large yellow wings, black-fringed,
were motionless

They say the soul of a dead person
will settle like that on the still face

But I thought: the rock has borne this;
this butterfly is the rock's grace,
its most obstinate and secret desire
to be a thing alive made manifest

Forgot were the two shattered porcupines
I had seen die in the bleak forest.
Pain is unreal; death, an illusion:
There is no death in all the land,
I heard my voice cry;
And brought my hand down on the butterfly
And felt the rock move beneath my hand.

232

MIXED METAPHORS

I love your poems, she said,
And kept stroking my thighs;
I love their intense thrust
And their hatred of lies.

I spend whole nights with them
— Your book's beside my bed;
For hour on hour I try
To keep them in my head.

I never felt the joys
Of poetry before,
Yet now I mean to know
Them more and more and more!

Your poems are lovely things:
So strong, yet sensitive;
Were they taken from me,
I would not care to live.

And yet because they're thrust
Into my soul so deep,
You must pluck them from me
That I may have my sleep.

FREE DJILAS

Friday. Nothing unusual.
  We drop out of the skies
with our picket signs
that read: Free Djilas!

The place: Ottawa.
  The astonished citizens
see us assemble
near the Rideau Canal.

And someone, incredulously:
  What is it?
Who is giving it away?
So I tell him to follow us.

As if sprung from the hot asphalt,
  a line of fierce Ottawans
is marching on the Embassy
for a free Djilas.

COURTESIES OF LOVE

You gave yourself to another
thoughtlessly:
out of lust or vanity.

Or was it perhaps pity
made you moan,
stretched out in his embrace?

O my trivial, empty-headed darling,
I remove myself
as your lover
that I may confer
on your piddling act
of baseness

A tragic dignity.

234

A PRAYER

My friend Alex,
a fine scholar and poet,
owes his landlady
a hundred and twenty dollars.

If seraphs split her skull
or she had a fall,
breaking her neck:
there'd be no one to collect.

When Alex has red wine
and no worries,
he writes deathless lyrics;
but she's common
as leeks
and of no account.

I shall pray for rains
to corrugate this land;
for a bright axe
in a celestial hand.

ICARUS

His friends drudged in an airplane factory.
The theory of speed was their sweaty talk;
And one who reclaimed rust machinery
Swore men hereafter would not run or walk.
Another crowed, pointing to his watch: "Feet?
As sure as I'm staring at Time's own face
Our offspring shall be a limbless race,
Hopping in crystal ships from street to street."
Icarus went on working on his wings.
Really he despised their tame discussion;
He'd fly, but as a god towards the sun;
And rubbing the strong wax into the strings,
He leaped into the air – to hear the chorus
Of dismayed cries: "You're bluffing, Icarus!"

235

MAGDA

At first you bared your soul to me.
Now you bare your body.

Your thighs are soft and supple.
Your breasts, bronzed and firm,
Are fragrant hillocks.

Corrupt is your soul, complex.
Your body knows many tricks.
In both there's ecstasy.

After the delights in bed,
This is what you and I said:
"Belovéd, you look radiant."
I: "It was the morning exercise."
"Don't be frivolous, don't."

I stared at you and thought:
Of the two, you are the more wise.

PRIZES

So well 'twas phrased
    I bagged a prize
Praising your thighs.

Immortal fame,
My cool-limbed queen,
    I might have won
Had I but praised
What lies between.

236

THE TRAGIC SENSE

You stand like sober Marxists, nose to rump.
Your tails beat the flies from each other's head;
This would've ravished a dead Russian prince
So I shall praise such glory in his stead.

And slowly the fields and fences crumble;
And the hills too, squat as your hooves;
And the slope under those elegant cows
With the startled faces of my wives.

Ah, Comrade horses, see their fine crescents
—Bone manacles that I pushed apart;
What! you've no wish for an exchange of views
When knives jab at you and make you start?

A constant stutter of protest, in vain
Your skins twitch and twitch, are never still;
Crossed by rhythm of pain, your exposed flanks
Humour in truth no god or devil.

Could he return from dust, Leopardi
Who made an inkhorn out of his humpback
Would weep poems in the air did he see
These pitiless flies forming to attack.

But I, stripped of children, a mere stump,
Stand bemused as you, as powerless;
Poor suffering brutes, at your neigh kneel down
And scrape my being from a spear of grass.

PORTRAIT OF A GENIUS

My friend Leonardo
gives himself real scars
with imaginary razors
that he tests on the pubic hairs
of his old nurse.
When the storewindows of the supermarkets
are unwilling to listen
he shows me his scars
and we use them to play Noughts and Crosses,
taking turns winning.
Nevertheless he's always one game ahead of me.

I know he has two or three corpses somewhere
but I'm much too proud or cautious
to ask him where he keeps them hidden.
When I follow my nose
it leads to the cold green glitter of his eyes
impassively watching the massacre of a city.
If I question him
he shows me they are only boys and girls
playing in the snow.
Those are red scarves on the snow . . .
The time of day is sunset . . .
When the noise gets too loud
he turns off his Hi-Fi
and crawls under the bed
to stare at himself in the mirror.
It reflects only his boyhood teeth.
He tells me he will deed it to the world
if the Secretary of the UN
promises to polish it each day.
Still, he's wary of the UN,
finding the initials inauspicious.

My friend Leonardo
seduces women with words
and vice versa.
When he can't tell one from the other
he changes them both into his mother
who plays Noughts and Crosses with him
with carefully blindfolded eyes.
She always loses because she cheats:
he always keeps an X in reserve
to mark the spot where the game first began.

The day he discovered the spot
changes places when the sky is below
a certain temperature
he fired a bullet into his father's grave,
splintering the decayed coffin
into two elegant heaps of ash.
He often dreams of them now,
but it's hopeless telling him what he sees
is the atomic dirt under his fingernails.
He says he'd like to deed them also
to the world
but he's afraid that after he's been buried
in his father's stained shroud
they'll keep on growing
and wipe away the boyhood smile,
leaving only the blank terror staring from the wall.

THE ARCHITECT

I put my hand through a hedge;
    the leaves of the roadside shrubbery stirred,
scattering immense grains of countryside dust.

The forest behind me began to sneeze,
    and blew into the quiet noon air
thrushes, sparrows, and red-winged cardinals.

They fell at my feet like coloured snowflakes;
    from their tiny, beautiful bones
I raised a city where the first bird had fallen.

The mayor's wife, resembling Alice B. Toklas,
    donated her most attractive smile
to decorate the flagpole of the tallest building.

On clear nights even dwarfs can see her dentures
    outlined against the sky as if
to snap at the moon or a moon man descending.

From a nearby swamp I came to another forest
    while humming the first faint banknotes
that came into my head and thinking of means

To squeeze the silver from the moon and stars.
    When I put my hand through a hedge
the forest just held its breath and gulped.

No bird dropped. A toad suddenly leaped up
    and looked me straight in the eye;
he remained suspended in mid air until he fell.

Yet when I pulled back my eager hand
    my wrist was thick as a porcupine
and ugly with huge unshaven bristles.

The toothless wife of the mayor, however,
    will not let me amputate:
my queer arm, she says, is a civic acquisition.

Together when we walk arm-in-arm on Sherbrooke St.
we make an intriguing pair;
tourists of all countries just stand and stare.

ADVICE FOR TWO YOUNG POETS

The idea's to drive *them* to madness and drink
– not yourselves;
or to suicide.
Consider well the lives of Crane and Poe
and that magnificent slob, Mayakovsky,
who played Russian roulette
with his genius:
then go and do otherwise!
Theirs is not the way. No. No.
In Apollo's name, don't panic.
Why? What for?
You have the choicest weapons – words;
and *their* wives and daughters
will always be yours for the taking.
Learn from Boris, a fox if ever there was one,
outliving Stalin and the other brutes.
That's it, that's the main thing, survival.
And do not be overfinicky here: steal
if you must; kill
if there's no help for it.
One miserable human more or less hardly matters
but the loss of a good poem does,
being irreplaceable.
God knows how many corpses
I have rotting neatly in my cellar.
I gave up counting long ago.

LIBRARIAN AT ASHEVILLE

She spoke of TOM
   OUR TOM
Did you ever see anyone
   flirt with a ghost?
a mere name? the name
of a great man?
What coquetry!

But this was something else again.
   It was fornication;
sepulchral, across a grave,
a warm live body with a shade;
   day in, day out; in & out
behind the desk, behind the stiff manuscripts
in black folders.
   Behind the bookstacks.

At the glass cabinet
   holding the famous first editions
she had her climax.

Wow!

His luminous semen
   was all over her;
her eyes were wet-grey streaks, her cheeks
opalescent.
Yes.

Gentleness: contempt-fostered.

Was I as great as TOM?
Could any man be?
   Nuns, I imagine,
feel the same way.
About men, I mean.
Look who's their sleeping partner.

Jaysus!

All the while smiling up to me
but not listening, not listening.
    It is someone else's voice
she hears, and hers
comes soft, comes soft.

The grey eyes are wet
    the cheeks, wet

It cd. be very genuine emotion
It cd. be the heat
It cd. be devotion

        It cd. be

Spiritual fellatio

HEY, WHAT'S GOING ON DOWN HERE

BETRAYAL

After an all-night session
of drink and turbulent sex
his lumpish mistress floored him
by espousing a new thought
in radical politics
– one he had not given her!

She spoke with such passion,
such self-consuming fire
he conjectured at once
she had the night before
with the same vehemence
pleasured a new lover.

OLIVES FOR JAY MACPHERSON

Two olives I have black as sin,
Where, proud maid, shall I put them in?
If I am ill and grow wan
No shepherd will want them, no unicorn.

For the lost boatwoman
Teach, Phoebus, my fruit to swim;
Or turn them into mythic fish
Or minotaur's horns. Anyway, something swish.

Nay, I'll bury them in a virgin's ground
And shout my hoarsest, yet make no sound:
There's a riddle, sweet not bitter,
To set a criticaster's heart a-flutter.

Call your bullocks, call your sheep,
And call all the maidens from their sleep;
Instruct them olives ripen, die
And in what soil they multiply.

For maidens who have never tasted
Of black olives go to waste
A dread god once decreed,
Peopling Babylon with his live seed.

244

The gay black olives ring like bells
They sound in cities and in dells
Their officious clanging will be heard
By man and beast and bird.

By lone fisherman and boatman
By satrap, child, and virgin
By the farmer's daughter in the dale
By every intense female.

In this freezing north
Black olives are nothing worth;
Eunuchs from their gaiety run—
Between their legs no olive stone.

List, a fable for your own ears.
I saw a maid who was in tears;
For she, the silly, had gobbled down
A venomed imitation.

Green olives in a cocktail glass
Are abhorred by each wise lass,
But green olives arc all you will see
In a grcen olive coterie.

The olives flaunted a dot of red
But the fruit, the fruit was dead;
Pimento, wise maids come to know,
Is the blush of the castrato.

The poor maid wept for she was sick
And nigh to dying;
Pegasus obliged and thumped her back.
She hiccupped and sent those olives flying.

BREAKDOWN

I knew him for a cultivated
gentleman,
a lover of operas
and a Latinist
who had annotated the De Amicitia
to the acclaim of scholars.

We were in Parc Lafontaine,
admiring the instinctual swans.
There was nothing in his behaviour
– in his walk or talk –
to make me suspicious.

As we passed
the blind woman sitting alone
on one of the benches,
he stopped suddenly before her
and plunged two pins,
one into each cheek.

I heard the blind woman's
terrified shrieks
as he said quietly:
"I can't understand her rage;
my ancestors would have pierced her
with javelins.
She ought to be grateful
we live in a reasonable age."

Of course they put him into the loony bin
where he shares a cell
with a distinguished anthropologist
and one other Latinist.

THE FOOL'S SONG

When I look back upon my life,
   What do I find?
   What do I find?
A single star, when I was seven,
That lit up earth and heaven;
   And here and there
   Some few wise and fair
But most, alas, unkind, unkind.

When I look back upon my days,
   What do I see?
   What do I see?
A thrush that sang from a windowsill,
Soul and ears to have their fill;
   But neighbours cried
   And my joy denied
And scared that bird, that bird, from me.

When I look back but yesterday –
   Ah, what befell?
   Ah, what befell?
A woman I told of bird and star,
Gleams and sounds that come from far;
   She brought me here
   Without sigh or tear
And bid me sing, but sing of hell.

LIFE IN THE 20TH CENTURY

He assures me
he likes my poetry
and has known grief.
Now he's all set

To turn my son against me
seduce my wife
or sell me an insurance policy.

IF I LIE STILL

If I lie still
the light from the leaves
will drop on my hands and knees

Fire will envelop me
yet I won't burn

I shall hear the silence plainly
while the stream flows into my veins
and out again

Small wild animals will no longer fear me,
but bring their young
to tickle my heels,
nuzzle in my armpits

I shall know love without disquiet
– without passion

For a thousand years
I shall lie like this
with my head toward the sun

Till knowledge and power
have become one;
then I shall write a single verse,
achieve one flawless deed

Then lie down again
to become like this shallow
stone under my hand,
and let my face
be covered with grass

To be pulled out by the roots
by what raging hermit,
his breast torn apart as mine now?

ON SPANISH SOIL

On Spanish soil how everything comes clear:
Trees that pain has twisted – but look up high,
Green leaves! The lizard with its tail snapped off
Thrusting its neck for the unswerving fly.
The stars extinct a million, million years
Burn brighter in the Mediterranean sky.

In the decayed villa of my mind, Love,
There are some playful ghosts, but most are drear;
They note the ruthless withering of the leaf
And toads straws shall tickle to death each year.
The wisp in the child's hand which once was grain
Has blown me up too beyond all joy and fear.

The mangled lizard, the caught fly, the toad
Splitting his sides in a sweet death, these seek
Me over an old trail of blood, then die.
Who'll show me I do wrong to mourn the weak
And win me from defiance and black hate
I'll take their censure though they be stones that speak!

PLEASURE

Saints and reformers are such awful pills
Who in the devil let them in
My glorious, glorious garden of sin?
And the social workers and analysts
And all their dreary kin
Of broken-backed conformists?
A leaky clap take them, one and all!

Religion and marriage can appal;
Even literary success and fame
Contrive a peculiar sense of shame.
One pleasure alone never grows less
But rather increases:
Love, your adulterous fingering
Of my overjoyed testicles.

249

EL CAUDILLO

In Spain,
Generalissimo Franco is top dog:
you know that
because in every village and town
there are at least
one *Avenida* and one *Calle*
named for him
– yet nobody speaks his name!
It's as if he didn't exist
but that some novelist
had given the alliterative title
– Generalissimo Francisco Franco –
to an obscure masterpiece
which no one reads any longer.
Still, it's this very silence
enveloping him
like the muteness believing Jews
offer their Tetragrammaton
that clinches the Caudillo's existence.
That, and the Civil Guards
wearing hats of shiny, black plastic
that hint at bull's horns.
At night, on the dark road to Denia
I saw one on a motorbike;
His back receding, the distance
made the contour of an idol's head;
and though I'm no bull worshipper,
remembering the obscene red mouth,
I can see how that grey apparition
out of the lightless groves of Crete
might turn a man's bones to water anywhere.

WHY I BELIEVE IN GOD

I was mad
when I wed
my first wife.

Plumb crazy.

Equally
was wife two
mad, quite mad,
who wed me.

Plumb crazy.

But the third
was not mad
(sane as grass,
as a bird)
nor was I
(sane as seed)
when we wed

That are now
(yes, alas)
two raving,
confounded

Lunatics.

SILLY RHYMES FOR AVIVA

A drop of viper's poison
Can still the brain of Einstein.

A stone coming down
Will break the fragile crown

Of Mozart, though behind it lie
The music of eternity.

Death with many hands struck Caesar:
Put an end to valour.

Don Juan who whored and sinned
Was turned at last to wind.

And where in all this sphere
Is the heart of Shakespeare?

Not even the philosophers can tell
What became of Hegel.

The common lizard of Spain,
The fig-tree and this field of grain

The cactus plant that appears
A parody on rabbit's ears

The grey, stone-faced mountain;
This Spanish earth, reddish-brown

The pebble under my big toe
Shall all outlast me. I know.

And someone else then come
And ere Death struck him dumb

Will think all day and write
Furiously into the night.

252

Brain, heart, valour, lust,
Thought itself fall into dust

Though Spinoza will have it said
The love of God is never dead.

Perhaps that sage man ought to know
Yet where is he to prove it so?

I, though witless, had rather be
Where I can touch and smell and see

And hear my name called
Though I'd grown frail and bald

And lacked a solitary tooth
For Death to yank out

But know my little one comes
To sniff at these silly rhymes.

THE WORM

The filthy rain
blackens the street

Knowing that you lie
this afternoon
whimpering in another man's
arms

I picture you stretched out,
a stiffened corpse

And your cold vagina
extruding
a solitary pink
worm.

253

THE LAUGHING ROOSTER

When his comb
was visibly reddening
in the early light
of the morning,
the solitary rooster
began to crow,
scattering the hills
in all directions.

When he saw
what he had done;
when he saw the crowds
of anxious people
on the roads
leading to the hills,
the rooster
– I alone heard him –
began to laugh.

To crow
would have been
out of place;
and besides
this rooster
wanted to be different.

BICYCLE PUMP

The idle gods for laughs gave man his rump;
In sport, so made his kind that when he sighs
In ecstasy between a woman's thighs
He goes up and down, a bicycle pump;
And his beloved once his seed is sown
Swells like a faulty tube on one side blown.

254

STONE-SPLITTERS IN ALICANTE

Under a dark olive tree
She dreams of a bronzed Conquistador
who'll kiss her eyes open
on hills of prefabricated homes,
this Spain that sleeps so beautifully
in the evening sun
like ripe muscatel grapes on the vine;
and that stirs herself and sighs
till the red tides of the Mediterranean
lull her to golden sleep again.

Yet not even the heavy mallets
of these coppered Spaniards
stripped to the waist and splitting stones
can hold her awake, it seems;
No, though the stones spring apart
with the violence of angered brothers
and the ringing blows
startle the underground worms.

THE CACTUS

I can imagine an airman
descending from the sky
into its dark heart and centre.

It persists there.
It stands there
beside my ripening fig-tree
like a sinister green mutant
– an eyesore
– a tenement on Third Avenue
– a fallen chandelier
– or a futuristic sculpture
Brancusi might have done,
having a green thought under a green tree.

Who can explain this thing for me
– this insane proliferation?
Mounting, mounting heavenwards
as if to crush the light
in its blind fingers,
immeasurably ridiculous
and awe-inspiring
like a corpulent tenor
flawlessly belting out an aria from La Tosca;
its misshapen conquest of space and air
its dry titter of derision
obstructing my clear view to the sea,
my neighbour's to the mountain.

From this odious ramshackle affair
of pulp-ponderous roots and shoots
will the airman finally appear,
his face torn under a comic crown
of spiky, fat-fingered polyps;
his bleeding feet, ah, shod
in the sandalshaped leaves of the cactus?

But where . . . where will he go?

BALLAD OF THE OLD SPANIARD

"Old man," I said, "it must be a trouble
To be bent as you are, nearly double.
So bowed are you, your forehead scrapes your feet,
Yet each day you parade along this street.

"Why are you not at home and in your chair
With wife or son to give affection, care?
What reason have you for disclaiming rest
When to stay by your hearth is wise and best?"

Slowly he straightened himself on his stave
And scowling, this passionate answer gave;
Though he spoke, it's true, with so muffled sound
His voice, I thought, must issue from the ground:

"You're not the first señor who on this street
Has informed me my toe and forehead meet;
Or bid me take my quiet rest at home
And leave the bright streets for *chicos* to roam.

"I shall have a long time for my repose
Where one's feet are kept away from one's nose;
I say, before the eyes are shut; the tongue, mute
One should be all fingers – the world, his fruit.

"Señor, I walked as though I wore a crown
Till Time's bandilleros brought my head down;
Yet I'm not bent with seeking for my grave:
When I meet Death I'll strike him with this stave."

He raised his stick as though to strike at me;
Then lowered it with Spanish courtesy,
And putting one hand on his shrunken thigh
With the other – stave aloft – waved good-bye.

There was a pain in my throat; in my eyes, mist
For Death's frail, quixotic antagonist:
This pair of scissors made of head and limb
That cut, as he walked, the minutes left him.

FORNALUTX

We came, sent by friends we respected.
The house, of course, was decent enough;
But heat and flies were unexpected,
Nor was water seen for cooling off.

The terraced hills made one think of hell:
I have in mind Dante's famous rungs;
Excrement, not brimstone, was the smell
When the foul air entered in our lungs.

And all winter we had planned for this;
In thought had made of it a place
Where running in paradisal bliss
We plucked the ripe fruit-bearing trees.

Who thought of the heat-stained cobblestone?
The damned who shuffled on the street?
And cheeks made pallid by a vile sun,
And rotting matter under one's feet?

We dreamed, yes, we dreamed of Fornalutx,
A fabulous realm, Oven of Light:
And indeed from shard and glass came shoots
Of numbing heat, so the name was right.

Or but half so, for the very dust
From plastered walls and the well-worn steps
Seemed buried in a film of green rust.
Light? O no! More like the dark perhaps.

But that too is not quite accurate:
I mean about the dark. The sun smoked.
That's the nearest I can come to it.
And no air stirred, and we almost choked.

Yet was it by chance that we came there,
And crossed oceans for a misspent day?
Or putting its foul breath to my ear,
What truth did Fornalutx wish to say?

ENCOUNTER

Seeing him pressed against the wall
-- an embossed aristocratic device –
why nevertheless
do I feel protective towards him
and his vulnerability
make me want to cry?

Is it because
I really wish to kill him,
to pierce him with a nail
and mess up his trim armorial?
Is that the reason why?
Is that it?

Go away, lizard, go away.
There are tears in my eyes.
It is dangerous for you to stay.

CREATION

I fashioned you:
Composed you between darkness and dawn.

You are my best-made poem,
The one I laboured longest over.

What does one do with a poem?
One gives it to the world.

Go, darling, delight others
As you have delighted me.

Bring your fragrant freshness
To lover and lover.

In their loins sow madness and fever
That my fame may endure forever.

259

THE MADDENED LOVER

At a gathering of Hampstead squires:
"I like that writer,"
said the bank manager
"he has a gentle satire
for the follies of mankind."

Idiot!
The one human I'd trust
is a deaf-mute paraplegic
– behind bars!

Monkeys and goats!
Deceit and vanity
– pitiless cruelty.
Cripples that rise from their sick beds
to beat each other
over the head
with their crutches.
Agh, filthy dogs!

With no words
terrible enough
to carry my loathing
I grab
the doting, bejewelled wife
of the eloquent banker
and screw her in the bathroom.

AT DESJARDINS

He: executive suite,
a moneyed lout;
she: a middle-aged harpy,
a hunk of powdered
and perfumed meat,
waiting for him
to clean his plate
and drop dead.

What amorous,
open-eyed poet
could be bothered
cursing them?
Look at them.
When all is said,
aren't they cursed
enough, my friends,
as is?

But the waitress
by their silence
knows the poisoned
meat they eat,
and with practised grin

Gives each a glass
of clear water;
and removing the dishes,
her good wishes
for a quick digestion.

HOMAGE TO LUCULLUS

Each year
the repressed virgins
bring me their poems:
sad epodes, quatrains
and from the more daring
free verse
shy and tentative
as the first puddles in spring
a warmer sun will soon blot out.

Ah, Lucullus is that sun!

For espying them,
before long
he's taught them the pleasures
of love;
they've other sheets for soiling
and they leave off
writing their empty
verses.

And you say
Lucullus
has done nothing
for poetry!

AT THE IGLESIA DE SACROMONTE

A death's head
from which falls away
a black soutane,
he conducts me
and the three withered nuns
from Pamplona
through his catacomb of horrors.

Complete with hairy lip
and decaying stumps of tooth,
the three withered nuns
from Pamplona
kiss relic and bloodstained bars
asking for intercession.

As they kneel and mumble
I hear reverberate
in cave and cell
the running bulls of Pamplona.

A LIFE

Thirty years, mused the pulitzered
    biographer
– the first volume of his fierce
extravagant life at last done.

I know what that fabulous man
wore on May 5, 1827
what papers he dictated with his breakfast
and why he regarded his eldest daughter
    with distaste.
I know his thoughts better than my own.

Were you impressed with his stature,
I was asked the following day
    by the curious sun-bathers.
Yes, I said, he was very short.

COAL

I no longer understand the simplest things.

When I loved that woman
and my nights were sleepless
for thinking of her kisses
that fell on my body live coals,
for all my great art
I was inarticulate
and I could not praise her
but moaned like a swollen filthy stream
under her amorous fingers.

Now that I loathe her
and hourly wish her dead,
the remembering of her lips
fires my heart, my imagination
so that I see her kisses
drop from her curved mouth
black coal from a filthy coalsack.
My thoughts flow endlessly
and I cannot stop writing for her
poem after poem.

AMBIVALENCY

I forsake my home
    and direct my steps
to the library
where poets and lovers
have left all their wisdom
    for safe-keeping.

Hell, some monstrous god
    twists my feet around
and turns me towards your abode:
I tell myself I won't ever come
    to see you
even as I ring your doorbell.

VICTORY

Only one woman I have met
with the humble and absolute dignity
of a turtle.

I can imagine
the sober wisdom of the earth
laid against her instep
and drawn as the sap is drawn
into her eyes
—so the women of Aeschylus must have looked once.

I can imagine undressing her
and staring all day
at her pudendum, dark in the fierce sun.

I shall set two caterpillars
on the white road towards her—
small Cyprian brushes;
and on her brown secreting skin
drop leaves the morning sun
has smeared with olive oil.

The plucked leaves will die;
the staring eyes, fail;
only the caterpillars, patient and hurried,
(O ripples of absurdity)
shall gain her thigh.

AMBIGUITIES OF CONDUCT

He was telling me
how important love was,
lamenting the atrophy
of human emotion
in our mechanical age.

It was apparent
he was well up
in Lawrence and Kierkegaard;
moreover, the man was sincere.

Even if, later,
he deliberately flicked
his cigarette ash
into a flowercup
where a black insect
was crawling.

But neither the sizzle
nor the scream
(which I alone heard)
interrupted his excited
words of love.

AT THE PIER IN DENIA

Three doncellas, three lovely criadas
– *hermosas!* – ripe-bosomed;
and three young men,
their skins darkened by the sun.

Such hair, such necks
for stroking;
such bosoms, which seen,
starving men might turn from melons;
eyes, *ojos*, that when raised
from the books they're reading
are clouded with love.

They sigh, reading *True Romance*
– Spanish version –
but ignore the suntanned caballeros
that squat behind them:
three stunned bulls.

What's between the thighs
is a baby-making device
– nothing else,
says the tough old priest
who rides to church on a motorbike
and speaks as if he knows.

So the doncellas
sit sighing on a pier
and the young caballeros, strong-loined,
simper – and glance
over the shapely, kissable shoulders
at *True Romance*.

With people this credulous
why should I work?
I shall sell flypaper
in the middle of the Mediterranean
and buy gold earrings
with sand or cork.

ENGLISH FOR IMMIGRANTS

Each Wednesday evening their knees
Pressed together like a pair of saints
They pivot on pencils and with eyes for aprons
Gather the lessonwords "books" and alien "hills"
While from the curve of their backs I take my flight—
A hawk, I exhibit the white grubs under my hand.

Then my birdcall scatters their eyes like chicks
And I am Caesar I cry I am Saint Francis,
I am this misty slate and a lump of chalk;
They only climb from their steep silence and stare.
So I call for the raven in their throats
And their cleft tongues toss on a bed of fever.

Yet from me, a hawk, they take whatever feather
Can start their heavy wishes under a stone,
When a May evening that is shaped by thunder
With gramophones and smiles shall graduate
Forty amphipods pointing flutes at heaven.

SUDDEN THAW

Icicles zigzagged across the page,
A ready graph for the winter's rage;
And sidestreets mock-heroically
Burned white like tusks of ivory;
The wind crowed through a million cocks—

    And thieves were picking at my locks.

As if a tyrant had changed his mind,
Told his subjects he wished to be kind;
Or like Charles V who took to a cloister,
The frost is nowhere—
Though I once heard Ravel on a saw,
Nothing unsettles like sudden thaw:

The snow shows darkly under your heels,
In places it looks like oyster shells,
The wakes of autos are like fat eels,
The sidestreets blossom with lovely smells;
Men are raising a shout in the town,
It might even bring the System down—

The thieves ran off with the wig of a clown.

QUESTIONS

Why is it
that when a man says
he's a realist,
his mouth, his eyes
at once
become fierce and ugly
and he looks
as if he's about
to wipe out
your whole family?
And why is it
when a woman says,
"I love you"
her mouth begins
to work curiously
as if she were getting ready
for a meal?
And why haven't the poets
made more
of the fact
that man is the only animal
who sings
and has hæmorrhoids?

269

OUR COMMON FUTURE

Ehrenburg wishes to know
What's happened to satire;
Clearly, the fellow's perplexed,
Paces his dacha, vexed,
Muttering, "Where did it go?"
Searches for it high and low,
Under the grey cement bags,
Under carpets—even rags! —
To turn it up with his toe.

Do pillows explode, and do
Dead ashes support a fire?
Unsifted, men wish to live,
Their thoughts sweetening the hive
While Sputniks float in full view
Like metal geese, two by two.
From cement bags, dear Ilya,
Is poured our common future:
A neutral dust with no hue.

ON THE ASSASSINATION OF PRESIDENT KENNEDY

When evil has become our normal climate
when madness stares from each ignoble eye
and the good develop a nervous stutter;
when husbands and wives devour each other
when sons pant to see their fathers die
or stalk their own shadows for the kill,
nullity from a cloud of dust zeros
to a rifle bore in forsaken Dallas.

My stricken coevals, say aloud with me:
The crackbrain with aim that might not miss
who made our noble prince crumple
like a withered stalk in his wife's arms
has but given the age its wanting symbol:
a Greek tragedy without catharsis.

270

WHY THE HARES STARE AND RUN

All summer long
I've walked this country road.
When I'm too near
the hares raise their hindparts
impertinently
and leap out of sight,
making enough turbulence
among the leaves
to let me know they're still there.
After a stretch of road
they reappear
and the same thing happens over again.
They look like shrunken deer.

But why is it
I never meet anyone
with a book of verse under his arm
and a walking-stick scuffing the stones?
What must I think?
Am I the last human
who still loves the smell of earth
– to feel the sun in his bones?
Is that why the hares
stare at me and run?

DISCOURSE ON CHRISTIAN LOVE

Frantic love of the Divine
Burns out common affection:
So it was that Augustine
Thinking concubinage sin
Abandoned child and wife
To essay the holy life.
And gentleman John Milton,
Regicide and Puritan,
Wrote a Christian epic
But turned his daughters sick.
Who would not walk in fear
Of one that camped this near
The precinct of Love and Light?
His harassed dame in fright
Prayed fervently no doubt
For sweet Christ to help her out
And bend his rod and fish in
One whose thoughts were all on Him.
Blaise Pascal, grown early sick
Of genius, turned ascetic
And fastening a girdle on
Fitted with spikes of iron
Punctured his erring skin
If appetite stirred in him.
From love's boon he made a sword
To serve his Master and Lord:
For though he praised the kind heart
Above science and mere art,
He railed at his kin Gilberte
And shrieked she wanted merit.
The cause? She showed affection
All mothers do for children!
Kierkegaard was another
Who made a noisy pother
About Love, Love, Love – though none
Had a heart so squeezed from stone.

Did he pen his books to prove
Anyone may write of love,
That even the loveless man
Should he set his mind to – can?
'Love' drool Auden and Eliot:
It's what neither one has got.
In each age cynics observe
Injunctions to love for love serve
– Writing them is less labour
Than to delight one's neighbour!
But when he lived Jesus
Won men's hearts through kindness;
And loved is the thoughtless boy
Who lives in the moment's joy.

INNOCENCE

How does one tell
one's fourteen-year-old daughter
that the beautiful
are the most vulnerable
and that a rage
tears at the souls
of humans
to corrupt innocence
and to smash butterflies
to see their wings
flutter in the sun
pulling weeds and flowers
from the soil:
and that all, all
go under the earth
to make room for more
weeds and flowers
– some more beautiful than others?

SECOND THOUGHT ON THE ARMADA

In immoral Spain
where there's no Liquor Commission,
no excited little Baptist,
no clean-jawed Methodist,
no Anglo-Saxon
with dirty sex on his brain,
I never saw a single drunk.

Cognacs and wines are that cheap
no Canadian would ever go to sleep,
but drink
as though he were back home:
the poor, miserable fuck-up!

Back home
in Calgary on a Saturday night
the drunks drop like flies
on their moral sidewalks.
In Toronto seething with alcohol
and Baptist virtue
they vomit and fall.
They do.

Have you ever seen a lush put it down
in Halifax or Saint John?

Immoral Spain
send us Philip II again!

274

THE TRAGIC POET

He affirmed life.

He affirmed it
as though it were an extraordinary
rock melon, ripe,
and his discovery.

And with yelps of gladness
he affirmed the brave toilers;
and affirmed the martyrs
whose burning flesh
sizzled hosannahs.

In despair
of ever equalling the courage
he had himself endowed them with
he stepped thoughtfully
before a chauffeur-driven car.

To the end
he praised the beautiful courage
of workers and martyrs,
and expiring at the finish
of a long siren screech
died as he had lived

affirming life.

INJUSTICE

Book in hand, tree-shade to keep off the sun,
I cried out from my comfortable fence:
"Justice, divine or human, there is none;
Look at these sweating Spaniards crushing stone,
Who reeling serve out a lifetime sentence
For a spasm in bed that was not their own!"

GIFT

Under the despoiled tree,
her park seat
soft with golden leaves,
the wrinkled
disconsolate woman
crimsons her lips.

A breeze
detaches the last
red leaf
and lays it
at her feet.

THE GIRAFFE

When I saw the sick giraffe
At first I began to laugh;
Yet scanning the rueful face
Laughs, I knew, were not in place.

One does not laugh at death
Even though the corpse draw breath;
Or gibe at a crippled man
Standing erect as he can.

Lives there one who will not weep
To see the cut worm still creep;
And who mocks at drunks who look
Morosely at their own puke?

Unsmiling I turned away:
What could I or the gods say
Who saw unhealed in the beast's eyes
The knit cut between the thighs?

276

AEROLITES

1. Up there, up there on high
   To all of us who crawl and die
   God shows his buttocks in the sky

2. My wife is sitting
   Demure and neat
   Knitting the socks
   For my graveyard feet

3. This is the world's acquired acumen:
   To sin privately and speak well of Good;
   Gumboil, the censor, who sees me with this woman
   Would be the first to rape her, if he could

4. Hear wisdom, my son,
   Hear wisdom and live:
   Heroes win medals
   That smart men give

5. I loved my city, my Montreal,
   But found the burghers monsters all:
   For seven percent or ready cash
   They would turn me quickly into ash

6. I was half in love with Death at night
   But saw a hearse stop for the traffic light;
   The light glowed like an inflamed eye
   And would not let the corpse go by

7. Married a woman with the face of an ox
   Yet she was much more sly than the slyest fox;
   I love you I love you I love you she said
   I'll love you I'll love you till you are dead

I SAW A FAUN

I saw a faun on Somerled Avenue;
a disc jockey had slipped him my address
under last year's Stanley Cup
because my countrymen were costive
from eating too many lies
as if they were waffles
with a side order of bacon.
He liked Mozart and Chopin
and held an unseen transistor radio
between his greenish ankles
as if the throbbing notes were nerve-endings.
He said he could foretell
when my mistress would take a new lover
if she climbed down a maple tree
dressed in nothing but my thoughts of her
– the material didn't matter;
and could make known the outbreak of wars
to Arab oil millionaires
and to politicians with oversized balls.
He called himself a star-mender.
His face made the air around him sweet.
I dipped my darling's maternity bra in it,
also my nylon jockstrap.
I noticed my department-store cufflinks
didn't tarnish
as long as he kept looking at them.
His laughter
turned insurance agents and social workers
into frozen potato peels at my feet.
Whenever he pranced
the snow really sparkled like snow;
even professors of Englit
when they pranced on the same spot sparkled.
In fact the whole street was lit up
with the sound of Xmas bells
and everyone confessed his fears
to his worst enemy.
The churches and synagogues told God
he was free to go whenever he wished.
I gave up cancer.

He wanted me to dance with him
but I was explaining just then
some copybook maxims
to a former Prime Minister
and the male's anatomy
to Charlotte Whitton.
He was killed uncrossing a street.
The rains melted him into earth and brown leaves.
The snows buried everything
except a silver fingernail
that kept glinting at me
like a slice of ice wanting to be noticed
until I closed the window
on some broken stars
and made myself a cup of tea.
Melba toast is good too
or a twenty-year-old virgin
if you can get her
to spread herself like jam.

MRS. POTIPHAR

The worst is at night when I lie beside him,
When the sheets are hot and sticky,
And it is all over with me,
And the vomit is forming at the bottom of my throat.

Then the room is quite still except for his breathing,
And he can't awaken for I've wished him dead;
Even the jackals are amazed
At his lumpish face and such quiet breathing.
They stare at him with greedy merchant eyes.

Only young lovers can be forgiven
A lumpish head and such easy breathing,
Their cool bodies
Twisting like black flames . . .
We are none of us what we seem.
Lies. Lies. Lies.

I'm a good wife. I keep busy. If he complains
I stop whatever I'm doing.

Then O his dead eyes open and you stare at me
From your dark rabbinical face
And your earlobes are like fine droplets of glass
As I bend to your lips with my open mouth.

Why don't you always kiss me like that . . .
Why don't you spit on me
On my adulterous teats

Try not to be afraid
Try not to hate me
O I have made you sad . . .
May Anubis forgive me
I have made you sad.

BLUE AND LOVELY, MY LOVE

Blue and lovely, my Love,
are the butterflies on your shoulders.
I heard you sing for them
when you were false to everything
including the snapshot of my grandmother
I gave you under the evening star.
They shovelled me into the cold earth
but I heard your singing;
I was bone and ash but I heard your singing;
I was ash but I still heard you.
It is no longer you or your voice
that torments me;
It's the blue butterflies looking for me
between the tall grasses
that grow from stilled desire and disdain
as if they were my hands reaching for your face.

HOMO OECONOMICUS

A whole society was reared
On Marx's carbuncles and beard;
The repressions of Herr Hegel
Interfuse the General Will
That seeks for each more liberty
By forcing all men to be free
And makes the heretic a foe.
His mad precursor was Rousseau.
The poet's visions or the saint's,
The mad ecstacies mystics paint;
Erasmus, Spinoza, the best
Of Leveller and Anabaptist
Have all by strange ways led to this:
A heaven of consumers' bliss
Where never the seed of Adam
Shall cry for conscience or freedom
But huge coupons to get and spend
On products produced without end,
Their one god reverenced truly
The insatiable belly
And their most radiant vision
A supermarket on the moon.
From everywhere comes up the stench
Of technology's *massenmensch*,
Not a man really, but a tool.
Frightened, alienated, dull;
A machine part, replaceable
Or thrown away as scrap; a null
Without brain, perplexity, heart,
Without philosophy or art.
The incitements of a great love?
What! Are you mad? In a bee-hive!
At the behest of the good State
Like insects he and his kind mate.
Their induced delights useful for
Enlarging the labour force or

Adding another voiceless shout
When a Leader is in or out.
O world where the chiefest concern
Of commissar, physician
Is to stock the proper drugs, smiles,
To prevent either cramps or piles!
Where zombies read their bulletin
And dispense with holiness, sin;
Where Mind's replaced by the Vozhd's speech,
The barked command, the radio's screech
Or the rebel's prophetic wrath
By smile & nod of bureaucrat;
And that which true men once named Art,
By some Ukrainian's burp or fart.

MY QUEEN, MY QUEAN

The rain falls on the street.
All this day I have passed
Thinking of your deceit:
Betrayals born of lust,
A woman's vanity.

If I rail who hears me?
Hearing, what man won't grunt?
Open a vicious eye
And say the world's a sty;
You – its prized ornament?

Shall I speak of honour?
Among liars and thieves?
He pants to get on her,
Warm nose in her cockmuff
That sneers the slut deceives!

The rain smashes the leaves
And blurs the windowpane.
Let poets say it grieves.
"Money and a good stuff"
I think is its refrain.

A modern man can't curse:
Lust is your best excuse.
Yet shall my speech be coarse;
My angry words a fuse
Smouldering in a verse.

There is no right or wrong,
Love is a madman's dream
And I must hold my tongue
Where pigs and pygmies roam
And you're my queen, my quean.

LUST

Desire
without reverence

is lust.

I know that
    by the way
my phallus stands up
at sight of you.

I could stab
you
    with it,
plunging it again
    and again
into the vile softness
    of your body
that I might see
your eyes glaze up
with death
    as once with sex.

Once the arms
that held you
    held glory,
held love and delight;
now when I leave
your embrace
    small vipers
fall from my moist armpits,
vermin,
and I am sick with hate.

LOGOS

If thinking of the mad things I've done
For your white shoulders and sapphire eyes;
How my hands across your breasts will run
Even as you mock me with your lies

Or that my soul lives between your thighs
Like a seed stuck to a moist furrow;
Or that submerged in Eros' narrow
Straits for its periscope it cries and cries:

I come suddenly on some bush, ferns,
Cove grass, or birds that flock after flock
Spring from the deep gorges the sun burns:
Lizards running into clefts of rock

I laugh and praise the Dionysian
Everywhere irrational thrust
That sends meteors spilling into dust,
This enchantment risen in the bone.

AFTERMATH

So composed you sit, and so ladylike;
Not blurring or slurring a single word
As you define for me Portuguese wines,
Africa, grief, and Napoleon III.

Are you that woman I gripped in my arms
Five minutes ago — eyes glazed, bubbling spit,
And moaning so loud the Pope must have heard?
You must be, but God, who would believe it!

PORTRAIT OF NOLADY

What does one do with a woman
   who when I send her a poem
praising her ears, her delicate parts,
reads it in turn

   to each of her lovers,
to scald them with jealousy,
to drive them further insane?

A woman, she's as evil as she dares be,
as cruel. No fool,
   she knows it's easier
to possess her
than be possessed
   by the finicky Muse!

I could have her whipped;
   with a safety razor
slash deep red trenches
from welt to welt.

No, she'd only display them
   to her maddened lovers;
taunt them mockingly
in this too to rival me.

Faithful to no man,
she must prove all men contemptible;
seeking to vindicate
   her betrayals,
each betrayal makes her more vicious.

THE SEDUCTION

First he knocks her down
    by assaulting her soul;
telling her she's vain, superficial,
and adding – to drive his point home –
    that she's frivolous
and terribly, terribly selfish.

She takes the bait
    like the blonde fish she is
and for whole weeks goes about
beating her lovely breasts
    till her niplets
look like congealed drops of blood.
O she's full of remorse,
    full of remorse for all
her past egocentric, thoughtless ways,
and she sighs and cries a great deal.

Remorse in women
    is a sure-fire aphrodisiac:
they can't bear to be thought less than perfect
and so their contrition
is actually a variant form of vanity
and vanity is a great quickener
    of the sexual appetite.
Everything about them, in fact, is false
except passion; only in their desire
for intercourse are they completely sincere.

This with a priest's cunning my rival knew
    as well as I myself now do:
Judging her sufficiently broken,
    humbled and contrite,
he thinks the moment exactly right
    to toss her some small compliment
    as one tosses a bone to a famished bitch.

(He praised, I think, her fidelity to friends).
The colour swoops back into her cheeks,
her eyes put on their fetching impertinence,
for the first time in weeks she laughs.

She's grateful,
    and when a woman is grateful
she has many ways of expressing her sense
of the occasion
but naturally prefers the easiest
    and most pleasant one.
In this, my Lucy was no exception.
Her gratitude is immense,
yet no greater than the provocation had been
which now stretches her out
    in perfect humility
while he rises beautifully to the occasion.
He dazes her with sweet, forgiving kisses
and all the long and lazy afternoon
    they're mutual as thieves in a cell
and, ah, tender as they come.

SUTRA

It is hard to keep the mind
evenly balanced,
said the Buddha.

But that is not so;
my mind
is evenly balanced
on the two buttock cheeks
of my beloved.

And poised perfectly
on what is around
and below.

289

THE LIZARD

Curiously, the light around him
makes an arc,
a broken halo.

Something has stumbled into it!

And the neat, heraldic emblem
on the wall of my whitewashed villa
is – presto! – changed into a miniature boat:
tiny oars of invisible galley-slaves
move it toward the waiting moth.

A pause: a sudden stretch of the neck
and the dark spot's gone. No dry cleaner
could do better.

The lizard rejoices because I read
Pascal and other religious thinkers at night
who've much to say about conscience and grace;
for the light by which I read them
brings the summer insects to his mouth:
gauzy-winged creatures
with wings like small sails.

Well, that's one won't go sailing any more.

Greedy lizard, you've bolted nearly a score!

AT THE ALHAMBRA

I sat where Grenadine kings
had once swept by,
thinking on Rey Boabdil
the last and unluckiest of them
– pleasure-loving, melancholy poet
unapt to defend himself –
and my heart went out
to those proud, indolent lovers of beauty
who had taken no cognizance
of death
but out of fountain and fern
had composed a poem
of living, perpetual praise;
and I arose, startling
the scented shadows from their flowerbeds,
and the painted birds from their bough
to cry from my desolate tower:
"I am a Moor
I have come home, I have come home!"

SUCCESS

I've always wanted
to write
a poem
with the word
'zeugma'
in it.

Now I've done it!

DAS WAHRE ICH

She tells me she was a Nazi; her father also.
Her brother lies buried under the defeat
    and rubble of Stalingrad.
She tells me this, her mortal enemy, a Jew.

We are twenty years removed from war.
She urges on me candied biscuits and tea,
and her face is touched by a brief happiness
when I praise her for them and for the mobiles
    she has herself fashioned
in the comfortless burdensome evenings.

Her face is sad and thin as those mobiles
moving round and round in the small wind
my voice makes when I thank her
and she bows her frail proud head into her hands.

The terrible stillness holds us both
and stops our breath
while I wonder, a thrill stabbing into my mind:
"At this moment, does she see my crumpled form
    against the wall,
blood on my still compassionate eyes and mouth?"

IN MEMORY OF STEPHEN WARD

I salute you, Stephen Ward,
England's last poet
asking: "What's wrong with fornication?"

After that, what forgiveness?
None. There never is
for the poet who's not
a blubbering liar;
who, unhinging the fatal door,
shows print of goat's foot
on the Embankment;
under the stiff, black bowler
horns of a distressed satyr.

In your comic masterpiece
the titled and rich, the Oxonian scholar
ran naked on all fours
to rub noses with a whore.
On scented sheets
you made class distinctions disappear.
Perfect your management
of conceit and measure
– poète maudit!
– ironist!

And you were great
in enjoyment
as well as craft;
your very leave-taking, yes,
in its elegant disgust and weariness
was that of a poet.
Mayakovsky would have understood,
Seneca, applauded.

"I shall disappoint the vultures."

With that you wrote your own epitaph.

An immortal one, as it happens.

293

EVERYWHERE, THE STINK

Everywhere,
the stink of human evil

Godlike men
in their zenith
are cut down by rifle fire

Urbanites pluck trophies
from their stricken Air-god
(128 killed);
around the smoking limbs
break into ritual dance

A fruit clerk smiling &
exposing two gold teeth
brags he severed
the arms of a Russian infant

Lesbians owning degrees
from Vassar, McGill
show colour slides
of the women they seduce

And one I loved, who knew glory,
washes her face
in the piss of her criminal lover:
says it makes her eyes sparkle

No wonder of late
I've taken to looking
at the sky
in impotent perplexity

In the black night
I hear a man cry:
"The world's coming to an end!"

Lacking his faith,
I go on writing my poems

FOR MY FORMER STUDENTS

Warning against the special poisons
   North America distils;
against the love of possessions
and the possible loss of selfhood:

I blew them into the waiting streets
   with words so fierce
the telephone poles came crashing down
and birds suffered from cracked wingbones.

Now they remember me, if at all,
as an embarrassing *lapsus linguae*
that one recalls
   with pleasure and fondness;
as a man might remember stealing apples
over a fence

And passing me
   in their expensive cars,
think they have left me far behind.

NEIGHBOUR LOVE

A grove
of tall offending trees
separates our cottages

Bang! Bang!

Jesus! how can I love my neighbour
when each morning, hour after hour,
even before the first bird has cheeped
he's out driving nails into boards and plinths?

What a racket!
Excusable only if he's building
his own coffin, a six-foot bungalow
by the placid lake

May the hammer fly from his hand,
his body suddenly shrivel
and a crazy carpenter hack off his tool
to use as a plug for a small knothole

Or let him live to be old as Nestor
and the hideous noise he makes
without let-up ring in his ears
but amplified a thousand thousandfold

No, may his next-door neighbour
drive a long shining nail into his skull
so that I can compose verses
and love my neighbour again.

FOR MY GREEN OLD AGE

Your eyes, lips, voice:
these I could withstand;
but when you unbuttoned your blouse
to show me the pink shapeliness
                          of your breasts,
my fingers like five sentinels
trembled with surprise;
warts and all my wisdom I sang away
and the cigarette's irresolute ash
splashed on my stiff trouser leg like water.

Was it a beautiful woman's malice
or her mockery
made you turn and say,
standing there like Eve's naked daughter:
        "Since you cannot find the ashtray,
how will you what's between my thighs?"

Whatever, and who cares:
when I am a greyhead full of years
I shall tell the priests and rabbis
about your gaiety
and of how to keep my hand from trembling
you pressed it between your thighs.

MAKE MINE VODKA

Change

There may be, comrades,
as you say, no God;
but there is death.
And the grass,
no matter what's buried
under it,
comes up smelling fresh and sweet.

Mysteries

Comrade Mikoyan,
why do you go on living?

Flower in a crannied wall . . .
but if I knew
why Comrade Mikoyan
wishes to go on living
(and goes on living)
I would understand
me, and thee, and all.

The Wave of the Future

The East Germans
are not running away
from Communism;
they're just coming
to tell us,
somewhat breathlessly,
how wonderful it all is.

Russian Intellectual & Collective Leadership

Now that the great Stalin is dead and gone,
He has five holes to smell instead of one.

Red Square

Evgeny Evtushenko,
fable-maker
and world-famous successor
to Pushkin, finds
angry young men
a phenomenon of the West.
COMRADES: bourgeois skin inflammations!

His own country
being declared perfect,
no one with eyes to see
would ever think to complain
—certainly no Russ poet,
great lover of life & freedom.

O SAY CAN YOU SEE

When I read somewhere
that Amerigo Vespucci
had been a pork butcher
and finance agent
in prosperous Florence,
I saw at once
the Muse of History
was a meticulous poet
with a fine sense
of the fitness of things.

299

MEXICO AS SEEN BY
THE REVERENT DUDEK

The jungle is, and is not, everything.
Culture is, and is not, everything:
but the buttocks
and breasts of the Mexican women
        have something to them; as have
the enormous frogs that made a mess
of our woven carpets, the dogs sniffing,
and the flies everywhere:
(Evil is in the woof of reality
yet the whole is good, is good!)

And when, ah, a young cow submerged,
for a long time
        I wondered what that meant.
The water rippled over the unseen tail
and I thought of eddies, and galaxies,
        and fierce reptilian orgasms.
O time flowing invisibly through wet hairs!
O constellations and death!

Nevertheless, we have arrived
        after looking death in the face
and giving money to beggars
(I give, therefore I am)
and finding, after much travail,
after much meditation
        in deserted village squares,
out of the jungle come the singing birds
and all turns by design
in my mind, O Love.

And the little hills are something
one travels up and down.

REDEMPTION

I murdered a bird
of rarer plumage
and delight
than the albatross.

Echoing
in the cold chambers
of the sky,
its final scream
has stunned my ear-drums
for ever.

Forgive, forgive me, woman.

Redemption comes,
but never
in the form
we think it will.

And we are broken
on no wheel
of our own choosing.

WINTER LIGHT

With you
I am negated and fulfilled

In you and through you
I am perpetuated and destroyed,
the child of our furious blood
a phantom hand touching
pregnant summer cloud
and perishing seed

Shiva dances on Somerled avenue
and in our bedroom

A million roosters cry up the sun;
at night when we embrace
we hear the silence of God.

ESTHETIQUE

Good poems should rage like a fire
Burning all things, burning them with a great splendour.

One wrapt flame at noontide blends
The seer's inhuman stare, the seaweed's trance.

And poems that love the truth tell
All things have value being combustible.

Out of rubbish burning and burning comes
Mozartian ecstasy leaping with the flames.

F. R. SCOTT

Drops his arm
on your shoulder
     like a heavy plastic;
drives a witticism
into your thick, dull skull;
waits for the smiles
              to start
in your eyes, roll down
your cheeks;
     espies
another: undubbed, virginal,
and leaves you gasping
     your delight.

For all that,
weary of his too clear sight,
his icy brain,
would rather be
     an ignorant Italian
grinding his hurdy-gurdy
for coppers
     under a lady's balcony.

Even if, friskily,
he lifts high
     his long, tailored legs,
and higher . . . so . . . so . . .
making one wonder
what tormenting ghost
has got him by the ankle
     and won't let go.

BAUDELAIRE IN A SUMMER COTTAGE

He sports his son's peaked cap;
Thinks, under his wife's prodding,
His dispraise of Baudelaire
Has somehow offended me
And blurts out at suppertime,
His glass of Chablis twinkling,
His blue boyish eyes twinkling:
"You . . . *you're* a fine poet, man;
Superb craftsman. Superb." Looks
Conspiratorially
To his wife for approval
And adjusts his son's peaked cap.
She, intelligent and French,
(Really, need one add to this?)
Who considers me – all men,
The vegetation itself,
A raging impetigo
Covering our sad planet,
Smiles therapeutically
At her husband, pats his hand;
While I again grieve over
The future of poetry,
I mean: communication
Passionate and unrehearsed
Between warm men and women;
Seeing the cancer spreading fast,
Destroying self-expression,
Destroying uniqueness, force,
And that which makes intercourse
Between humans sweet and good,
I mean: authenticity.
So I say, "Yes, Baudelaire
Though mad was free as the air
And so's every true poet."
And look at the jerk's burnt face,
Thankful he is not quite dead
Who has one ballock snipped off
And one hanging by a thread.

A DEDICATION

Somewhere, alone in a rented room
a man is smoking a pipe under an orange lampshade.
His glasses, mirroring an empty wall, are blind;
the book under them has already declared bankruptcy.
Below his window, gabled roofs have put on their astrakhans
    for the winter.

A modern, complete with briefcase and fountain pens,
he's dogmatic as a parade sergeant though uncertain
whether the voice he's just attended to
was that of God or Satan's.
The church spire fronting him is of no help,
pointing in one direction only like a jammed compass
    needle;
and the wind's noise open to conflicting interpretations.
Like bankers radiant at convention tables
    the lights of the city blink their unconcern.

He only knows, this strange man,
that through dense Nothingness somehow he must open
a path to power and insight – to freedom
though he and his brief azure soon afterwards
be swallowed up in the night air for ever.
When all the lights are put out, the buildings darkened,
he blesses a snowflake – a solitary particle of light
expiring on the black fire escape
    and gladly dying in its death, lives.

Therefore I've written this poem for him.

EL GUSANO

From the place where I was sitting
I watched the weary stone-splitters
Building a road to blot out the sun;
And seeing their sweating bodies
In the merciless, mid-day heat
I wished I could do it for them:
Turn it out like a light, I mean.
And I almost rose up to do so
When my eyes suddenly picked out
A strange, never-before-seen worm
Making its way on the dried leaves.
It had a rich, feudal colour,
Reddish-brown like the Spanish soil
And knew its way among the stones
So plentiful in Alicante.
I love lizards and toads; spiders, too
And all humped and skin-crinkled creatures
But most in love I am with worms.
These sages never ask to know
A man's revenue or profession;
And it's not at antecedents
Or at class that they draw their line
But will dine with impartial relish
On one who splits stones or sells fish
Or, if it comes to that, a prince
Or a generalissimo.
Bless the subversive, crawling dears
Who here are the sole underground
And keep alive in the country
The idea of democracy.
I gave it a mock-Falangist
Salute and it crawled away; or
Was it the stone-splitters frightened
The worm off and the brittle noise
Of almond-pickers? It vanished
Under a dusty dried-up leaf
For a restful snooze in the ground
But I imagine it now tunnelling
Its hard way to Andalusia
Faithful to the colourful soil

Under the villas and motels
Of those whose bankers let them stow
Ancient distinctions and treasure
In the rear of their foreign cars.

O plundered, sold-out, and lovely
Shore of the Mediterranean:
This worm shall knit the scattered plots
Of your traduced, dismembered land;
And co-worker of wave and wind,
Proud, untiring apostle to
The fragrant and enduring dust,
Carry its political news
To Castile and to Aragon.

A POCKETFUL OF RYE

Poets praise, I pray you, Nancy
Who bends her limbs to suit my fancy;
O the road to heaven lies
Through her cool accustomed thighs.

Poets leave, I pray you, reason;
Put thought behind you for a season:
Let my blessed Nancy show
How I make her nipples grow.

How I make her nipples grow
Let my blessed Nancy show;
Poets leave, I pray you, reason
Put thought behind you for a season.

Through her cool accustomed thighs
O the road to heaven lies;
Poets praise, I pray you, Nancy
Who bends her limbs to suit my fancy.

307

ZOROASTRIAN

I want nothing
to ever come
between me and the sun

If I see a jetplane
I shall shoot it down

Philosophies
religions:
so many fearful excuses
for not letting the sun
nourish one
and burn him to a cinder

Look at the skeletons
of those oaks:
the proud flame of life
passed through them
without their once having heard
of Jesus or Marx

VARIATIONS ON A THEME BY SHAKESPEARE

We're all psychic scavengers
and so much rubbish;
this makes work for all hands.

My darling,
praised for her adorable ass,
grown suddenly perverse
adorns it with a pair of long ears;
and Lelia thinks my body
a towel to wipe her hands on;
women are hopeless
—the worst offenders.

My brother,
now mean and rich
after a lifetime of struggle
says, "I shall never let you starve."
There are real tears in his eyes.

And the poor shits
that make up the world
—vicious and blind—
with the stones they've flung
build monuments
to the slain prophets.

Taking the hint,
I've invested my money
in property
that yields seventeen per cent.
At last I know peace of mind;
sleep like a narcotized nun
dreaming levi'd apostles.

ON REREADING THE BEATS

If only it were *that* easy to write poems

Look at me, I'm standing on my head
Look at me, I'm whacking my doodle
Look at me, I'm making paste out of earwax
Look at me, I'm pissing into a flowerpot:
    the steam rises and hisses, "Saint-Saens"

O if it were that easy

To take American brag, American ignorance, American
vulgarity, American provincialism & superficiality,
American prevarication & hucksterism, and watch them
expand & expand like a non-illuminating gas till they
filled up the largest warehouse in San Francisco or the
biggest emporium in Chicago; and then to paste a label
on the forehead of the building in large block letters
for everyone from the President down to see:

POETRY ADMISSION FREE

If poetry cd. forget its origin in song & metaphor; cd.
forget it was genuine like Alp snow or childbirth; cd.
be sold over the counter like olives booze; held up
like a stagecoach in a phoney Wild West and made to stand
& deliver; or become the nation's official con game like
Italian Enalotto or our own Bingo before the cops stepped in
and scattered it to the outlying paroisses.

DeTocqueville, you are justified
De Tocqueville, you are vindicated
De Tocqueville, you were dead right

From the debased amorphous mobs pouring out
of the American megalopoli like exhaust fumes
blackening kiosks & storefronts what else but:
megalomania, narcissism, hysteria, effeminacy,
coarseness, ignobility, and the mindless iteration
about LOVE ad nauseam
                              Faugh!
And COMRADESHIP and BROTHERHOOD

O these swine that need collective showers for cleansing!

They almost make me prefer
    the Eton boys & eunuchs of England
—almost I said almost
At least the Beats have vitality!
Yet vitality proves nothing except that something is alive
So is a polecat; so is a water-rat
Excitation is not excitement; and energy is fine, boys,
but who admires the energy of a self-flagellant or sadist?
Consider the animation of a garbage heap in mid-August: its
    seethe & flow of maggots; you may never hope to equal that,
and be advised the frenzy of a trapped bluebottle is not poetic
Moreover you ought to be ashamed to hide between the flowing
    robes of Plato & Buddha
    with evil-smelling dung on your fingers
If you must retch at the sight of your smeared fingers
    do so decently, in privacy & in your own sinks
Above everything, do not hold a pen with them and write about
    your lovely desires. No one will believe you,
least of all your comrades
    who will measure and know you, quite naturally,
by their own feculent selves.

WHY I CAN'T SLEEP NIGHTS

From the garden
where I had seen nothing growing,
nothing green,
only stiff, mechanical birds
on fragments of chromium

The host led me into his house,
speaking like someone
who does not care to be heard,
certain his words are true
because they had been spoken

Pipes, cylinders, levers,
were all his furnishings,
while circuits of amazing wires
lit up corner bulbs
when I coughed or sneezed

I felt odourless, without weight,
as if my body
was moving independently
between my host and me
though a mirror on each wall
showed me gross and tall

The floors, I recall, were bare
and glistened like polished steel
reflecting my host's skull,
the skin and flesh not at all

There was a white light
behind each socket,
and the shadow his person cast
lay on the floor like a soft carpet

A needle came out of the air
and pierced my blue eyes,
spattering the blood
on the bare, polished floor

"This is what the house was made for,"
said my host
as he took me gently by the arm
and led me back into the garden.

CONCOURSE AT CATARAQUI

There were of course those whom ease
or a default of imagination
had made optimistic:
the backbone of the country
but slightly bent with perplexity.

There was the Muse's stepchild,
an amuser:
a price on his English beard,
on his viewable grimace.

Also the hack fabulist
with no gift of words
for us: gain
his criterion.

And one, a one-lunged
trumpeter
who denied
long, long before cockcrow
– hollow-chested.

And Cowardice hiding out
behind a circus show of reason:
hardest he was to smoke out.

ARBOREAL NATURE

Daughter to mother; son to father, cleaves:
Yet the tree has one sap for all its leaves.

313

THE WAY THE WORLD ENDS

Before me on the dancestand
A god's vomit or damned by his decrees
The excited twitching couples shook and
Wriggled like giant parentheses.

A pallid Canadienne
Raised a finger and wetted her lip,
And echoing the nickelodeon
"Chip" she breathed drowsily, "Chip, chip."

Aroused, her slavish partner
Smiled, showed his dentures through soda-pop gas,
And "chip" he said right back to her
And "chip, chip" she said and shook her ass.

Denture to denture, "Pas mal"
They whispered and were glad, jerked to and fro;
Their distorted bodies like bits of steel
Controlled by that throbbing dynamo.

They stomped, flung out their arms, groaned;
And in a flash I saw the cosmos end
And last of all the black night cover this:
"Chip, chip" and a shake of the ass.

DONE ON BOTH SIDES

First on your belly, a babe, you lie;
And then on your back, a corpse, you lie.

Prone on your belly it's wet you give;
And prone on your back it's dry you give.

Time like an egg has turned you over;
Done on both sides your life is over.

314

BERRY PICKING

Silently my wife walks on the still wet furze
Now darkgreen the leaves are full of metaphors
Now lit up is each tiny lamp of blueberry.
The white nails of rain have dropped and the sun is free.

And whether she bends or straightens to each bush
To find the children's laughter among the leaves
Her quiet hands seem to make the quiet summer hush –
Berries or children, patient she is with these.

I only vex and perplex her; madness, rage
Are endearing perhaps put down upon the page;
Even silence daylong and sullen can then
Enamour as restraint or classic discipline.

So I envy the berries she puts in her mouth,
The red and succulent juice that stains her lips;
I shall never taste that good to her, nor will they
Displease her with a thousand barbarous jests.

How they lie easily for her hand to take,
Part of the unoffending world that is hers;
Here beyond complexity she stands and stares
And leans her marvellous head as if for answers.

No more the easy soul my childish craft deceives
Nor the simpler one for whom yes is always yes;
No, now her voice comes to me from a far way off
Though her lips are redder than the raspberries.

WHATEVER ELSE POETRY IS FREEDOM

Whatever else poetry is freedom.
Forget the rhetoric, the trick of lying
All poets pick up sooner or later. From the river,
Rising like the thin voice of grey castratos – the mist;
Poplars and pines grow straight but oaks are gnarled;
Old codgers must speak of death, boys break windows;
Women lie honestly by their men at last.

And I who gave my Kate a blackened eye
Did to its vivid changing colours
Make up an incredible musical scale;
And now I balance on wooden stilts and dance
And thereby sing to the loftiest casements.
See how with polish I bow from the waist.
Space for these stilts! More space or I fail!

And a crown I say for my buffoon's head.
Yet no more fool am I than King Canute,
Lord of our tribe, who scanned and scorned;
Who half-deceived, believed; and, poet, missed
The first white waves come nuzzling at his feet;
Then damned the courtiers and the foolish trial
With a most bewildering and unkingly jest.

It was the mist. It lies inside one like a destiny.
A real Jonah it lies rotting like a lung.
And I know myself undone who am a clown
And wear a wreath of mist for a crown;
Mist with the scent of dead apples,
Mist swirling from black oily waters at evening,
Mist from the fraternal graves of cemeteries.

It shall drive me to beg my food and at last
Hurl me broken I know and prostrate on the road;
Like a huge toad I saw, entire but dead,
That Time mordantly had blacked; O pressed
To the moist earth it pled for entry.
I shall be I say that stiff toad for sick with mist
And crazed I smell the odour of mortality.

And Time flames like a paraffin stove
And what it burns are the minutes I live.
At certain middays I have watched the cars
Bring me from afar their windshield suns;
What lay to my hand were blue fenders,
The suns extinguished, the drivers wearing sunglasses.
And it made me think I had touched a hearse.

So whatever else poetry is freedom. Let
Far off the impatient cadences reveal
A padding for my breathless stilts. Swivel,
O hero, in the fleshy groves, skin and glycerine,
And sing of lust, the sun's accompanying shadow
Like a vampire's wing, the stillness in dead feet –
Your stave brings resurrection, O aggrievèd king.

PRUSSIAN BLUE

What shall ignorant men say:
Was it Accident or Fate
Or some powerfuller thing
More sinister than they
Which ordained Frederick the Great
Choose for his regal bedmate
Queens whose names commence with K
—Keith, Katte, and Keyserlingk?

317

THE WIDOWS

Up from the pale grass
The widows came
Sporting grey mantles,
Admonishing me of time
And saying, "They lie slain
Who were our lovers;
Now we make bibles
Out of their lime
Black as the flies
We killed all summer."

Ah, these widows.
Ah, like grey spiders
They came up from the grass
Dropping between
Their slender outlines
Shadows upon my face.
"Wicked persons," I shouted,
  Scaring a mite from a leaf,
"You are deceivers
  They are not slain, your lovers.

"They are not slain, but sleep.
  Your shadows quelled them
  Till their limbs grew stiff,
  Grew stiff with sleep
  And impotent,
  And now you keep
  As a talisman between you
  Their whereabouts of grief
  Enabling you to go
  Row behind even row.

"Step back, sucking spiders,
  Dire conquerors,
  And let Diogenes' great sun
  Shine on my form of man.
  Your lovers shall rise with me.

See through the bunching air
Their limbs begin to stir
And a froth falls from the youngest.
Go, hang your sad cloaks from a tree
For now is all nature blest."

Like stricken shadows
The twilight folds together
They fell, their faces pale,
Into one another.
Then I roared and a wind
Out of the centuries
Hurled them sadly shrinking
Against a blasted tree
To mark – O grey diminutive rag –
My green and fertile sea.

MR. BEUTEL LAYS A CORNERSTONE

Near forlorn beaches
Turtles drop their eggs;
So do ostriches
And great blue herons
With delicate legs.
He so proudly furred
On his large estate
– No reptile or bird –
Lays his cornerstones
Stamped with name and date.

GIFTS

I left two dollars for a taxi.
I did it discreetly.
I placed the money on a chair,
Knowing she would find it there.

The next day my darling flew at me.
"You hurt me terribly.
Gifts: as many as you please
But not . . ." I stroked her knees

And waited. "Who'd be upset,"
She sobbed, "by a bracelet?
Or even dismayed
By earrings, pearl-inlaid?

"An alluring perfume,
Or some small thing for my room,
A vase or silver dish?
Gifts: as many as you wish.

"But not, mon chèr, money.
That dishonours both you and me."
In Cosette's swimming eyes
I could see the fleshly compromise:

Where sharpest knife won't cut
Wounded honour from appetite,
And self with the first kiss
Turns love into a casuist.

HOMAGE TO BEN JONSON

Legend says a drunken churl
Did for Villon in a brawl.

The dagger of a lout
Squeezed the brains of Marlowe out.

Pushkin was slain in a duel
By an aristocratic fool.

Another poet, I forget the one,
Ran from a pointed gun.

But ~~soldier~~ *solider* Ben Jonson
Very fitly killed his man

Lest the merest worm's food
Presumptuous grown and rude

Establish beyond discord
The pen inferior to the sword.

SUPERNATURAL EVENT AT CEDAR POND

"The flowers," I said, "in the hollow where we lie
Take sun and moon with a fine natural aplomb;
Don't whine, never hold up their cold extremities
As a reproach to the State of New Hampshire
Or look as if their fate was anyone's concern
—Not even their own, my fretting pet;
And certainly not that of the cosmos."
I was about to say more when Dorothy Wordsworth
I discerned, a bright look in her mad eyes,
And Emily running free across the heath.

I saw them, I aver, up there ahead of me
On that not-too-distant, fragrant hill,
Turning their visionary heads to glance back, shy,
As if to say, "Walk here between us, if you will."
And I would too, you know, for women ghosts
Who love the hills and clouds, rain and mist,
The purple look on mountain and sky,
Wind and late evening birdcall
Hold for me no supernatural dread at all
—Far less than young wives that fret all day and squall.

Yet all I said was: "Come here, poor devil,
And let me kiss your damp fingers
More limp than last week's cut celery;
Perhaps my lips will suck up their frost,
Dispel the conspiracies of cloud
That've kept you hovering over the fire, a sad
And shivering bride: the bad weather scramble finally
Over the famous beechtrees and get lost,
And the ragged curtains of mist for your sake
Lift from this region and this rented lake."

She was silent. I said, "My Strange One, hear me:
That very night before we met and wed
I walked into an expected storm
And though later the winds shook the trees and me
And the skies bled, I sang like an Italian tenor
Into the wild, electric darkness for an hour
While all about me enormous flashbulbs went off.
Someone up there was taking the picture,
Front views and profiles, of a solitary happy man
—You may scoff—was snapping it again and again.

"My Love, they say God himself asks to see
These photographs from time to time;
It must give him a most heavenly lift
To know someone like me walks the earth,
A single ecstatic man on his planet.
(Imagine me with face and hair all wet,
My mouth open, and one soaking foot
Thrust out defiantly before the other!)
Yet now that I consider it, I wonder
At the antique photography that still needs thunder!"

Her face grew more unsmiling; I saw her frown
And felt as when clouds suddenly darken
And a chilling wind blows on heated limbs.
So to humour her, lift my own unease, I laughed:
"Perhaps when Lucifer visits heaven again,
The Almighty flourishing a snapshot of me
Will say, 'Forget poor Job, dear Satan,
See if you can topple *him*, this joyous one.' "
My darling's eyes grew green as moss, then baleful red.
Her hands furred, I swooned and was left here for dead.

323

CAIN

Taking the air rifle from my son's hand,
I measured back five paces, the Hebrew
In me, narcissist, father of children,
Laid to rest. From there I took aim and fired.
The silent ball hit the frog's back an inch
Below the head. He jumped at the surprise
Of it, suddenly tickled or startled
(He must have thought) and leaped from the wet sand
Into the surrounding brown water. But
The ball had done its mischief. His next spring
Was a miserable flop, the thrust all gone
Out of his legs. He tried – like Bruce – again,
Throwing out his sensitive pianist's
Hands as a dwarf might or a helpless child.
His splash disturbed the quiet pondwater
And one old frog behind his weedy moat
Blinking, looking self-complacently on.
The lin's surface at once became closing
Eyelids and bubbles like notes of music
Liquid, luminous, dropping from the page
White, white-bearded, a rapid crescendo
Of inaudible sounds and a crones' whispering
Backstage among the reeds and bulrushes
As for an expiring Lear or Oedipus.

But Death makes us all look ridiculous.
Consider this frog (dog, hog, what you will)
Sprawling, his absurd corpse rocked by the tides
That his last vain spring had set in movement.
Like a retired oldster, I couldn't help sneer,
Living off the last of his insurance:
Billows – now crumbling – the premiums paid.

Absurd, how absurd. I wanted to kill
At the mockery of it, kill and kill
Again – the self-infatuate frog, dog, hog,
Anything with the stir of life in it,
Seeing the dead leaper, Chaplin-footed,
Rocked and cradled in this afternoon
Of tranquil water, reeds, and blazing sun,
The hole in his back clearly visible
And the torn skin a blob of shadow
Moving when the quiet poolwater moved.
O Egypt, marbled Greece, resplendent Rome,
Did you also finally perish from a small bore
In your back you could not scratch? And would
Your mouths open ghostily, gasping out
Among the murky reeds, the hidden frogs,
We climb with crushed spines toward the heavens?

When the next morning I came the same way
The frog was on his back, one delicate
Hand on his belly, and his white shirt front
Spotless. He looked as if he might have been
A comic; tapdancer apologizing
For a fall, or an Emcee, his wide grin
Coaxing a laugh from us for an aside
Or perhaps a joke we didn't quite hear.

A WORD FROM DIOGENES

You're answerable to no one, poor human clod.
Not to your forbears; neither to State nor a God.
Shameless always, give them the stink of your armpits.
Rather than a lump, be a dog and howl in fits.

NEW TABLES

I do not want power
And great wealth I never cared for;
Most people, when I see them running after these things,
Fill me with anxiety and compassion;
I am anxious about them
And about myself who must unavoidably deal with them
These sick people whom no one loves or understands,
Whom even the gods
        with their lovely waterfalls and mists
Have completely expunged from their memory

These ailing people are each other's death
Sooner or later they fall upon each other's swords
They die into each other without valour or pity
Or fold noiselessly into each other like grey shadows;
They expire quietly like poisonous mushrooms
On a forest floor
And are shrivelled up by the sun
Into a fine white powder waiting to make greater sense
In some other, more fortunate duration

For myself I like nothing better
Than to go walking down the unpaved streets
With the sun for my constant companion;
I like the way the dogs greet the two of us
With plenty of tail-waggings, rushes, innocent barkings.
When the children lift their faces
Like delicate flowers to be touched lightly
I feel an emotion no saint, no, nor mystic
Ever felt before me at this arrangement of sudden glory;
Perhaps the humble grasses in the fields
Understand this whitest ecstasy,
And the bare trees in late April
Waiting patiently for their gift of leaves

At such moments, poor and powerless,
I am so full of blessing I think I could babble
The meaningless religious words, the formulas of contrition,

The bewildered ghost-sounds, ghost-meanings of old men;
And if I do not it's because I wish to startle the earth
Bored to death by the prodigal centuries,
Their white ashes combed by fierce winds
Like the streaming hairs of frenzied anchorites,
The yea-sayers of hammered conviction;
And because thereby, decked out in green and gold,
She gains a greater glory –
The finer triumph – to force this praise from me,
An atheist, shivering with blessed ecstasy

LYRIC

The rains will come and pass away,
The brown buds hanging from the bough
Must soon adjust their twinkling fans
—Will you love me now?

Their songs are to the season sweet
And I must wait their potent prayer;
When grasses climb that bitten hill,
I will kiss you there.

A ROMAN JEW TO OVID

Amaryllis has a white bosom.
I adore seeing her bosom swell.
Of the art of love she understands
Everything. She has expert hands.
I know it to be impossible
To stand covered in her bright presence;
I remove trousers, cufflinks, tie
And the night long with her I lie.
And all night I ply a lover's arts
And pump seed into her sweetest parts.
O favoured for delight I am blessed
Beside my sweet girl Amaryllis,
For when kisses me and her exhaust
Her adored bubs fan me to my rest.
I sink, yet soon restored, am saved,
And dying, am no dying David
Since such revivifying flames pass
From her perfumèd limbs and small ass
Dead Pharaohs start up and cold metal
Turns shooting fountains; O marble,
Marbled statues melt, the most famous
Happiest t'exchange in her embrace.
Yet what imports it thus to flow if
Apprehension has made me costive?
I die to see the girl's breasts swell
But hang it I do not purge well;
The very joy of my flooding front
Is to my backside reproach and taunt;
Or as if by captains I were mocked
Here I have exit but there I am blocked
Till baffled, should I escape to woo,
I escape no longer one but two;
Yet so bemusing's my prurient itch
That halved or doubled I can't tell which.
O believe me, returned to spouse and home
I am a Hannibal hot for Rome;
Willing are my loins, straight is the blade,
The force assembled for the final raid;

The ancient plains are taken, the rest
Lies before me an easy conquest;
Then such pains take me, not leaving off
Till I've outhowled the loudest wolf;
Away I roll from my good dame's side,
She more troubled than a virgin bride
Haply grieving when her body's charms
Bring her heated spouse perplexing harms.
O pathos! she tells the gods my ills,
Feels my flick'ring pulse and feeds me pills
Till touched by her devotion I curse
My wandering lusts, my Amaryllis;
Call myself a wretch and now resolve
To give lawful hairs and breasts my love.
How mixed the elements in our blood,
How all is overborne by its flood;
E'en as she strokes and restores my pulse
She awakens lust, makes fly remorse;
My merry glances she misconstrues
And takes for herself another's dues;
She joys in my reviving spirit
While I disdain her for reviving it;
Tell my quiv'ring soul hers the blame
And reproving her excuse my shame.
I fight the injustice in my breast;
This only maddens: the hate's increased –
So the guilty Athenians gave
Carping Socrates a poisoned grave
And, offended, banished from their midst
Aristides, a man – yet nobly just!
Ah, past our wisdom, and most subtle
Is evil, dear friend, in the human soul:
For 'tis her blindness makes me despise
Those minist'ring hands, that careworn face
As 'tis oft the innocent eyes that make
Butchers, moved, the lamb more harshly strike;
The kindled master kill the pleading slave;
Grace, abashed, doom the helpless captive.

So, contemning, at her feet I kneel
And hate, pity, in one heart-throb feel.
(O the gods who apportioned me thus
May their semen turn a milky pus;
Or may there come a cooling waste of snow,
And I and all my fevered bones below)
I rail! Yet railing feel – most wise, most dear –
Betrayed like bold Hannibal by his rear.

REQUIEM FOR AN AGE

We that have troubled long and laboured hard
And counted each bare doubt a separate fang,
Where shall we take the thirst the world disowns;
What nameless race of men, untamed, receive
The breath that is the symbol of our lives;
In what new bracken must we bury now
The muted fragment that will hint of gods?

This is the final wretchedness, to know
Of some fairer land, and yet to bow
To idols long decayed and old and blind
Whose diseased breath makes grey the world we love.
How shall we meet the burden of our times,
Or make profession of our tongue-tied faith
When all the lamps are gutted, one by one?

FRIENDS

The person I most admire
is Kathe Anne.
She has blue eyes, blonde hair.
I met her one day
at a park.
I was at the park
and there was no one
to go on the seesaw
with me.
So Kathe did.

She has strong feelings.
Sometimes she is a tomboy.
We climb fences together.
We sell things and make clubs.

Kathe is ten.
She has two older sisters.
She lives on my street.
She is a Prodasstint.

Her telephone number
is almost like mine.

FIVE WOMEN

I

You are grass.
You are earth and water.
You are sunlight on a rock.

Out of the burning air
you place your lace panties
on my hidden altar.
What a queer incense now arises!
The lighted tapers snicker.

Like sands thrown at a ruined door
your lips scrape at my ear:
"Love sees better in the dark."
Your mouth blows out the dying taper
and I lie down on the starlit bed
and hold your perfect breasts like water.

II

The mother of seven children,
six daughters and a grown-up son,
she still finds sex distasteful
and walks like a somnabulist,
unawakened and virginal,
saying, "Whose children are these?
Where do they come from?"

Sex is beautiful as the earth.
In her it has crumbled into dirt.

III

I love water.
Not this thin drizzle of pleasure.

IV

The earth is beautiful.
The grass is beautiful.
But she covers them both
with a picnic tablecloth
and sets wines and comestibles before me.
Before making love, she says,
one should eat well,
being careful of the digestion.

Seeing the sausage grease
on her honest hands and neck,
I half expect to find love
explained in a cook book.

V

I love earth.
I love grass.
I love water.
I love the sun,
and death
as final consummation.

But a sexless woman is not death;
is the odour of death,
of cerements and coffin wood.

Why doesn't this unlovely woman die,
instead of uselessly brushing her teeth
and polishing her fingernails?
When she smiles I see bits of cerement-cloth
between her teeth;
when she bends her fleshless arm
it is as if a coffin lid came softly down.

WHAT DOES IT MATTER?

This has been a rainy summer.
Once or twice we quarrelled.
What does it matter?
The main thing as we say
when we embrace
is that we love each other:
that, mutatis mutandis, we know
with the finality of calendar
and equinox
the summer's here
though the days are sullen and wet
and our teeth shake at night
louder than wooden windowframes.

Yes, I have known loose garrulous women.
What does it matter?
And restless, beautiful ones
that intoxicated me with flattery and drink.
What does it matter?
And sad helpless ones
that reached out for love
no one nowadays gives
and the pinheads sneer at and besmirch.
Again, what does it matter?
A poet lives in a special hell
—it has a view opening on heaven;
and whether it is digust, hatred of death,
concupiscence, love, or aspiration
that broils and blisters him here
not even the Devil can tell
though he's seen many queer ones in his time.

The price comes high
for the kind of immortality I want;
still, I am shamed by your greatness,
your savage pertinacity.
You have earned your own coign in hell,
with me (what a crazy paradox!)
your small glimpse of heaven.
So be it.
There have been other strange pairs in history;
and anyway what's this life for
if not to proliferate conundrum and mystery
for the journalists to be amazed at?

Yet believe this:
it is my destiny
from any ditch
to walk out clean;
and though I lie drunk with poetry and wine,
my back is never to the stars,
my face never in the muck;
and always I feel your presence
brooding over me like the summer sky
where your face, a star,
is clearly seen
(Ah, I am really sloshed!)
and multiplied in the million lights that shine.

MARIUS

Believes women exist for one purpose only
High or low, rustic or perfumed suburbanite
– Bellying, to spread their legs.

He thinks that I
Am a dumb waiter: my approach
Is too slow and fastidious –
                                        His is not so.

He says when he shuts his eyes
He can see assorted maidenheads
Winking in the violet air:
                                        that, for this,
His shopfellows, hair greased, their teeth
Picked clean, envy him.

He says his schooling enables him
To read the paperbacks, to mark
In red ink the requisite passages.

On hot extravagant afternoons
He likes nothing so much as to lie
On his back like a Breughel peasant;
Or as one limp, with eyes shut, under
The masseur's warm and expert hands.

If I ask him, Marius
At what do you stare, at what nod,
He invariably smiles.

Two other details: his nails are always cared for
And his manners adequate.

IF YOU CAN'T SCREAM

Insanely
the decapitated
cigaret
puffs in the dull
ashtray.

Your gloved hand
on the door,
my stoned eyeballs
tighten
in the neat slingshot
of your posterior.

I know you hasten
to another
to bring him
on barbarous feet
the self-same torment.

The composure
of the two couples
in the open-air
restaurant
makes me sad.
I must bone up
on Parmenides.

DIVINE IMAGE

Swiftly darting in the setting light,
The doomed sparrow feels the falcon's wings.
How beautiful are they both in flight.

337

HOW DOMESTIC HAPPINESS IS ACHIEVED

Here, Sir, is the way it was.

There were clouds; unmenacing, white,
that kept dropping in and out of the sky;
on the mountainside,
a fearsome phalanx of trees;
but they had never read Macbeth: I had;
there was no cause for alarm or worry.

The grass was full of tipsy poets
repeating again and again their single good line;
several thistles, that's true, raised
their sullen misanthropic faces
but I am married, Sir –
I did nothing to provoke them.

For compensation,
the goldenrods spilled over in yellow friendliness,
the flies stayed to be killed,
and overhead the sun took its time.

And behind me – mark this well –
a battered sign in two languages
outlawed shooting;
yet all day peaceably I sat there alone
and observed neither animal nor quail.

POETIC FAME

Best of all are the supporters
who now reach me their hands to put money in,
their collateral being their good opinion of me;
and the neighbour who gave my name to the police.

At my approach
the ladies, unsubtle and ugly,
rush their adolescent daughters upstairs;
insert a table between themselves and me
and leer sensuously across the waxed surface.
I do not understand their discordant hints
    and manœuvres.
Do they expect me to sire tables?

And to turn away from their unease, the men
keep my glass tumbler filled;
in this unroyal kingdom a child knows
all poets are dead or they're Englishmen.

(When an armoured insect ran across
my darling's naked knee
she made a curious mouth and trilled:
"Was it from an alien planet?")

Lights for this Venusian
with the twisted nose and fierce eye!
alcool and bawdy stories . . . .

PAGING MR. SUPERMAN

I myself walked into the Sheraton
And after remarking his raw nose
Was part natal umbilicus I told
The clerk in the loudest voice I could bear:
"Page me Mr. Superman." He looked
Diffidently at me but acceding
My tie-pin, made of the rarest onyx,
Belonged to neither a sour fanatic
Nor one sick in the head from eating
Shrimps canned in the Andes and contraband
Here, he signalled for a call boy who came
Running all spongy with awareness,
His cheeks flapping in the air-conditioned
Air and his white dentures extended in
Warmest greeting. "Page Mr. Superman,"
The uneasy clerk said eyeing my pin
To re-assure himself and in his mind
Recapitulating the small number
Of paid two-week vacations he had had.
Luckily the grey-haired call boy was one
Of the ignatzes the cities now breed
Reliably and with a more exact
Efficiency than former days.
                                        He saw
Nothing remarkable in the clerk's request
And sent his voice through the loudspeaker
Of his imagination constructed
In the faraway days of childhood in rooms
Alone with Atlas and the last pages
Of boys' magazines. I heard the glory
Of it that afternoon like the closing
Chords of Handel's Messiah. "Superman"
It rang out clear across the floor polish.

"Mr. Superman." There was such triumph,
Such wildest exultation in his voice,
The pale cigarette girl at the counter
For the first time in her life gave wrong change
And all the elevators raced upwards
As if a pistol shot had startled them;

They did not stop till they had crashed the roof
Where one can see their solemn closed cages
Side by side and standing pigeon-spotted
Like the abunas on the cathedral
Dazed-seeming by the wildest flight of all.

This was the cocktail hour when love
Is poured over ice-cubes and executives
Lay their shrewdest plans for the birth of twins
With silver spoons; when one forgets the ships
Aground in fog, the pilot with letters
For mountain peaks and snow; the silent poor;
Or the wife with pre-menstrual tensions;
When Asia is rubbed out with an olive,
A truce ordered to the day's massacres.
I saw only six in the large lobby,
Five men and one solitary woman,
Who hearing Mr. Superman called
Looked up at once from the puddle of their
Lives where they stood at the edges making
Crumbling mud pies out of paper money.
While the stout woman adjusted her bra
And studied the door of the Gents' Room,
The men had risen to their feet watching
Scared and breathless the quick revolving door
As if they expected the flashing blades
To churn him into visible substance.
But no one emerged from either place;
The unusual name was finally
Lost under the carpet where it was found
The next day badly deteriorated.

The condemned six returned to their postures
And the hour rained down the familiar
Wrinkles and the smiles cutting like glass.
The call boy gave it as his verdict
Superman was nowhere in the lobby,
And the tall clerk now regarding my pin
Mistrustfully rubbed the umbilical
Part of his nose that was raw and itchy.

341

"He has not yet arrived," he said. "Perhaps
He'll come later." For a split second
I thought he was making game of me
But his eyes were steady as if fixed
On a T.V. serial. I thanked him
And smiling amiably in all
Directions of the bell-shaped womb, I walked
Out into the ordinary sunshine.

BLACK, BLACK

Black, black did I see today
As on the cold ground I lay:
The flowing dress of two nuns
At their mild devotions
And a small, most savage dog
Harrying an age-felled log.

And the unceasing fall of
Leaves – ochre, vermilion, buff –
That kissing the grass died
The blackness intensified,
Till I fancied the swart gleam
Weakness that lets evil in:
The mortified heart, unfree,
And black, more black than all three.

INDIVIDUALISTS

I'm not good at giving
the names of bushes;
                      anyway
this was not a bush —
a plant
        that had taken root
away from its fellows
            on the safe ledge;
It was built
                    stubby,
close to the ground
like certain kinds of boxers
           — tenacious —
but it was going somewhere:
           it was on the road.

It did my heart good
                  to see it,
like the white leghorn
                I watched
crossing the wet field,
           small and arrogant,
his comb a red taunt
           at the vicious weather
— artillerist!

RAIN

The wind blew hard in the trees
And palegreen was the wet grass;
I love you, Love, my Sweet said
And gave her false mouth to kiss.

Huge leopard spots the rain put
On the stone near where we sat;
An obscure song at our feet
Sang the troubled rivulet.

In front the black road went by,
A panther in search of prey;
Between some mouldering firs
I lay down her bleeding corse.

The wind blew hard in the trees
And screeched in the low briars;
I loved you truly, I said
And kissed her false dead mouth.

The rain fell, decaying eyes
And small ears: how green the moss!
Let her red lips kiss the rot
In their last quiver of death.

The white rain shall knit her shroud
And clean my hands of her blood;
The cottage on the round lake
Blind that eye like a cataract.

GARTER SNAKE

Defiantly, as if
with the will to hold back,
the yellow guck
disappoints by its paucity:
is, O irony, a useless glue.
The black works its way
from the cut. So do the flies.

And rising from the hard road
under the massing clouds,
the hills turn toward me
their coloured fleece.
They are not going anywhere.
You would say they were innocent.

So I have seen a rowboat
in a summer resort
a small boy had fallen from and drowned:
a white smile on the face of the lake;
and my father's black beard that never spoke
and became a volley of red tongues.

Return, return in a week.
The grass snake, a strip of hide,
makes in its last contortion
upon the road
a calligraphic S: the fine print
of a Chinese dragon: parody of one.

Now gaze up at the sky
and at the innumerable Rorschachs;
no specialist shuffles those clouds.
Riven like the garter snake
what do they mean? what do they signify?

DANCE, MY LITTLE ONE

Little one, the men are loonies
Who'll cart them to their loonie bin?
Some have seen you on the street,
Yet they prate of God and sin.

And God, their hideous women!
Evil gossips, mean-souled trulls.
Sniff with me the ocean,
How clean and handsome are the gulls.

My little one, they're loonies
Who'll bring them to the loonie bin?
Who'll give to each a rattle
Who'll listen to their din?

Their foulness shall not touch you
Their corpselike stench I'll hide;
I shall build a golden pigsty
I shall put them all inside.

And only if you are stubborn
Will not dance or sing for me
Will I a small door open
And let you hear & see:

How the loonies hate each other
How they jeer & grunt & swear,
Their sullen faces happy
When another's wound they tear.

How they storm & rage & batter
How they roar & sweat & push.
Have I frightened you, my pretty?
Do not whimper, silly. Hush.

O like a fire that flickers
Sometimes low in greyest ash
Late, late, my Sweet, I found you
Now I hold you like a mesh.

A mesh of mad and kissing verses
That I pluck from out the air;
The writhing of your hips
Only serves to keep you there.

So dance, my little one, dance
I shall not slide that door!
Think the noise below your feet
One long applauding roar!

And sing, my little one, sing
Let the loonies hear your voice;
Under the gold-leafed ceiling
Their crazy eyes rejoice.

Into song shall turn their shrilling
Into music turn their grunts;
Then sing, my pretty one, sing
Then dance, my little one, dance.

CHATTERERS

Pressing forwards to the Finland Station
and the blood of the Romanovs,
Bolshevik Lenin
on the civilized Kautsky et al:
"chatterers."

Epithet which clear-eyed history
in love with the real
translated into their echoing epitaph.

How similarly mock these writers
Joyce, Rimbaud, Crane –
fanatics without remorse whose pen
scraped their own and their age's pus –
the distinguished & amiable men-of-letters!

THE TOY GUN

Where not one year ago grew
Whin and chokecherry bushes
A small boy thumps, fires a gun.
BANG, BANG. But it's not dangerous.

His tall papa who in repose
Is a sphinx with a broken nose
Now secretless however
Pushes an electric lawn-mower.

The din does not disturb
His wife, sleek and imperial,
Who lazily lets the sun
Make her beautiful.

Do they care much if poems
Are never again written?
The bungalow lobs its shadow
On a new civilization.

Morose Schopenhauer
Was a philosopher:
But I'll lie hid at the Riviera
For a wet snatch from Trafalgar.

Its begetter owns a broadhipped car.
Think, a twelve-year-old can blow a man.
Everything's for pleasure.
What a civilization!

The eupeptic innocent boy
Discharges again and again,
Levelling at his parents
His merciless toy gun.

MONTREAL

Thérèse who died of that or this
Hath made a miracle for us:
Her blood now prinks in every arc
And neon crescent after dark.
Her soul, a glass bead, lights the sky.

And like a swarthy Jesuit
Mount Royal grips its burning cross
Where every sacred bulb is lit
By some pure soul who dwells in it.
Sparrows and virgins glorify.

Observe the stricken—bent in prayer—
Like glistening snails upon the stair:
Mute fifty years, the voiceless talk,
Old cripples dance before they walk
The stone-blind see
And only poverty
Finds no cure there.

Hush, the jewelled hour has come
When saints and birds are dumb
—After a famine or a fire
God for a toothpick plucks a spire!

LAURENTIAN RHAPSODY

Tomorrow my little one will come.
She alone reckons me as I am:

Sensual, argumentative
(Only when sober) lazy and naïve.

And she's wise in other ways: she's neat
And her small body is fragrant sweet.

And it's a miracle one this young
Should have the mastery of her tongue.

She say she loves my distinguished ears
And I have likened her breasts to pears.

Well, she'll bring books, Bacardi rhum
And her own irreplaceable bum.

And I'll pretend I am Bliss Carman,
That tramp and terrible bohemian.

And Kit – but what native poetess
Was other than over-virtuous?

So to our own act: we sit near the stove;
When it grows too warm – why, we make love!

Should the paraffin fire die down
We skip out on love and zip to town.

Our game? She asks the bartenders there,
Do they know a sweetheart that's more fair.

Since they don't they must give Kit and me
A double glass of Irish whiskey.

Then off we zoom to the next village
To find a priest who can guess my age.

As much as he tries, he cannot tell.
His forfeit: he must ring his church bell.

Ring out to the cold Laurentian sky;
They sweep to the grave grey hair, bright eye.

O ring out, harsh bells, ring out my years:
In a young girl's arms there are no tears.

And they who smile, say the moral's old,
Had best apply it before they're cold.

Let's lose no time but make a fine feast.
Invite the bartenders and the priest.

Let them come, be merry for our sake
In this rented cabin by the lake.

The bartenders can't leave, they've business;
But the young priest will send his mistress.

And since you're fair and I am forty-six
We'll – forgive the rhyme – we'll teach her tricks.

And we'll make such noise the fish shall come
To lead us out in a moonlight swim.

On a rock the priest's girl will preside
While Beauty and Age swim side by side.

Bless the mistress, bless her young priest,
Bless my grey hairs and your lovely breast.

Bless the village, O bless this cabin,
And bless the waters where ends all sin. Amen.

SHEEP

Like a socialist I knew, a simple soul,
These two sheep, male and female, stare at us
        from their fold;
And their faces are fine, fine and sensitive
With the proper intensity of reserve.
Even the credulity, so water clear in them,
        is attractive.

Yet, indifferent to the impression they make,
They crouch on their mat of dung or with the poise
        of a philosopher seek
The rough part of the post which they know well
To scrape against it their purloined fleece and fell;
Staring, warily staring, wearily staring, with a mien
        silly and gentle – and cynical.

Amazed? No, but look at those fine musicians' faces again;
More particularly, the ebony line of the mouth
        curving long and thin.
Do you see it? Would you not say that's the smile
You've caught and watched on the face of someone
        who, while he's too meek to defend himself,
Sees through and despises your guile?

I'll tell you something else about sheep
You haven't noticed, see them as much as you wish
        in your sleep;
They're neither-this-nor-thats, half-and-halfs if you prefer.
I've asked you to take in they scrub their fleece,
        standing wrapt like a philosopher;
Their itchy, bulky, dung-matted, grey-dirty fleece
        yet, look down – what feet! the trim feet of a dancer.

And there's also this: they're practical, prudent.
Or they seem so, yet they also somehow contrive to appear
        gullible and vacant.
Here again is that unsatisfactory, disdain-making quality:
        that of the half-and-half, the in-between.

I should expect my gifted and temperamental daughter
If she flew high, then came down to failure
    to look afterwards as silly and circumspect
As this sheep and his dam.

But Christ, the whole world moves in on this fold.
All, all, have become mixtures: alloys, neither
    pure tin nor gold.
Integrity's gone. And I myself at my wife's deathbed
Shall, I know, weep: weep like Othello, be
    grief-rent and troubled
Yet note the small cost of some extra flowers or bulbs.

SPRING EXULTANCES

Exulting that I am I, not one
whose mind envy darkens;
the body healthy, my senses swift as a boy's;
that I love, am loved,
and in a world of Jacobean murders,
witty, appetitive, playful,
I flourish while others bleed;
I pity that reckless Italian
who carved out a sister's heart when,
her bright rebellion spent, she broke
their compact of loving flesh
against a cross-eyed fate, a pigsty world.
Rather, a gifted soloist I melt
into the laughter and white arms
of my dove when I tell her: "Love,
you shall surely die poor
for puritans have put a tax on beauty."
—certain moreover the best in men,
beyond folly and the corruption of thighs,
lies with me here under this giving sun.

AUTUMN LINES FOR MY SON

Like a rag, an immense sleeve on which
Eternity wipes its nose – the crowds!
      Inflamed imbeciles whom pleasure torments;
Soiled dust and bits of straw the wind
Pounds murderously against the walls of cities.

Turn from these. Turn, my son, from their hideous
Warts, their welts: fate keeps an especial whip
      For them. And turn from the women yearning
To become wives, and their encircling arms:
Monstrous circle where Love's garrotted.

Never forget the concupiscent and corrupt
Deserve their ends: wait from afar off;
      Let the wind bring you the heavy death rattle.
This age like a slit and twitching rooster
Spills its bright blood down the flaming hillside.

In death's flaring athanor how beautiful
The trees! Look, the October landscape is
      Lovely and dying like a consumptive
Keats – O red-haired runt, I would have poets
Hard as munition-makers, pitiless.

Be strong, be joyous. Do not believe lies.
When gelded men speak violently
      Of virtues (bistoury & scission)
Observe, son, inept behind the gloating arras
The shuffling schoolmaster, abba of all their lies.

And in that moment of immortal joy
When you are most like a god recall
      Your pale friend, how ineluctably he wills
Your ill-fortune: and this dark sense keep
As once the feasting Borgias their drop of poison.

354

CÔTE DES NEIGES CEMETERY

As if it were a faultless poem, the odour
Is both sensuous and intellectual,
And of faded onion peel its colour;
For here the wasting mausoleums brawl
With Time, heedless and mute; their voice
Kept down, polite yet querulous –
Assuredly courtesy must at last prevail.

Away from the markings of the poor
On slope and summit the statuary is vain
And senatorial (now the odour's
A high-pitched note, piercing the brain)
Where lying together are judge and barrister
And some whose busts look on a shrunk estate.

Persuade yourself it is a Warner set
Unreal and two-dimensional, a façade,
Though our mortal tongues are furred with death:
A ghost city where live autumn birds flit
And small squirrels dart from spray to spray
And this formal scene is a kind of poetry.

Especially the tomb of Moise Wong, alien
And quaint among French Catholic names
Or the drainage pipes inanimate and looped
You may conceive as monstrous worms.
Undying paradox! Yet, love, look again:
Like an insinuation of leaves in snow

And sad, sad with surrender are the tablets
For the Chinese nuns; or, a blade between, the rows
Exact as alms, of les Sourdes et Muettes
And of les Aveugles: – and this, dear girl,
Is the family plot of Père Loisel and his wife
Whose jumbled loins in amorous sweat
Spawned these five neat graves in a semicircle.

FAMILY PORTRAIT

That owner of duplexes
has enough gold to sink himself
on a battleship. His children,
two sons and a daughter, are variations
on the original gleam: that is,
      slobs with a college education.

Right now the four of them
are seated in the hotel's dining-room
munching watermelons.

With the assurance of money
in the bank
they spit out the black, cool, elliptical
melonseeds, and you can tell
the old man has rocks
but no culture: he spits,
      gives the noise away free.

The daughter however is embarrassed
(Second Year Arts, McGill) and sucks harder
to forget.

They're about as useless
as tits on a bull,
and I think:
"Thank heaven I'm not
Jesus Christ –
I don't have to love them."

CLIMBING

Along the road I walk with my son
Noting the damp ferns, the confusion
Of goldenrods, mulleins, chickories
That grow by the road's side. But he sees
A sandhill to the left and he's gone,
His high voice urging me, "Quick, come on!"
But he does not wait to see if I
Have reached him and his excited cry,
Nor does he care overmuch whether
The sand-dust from his quick feet cover
My head and neck, the face turned away.
There'd be no point shouting, "Hold, son. Stay."
He wouldn't hear me for all the noise
He makes: yet supposing he did what's
Gained asking a boy that's lithe-limbed
To stop midway an important climb?
So I let him go on till his feet
Are bravely planted on the summit.
From there of course he at once looks down;
He laughs when he sees my past concern.
How can I show him my relieved face
Is for more than a boy's morning race?
So I grin and wave up to him there
(This poet, lover, frail Balboa)
The goldenrod I hold in my hand,
While white sprays of dust still drift on
Forcing me to shade my eyes and frown.
But son capers on his hill of sand.

CAT DYING IN AUTUMN

I put the cat outside to die,
Laying her down
Into a rut of leaves
Cold and bloodsoaked;
Her moan
Coming now more quiet
And brief in October's economy
Till the jaws
Opened and shut on no sound.

Behind the wide pane
I watched the dying cat
Whose fur like a veil of air
The autumn wind stirred
Indifferently with the leaves:
Her form (or was it the wind?)
Still breathing –
A surprise of white.

And I was thinking
Of melting snow in spring
Or a strip of gauze
When a sparrow
Dropped down beside it
Leaning his clean beak
Into the hollow;
Then whirred away, his wings,
You may suppose, shuddering.

Letting me see
From my house
The twisted petal
That fell
Between the ruined paws
To hold or play with,
And the tight smile
Cats have for meeting death.

LETTER TO A LIBRARIAN

Mr. P. – I have heard it rumoured
That you, humanist, librarian with a license,
In the shady privacy of your glassed room
Tore up my book of poems.

Sir, a word in your ear. Others
Have tried that game: burned Mann
And my immortal kinsman Heine.
Idiots! What act could be vainer?

For this act of yours, the ligatures
Pest-corroded, your eyes shall fall
From their sockets; drop on your lacquered desk
With the dull weight of pinballs.

And brighter than the sapless vine
Your hands shall flare;
To the murkiest kimbos of the library
Flashing my name like a neon sign.

And the candid great
Of whom not one was ever an Australian
Cry dustily from their shelves,
"Impostor! False custodian!"

Till a stunned derelict
You fall down blind, ear-beleaguered,
While Rabelais pipes you to a wished-for death
On a kazoo quaint and silvered.

359

VENETIAN BLINDS

To remember me I gave you Venetian blinds
Bought from a merchant corner Craig and Main;
I had my face painted on the wooden slats
By a poor artist who did it for a song
My sister taught him; the face, moreover,
Changed with the changing seasons: In summer
It was gay and self-possessed, the face
Of an Uebermensch living on a small pension;
Autumn saw the cheek lines in a charade
Of leaves falling: the Pathetic Fallacy:
And then it blended with the white paint
And was gone, a smile only remaining
(It may have been a dent in the wood) a
Finger laid on the negligée of your
Affections. When breathing hard spring arrived
My face stared down at you lecherous
And like a famished goat. This was the face
You liked best, especially when April winds
Moved the wide slats that composed my visage
And made it ripple like an uneven screen
In a movie house, my gaunt jaws opening
To snatch your small ears and small firm breasts.
In the dream which followed after you saw
A bright key laid on a cushion of air
Which your mother's cries moved a mile each way
And Stalin who threw himself boldly
Beneath it offering you a Five Year Plan
Which of course you turned down, my Love.

POEM FOR THE NEXT CENTURY

The old lights are broken.
Politics, religion,
Conscience, the perplexity
Of right and wrong – O pity
The baffled heart of Christ!
All fug, all hovering mist.

Will from individual truth
Come charity or death?
Like a sick lamp the Faith blinks.
We ask and ask while hearts shrink
To fibres and cells, our loves
Ridiculous as brief.

This is the house the jacks built
Out of hemlock and gilt:
The saints and lovers are dead
And all is common as bread.
Now none believe in greatness,
The dwarfs possess the bridges.

Crushed is the light, yet chromium
Neither shines nor warms as sun.
Cunning eyes gleam in the murk.
Points of light? Perhaps. Who'll walk
Into the sunlight and air,
Pitch and build his folly there?

And praise the stellar night,
The made-human infinite;
In the burning cosmos find
The lineaments of mind,
The throbbing of space akin
To the heart and not alien?

PARTING

What's the use if we should walk
Arm-about-the-waist and talk
Our married foolish hearts out;
Nor you rage, nor I shout
Out of grief, vexation
For the dusty road taken,
And that wound that's worst of all
Because unintelligible –
The passionate will to hurt;
And the recollected mirth,
And the intolerable pain
Of bright well-favoured children
Growing, fed on our evil,
Sullen, asymmetrical,
Their unformed unattached cry
Blood on our eardrums till we die:
For all that, troubled wisdom,
Experience and that dream
Of courage by which we live
Though the living be fictive,
Stony, a waste of breath,
And poor excuse for shunning death
Would make us give hands and part;
Reteach to cold lips an art
Of smiling they one time knew
Tender and lovely as the dew;
And drop from them a wry kiss
Into our growing emptiness,
Implanting there compassion
Beyond charity and reason
For the stubborn human fault
Brought from that fashionable vault
Men say floats invisibly
In a hollow of the sky,
But theologians reason well
For a thick basement in hell.
Yet it's the business of none
To say whether up or down;

Enough to know the human
As a mixed constitution
Imploring and fallible,
Choosing and despising ill;
Enough that we two can find
A laughter in the mind
For the interlocking grass
The winds part as they pass;
Or fallen on each other,
Leaf and uprooted flower.

ANTI-ROMANTIC

You went behind a bush to piss.
Imagine Wordsworth telling this!
About Lucy? And Robert Bridges
About his dear lass?

The poets are such bad liars.
Damn them and all their admirers.
The stars, the moon, for all their talk's stone –
Coynts, not always clean.

Yes, and they've solid interests
In mournful birds, in clouds, in mists.
Did La belle Dame sans Merci a-shit?
Keats nowhere says it.

But read the Oxford Book of Verse
By whatchamacallit, and curse:
Second-rate thoughts, weakness, groans, laments,
And soft sentiments.

You, Love, fat, fat-assed, pissed away.
The odour was that of cut hay;
The flood came towards me with brown mirth
O waterfalling earth! O Light!

MAN AND WIFE

If I do not hold on
to my maleness,
my individuality,
I shall become her son
I shall return to the womb.

I shall surely die.

The womb
is such a diminutive room
in which to lie.

Ah, anywhere but there:
In the field, the filthy ditch,
the busy metropolitan street;
best of all, on an Alp
babbling to the free air.

Time is my true mother,
Space my father.
I was made to batter doors,
and my attentive phallus
prods her and points to the stars.

Rejoice, O woman, in the pointer!

OBIT

The hour when I lose life
My friend made ill by grief
At once takes to his bed
With my poor darling Kit;
Laments in her white arms
My cold expired limbs,
And since her naked flesh
Such perfect marble is
Erects betwixt her and him
A towering headstone.

Alas, his mind is grief-crazed
(Interment all its image)
And into her roomy crypt
His rude memorial
With no delay he slips
While kissings ring its knell.
More! Writes on her mound of tit
A friend's flowing tribute
Spurred on by her frequent sighs
And praise of his fine merit:
Till he too all distracted
Groans and with a shudder dies!

THE WARM AFTERDARK

And leaving the city for the country
and man's ungovernable appetite
for malice and his evil wit,
I am more at home among dead moles,
twigs and fallen pinecones
strewn like the hard pellets of goatdung;
or where my wet limbs cannot be seen
when under the firtrees I sit out the rain.

There think how the mindless rain
will spill me into the sands of the road
or disperse beneath portentous skies
all men's images of wisdom and good;
and that large recurring image
of fields withdrawing from the sun
when leaves and blossoms blurred
into the stitchless colour of black
and you, Love, exclaimed:
The warm afterdark, this is the sweetness of love
This is the sweetness of fame.

DIVINITY

Were I a clumsy poet
I'd compare you to Helen;
Ransack the mythologies
Greek, Chinese, and Persian

For a goddess vehement
And slim; one with form as fair.
Yet find none. O, love, you are
Lithe as a Jew peddler

And full of grace. Such lightness
Is in your step, instruments
I keep for the beholder
To prove you walk, not dance.

Merely to touch you is fire
In my head; my hair becomes
A burning bush. When you speak,
Like Moses I am dumb

With marvelling, or like him
I stutter with pride and fear:
I hold, Love, divinity
In my changed face and hair.

YOUNG GIRLS DANCING AT CAMP LAJOIE

Through the rainspecked windowpane
I watch them wind their shiny gramophone;
The flies, trite and noxious as humans,
I lunge out at when I can.

And some I slay. Those I can't
May get around my flailing fist for now
And stuff my ears with momentary rant,
But not December's crate of snow.

I have with aching fingers,
Heart moved and green, touched men more gently:
Alas, a buzz of soiling laughter
Lies mined behind each docile eye.

There at the pool's black margin
I thought of Nietzsche's *No more great events*;
Now watching these Catholic girls spin
I see with a fine clairvoyance

Not gold, not gold, Lord Timon,
But medallions swivelling with heated breasts
Shall level old and splendorous kingdoms
And fell two thousand years of Christ.

LOVE IS AN IRREFUTABLE FIRE

The self-effacement of the dead.
These logs, stiff
And as if mute with embarrassment;
Eager to be gone, to be fire and sun.
But this, this is mortification.

And the lightning-blasted trees,
The fires blown out;
Even their sad hauteur is absurd
                            and does not please;
The twigs, accusatory fingers in the air
Or smirking like a wife's infidelities.

The moon alone is lucid
And its circle perfect, needing
No intervention of lake-created
Cloud.

As does the living sun.
But beauty to be beauty
Should be flawed
                    not dead;
So I, a formal creature
Of fiery flesh and bone
                    declare
Streetlamps are the exact circuit of despair
For light imprisoned in the black air.

And only love is truly perfect, a fire still,
And though partial from excess of joy
        nevertheless, like genius, irrefutable.

MY FLESH COMFORTLESS

My flesh comfortless with insect bites, sweat,
I lie stretched out on my couch of grass;
Chipmunks break like flames from the bleak earth.

And the sun's golden scarabs on the surface
Are aimless, nameless, scintillant;
Unmoving, or darting into pools

Of dark, their brightness gone. But the frog sits
And stares at my writing hand, his eyes
A guttersnipe's, leering. Or lecherous

As though an underworld savvy swelled
Those heavy-lidded eyes, xanthic beads,
They're desolation's self-mockery,

Its golden silence! Vacancy expressed,
Stressed by unblinking eye, fulvid lid!
And this vile emptiness encloses

Makes me too its rapt pupil. I goggle
At the quiet leaper, wondering
Will he rise up slim fairytale prince

At the first thundercrack. Will flash reveal
The universal lover, my Jack
Of hearts? A royal maniac raving,

Whirlwind's tongue, desolation's lung? Or flung
At the edge of this drear pool – mansoul,
Privity of evil, world's wrong, dung;

A cry heard and unheard, merest bubble
Under the legs of sallow beetles?
O, Love, enclose me in your cold bead

O lift me like a vine-leaf on the vine;
In community of soil and sun
Let me not taste this desolation

But hear roar and pour of waters unseen
In mountains that parallel my road –
Sun vaulting gold against their brightest green!

MUTE IN THE WIND

At the Lookout, leaning
against the white balustrade
a man was muting freely.

– Why do you mute
against the wind, I asked.
Though the city burns it is cold here.
Your stint in any case is futile.

He looked at me
as though a post had spoken.
His little eyes glittered.

– I have no fiddle, he said at last.
In a world of significant form
and the fashionable timelessness

of the moment my gesture
like that of Rome's emperor
may endure forever.

I deduced from the odd rhymes
he was a diseased poet and turned
from a too careful scrutiny

of his features to decipher
on the canvas of snow below
the cold balustrade: PERENNIS

TWO SONGS FOR SWEET VOICES

1.

It was a late November day
Or so I dreamed a dream;
The fog descending on the banks,
The sun a frozen gleam.

No living thing survived except
That like a frightened thief
There quivered on a barren bough
A single, wind-torn leaf.

And only you and I, my love,
Remained to see it fall;
And you were very beautiful
And I was straight and tall.

And as the sunlight ebbed away
We danced around the tree,
Until the snows came burying
The leaf and you and me.

2.

Now all the fields are lying bare
And desolate;
The road, the gate
Address a sadness everywhere.

And you have pretty eyes to see
When Autumn comes
The lovely plums
Are taken from the crowded tree.

Yet should a kiss end my pursuit
I'd see again
The ripening grain
And all the trees bowed down with fruit.

PIAZZA SAN MARCO

They have already consumed the Doges' palace
And it goes without saying the Bridge of Sighs
Misery and a club-footed poet made famous.

Pert and clumsy as the pigeons they feed,
They photograph each other endlessly.
Beer-garden gemüthlichkeit. Also Belmont Park.
The orchestra spiritedly plays the overture
To La Traviata.

Where have I twigged this before?
Ste Agathe? Some other Laurentian resort?
It does not matter.

This is Venice. This is Europe.
And these are Nietzsche's "good Europeans."
Tomorrow they will sprawl on the Lido sand
Getting their legs and torsos tanned.
So greatness is digested. Saint Mark's lions.

Their overtired eyes will close in sleep.
Sleep. Sleep. The sleep of the just cultured.
To eat. To eat palazzos and monuments,
Menu in hand.
"Mesdames e herren, you must eat first
That fine piece of sculpture
And the rest in this order."

While hangs Il Duomo in miniature
From burnt neck or wrist.

WOMEN OF ROME

The most beautiful women in the world
    Go past the Piazza Venezia.
Relics of the Risorgimento are stored there
Gathering the tourists' purchased stare.
They might gather dust for all I care.

Benito, Benito, where are your bones and thugs?

City of Caesars and Popes,
    Rome's imperial statues split and crumble.
Time and the rains that called their bluff
Have stood them there useless and formal.
My friend who knows the clever dupes we are
    Would call it elementary stuff
Sticking one's image in a public square.
Still, it worked. Look at Caius' metal finger
    Pointing to – where?

Italia, Italia, land without a recent past.
    There was a time when all went suddenly black:
How should you remember it? But that Roman girl
With the voluptuous neck and back
Is real enough in a shifting world.
I'd like to lie with her in vineyards plucking
    Grapes for her under the sun;
Or lie in orchards and pluck oranges.
Plucking is good for my complexion.

Or that beautiful lady crossing the square
    Who once lent her eyes to Raphael, da Vinci:
The fountains of the city flying
Upward in the illusive act of dying
Shaped the dark rondure of her body.
    I'd follow her to the Via Ostiense where
Perched on a pyramid Death, the arch-romantic,
    Holds court among tombs and sarcophagi
Conferring on prince and pastyface alike a tragic air.

374

Cities and skylarks perish, molluscs on a column:
    Her loveliness will never die.
Beside an English poet's grave, fertile
With sunlight, we'd there embrace
    Or any other convenient place;
Kicking, if needed, epitaphs out of the way
    – Stanzas of dejection.
The agonized stance, beloved of schoolmistresses,
    Is out of fashion and of another day.

Among ruins and travellers' cheques
    Stay always lovely, my Italian lady;
Though tomorrow the heart of Jesus
Bleeds into a garish night
Where St. Peter's keys blink green and red
    And the mad bicyclists are everywhere.
In the pale palazzos of my mind
Dance on a marble terrace floor
    Lie down on my ghostly mental bed.

AFTER THEOGNIS

Theognis prayed: "Let me drink the dark blood
Of my spoilers." – Through your veins flows black mud!
If I killed you, spilled out that evil stuff,
Where it fell, no grass would grow and no leaf;
Since I love fair earth more than I hate you,
I'll grant you years, praying they might be few.

BECAUSE MY CALLING IS SUCH

Because my calling is such
I lose myself whole days
In some foul cistern or ditch,
How should mere woman's love reach
Across the lampless silence
For the sake of that craze
Made blind Homer dance –

I, crouched in the rainless air
And choking with the dust?
Yet so bowed, the readier
To kiss your palm, my finger
Touching your fabulous face
Beyond all error and lust
In all that dark place.

For the trove of images
One gathers in the dark,
The dark that's piled with refuse
I shall not curse the bright phrase,
Coronal of my eclipse;
Though had you wed a clerk
He'd have your red lips.

Not driven like a lazar
From his house and children,
His embraces as he were
Frog on your white sheets, my dear,
Made mock of and rejected:
Who'd turn had you chosen
A prince on your bed.

SONG

For you I want the world good.
To be here and in Peking.
For the skies to open wide
And let fall a radiant thing.

The sun to be twice its size,
And the moon so red and small
That men will look up and say
It's your lip or fingernail.

And the happiness I feel
When I think of your small feet
Be that part of the rainbow
Where prayer and sunlight meet.

But that's nonsense. What I want
Are ears for your lightest tread
When you are in the market
Buying olive oil and bread.

And eyes, such eyes in my head,
So clairvoyant and so clear
That let me but close them once
I can touch your breast, my dear.

THE DAY AVIVA CAME TO PARIS

The day you came naked to Paris
The tourists returned home without their guidebooks,
The hunger in their cameras finally appeased.

Alone once more with their gargoyles, the Frenchmen
Marvelled at the imagination that had produced them
And once again invited terror into their apéritifs.
Death was no longer exiled to the cemeteries.

In their royal gardens where the fish die of old age,
They perused something else besides newspapers
– A volume perhaps by one of their famous writers.
They opened their hearts to let your tender smile defrost
    them;
Their livers filled with an unassuageable love of justice.
They became the atmosphere around them.

They learned to take money from Americans
Without a feeling of revulsion towards them;
And to think of themselves
As not excessively subtle or witty.
"Au diable with Voltaire," they muttered,
"Who was a national calamity.
Au diable with la République.
(A race of incurable petits bourgeois, the French
Are happiest under a horse under a man)
Au diable with la Monarchie!
We saw no goddesses during either folly;
Our bald-headed savants never had told us
Such a blaze of pubic hair anywhere existed."
And they ordered the grandson of Grandma Moses
To paint it large on the dome of le Sacré-Coeur.

My little one, as if under those painted skies
It was again 1848,
They leaped as one mad colossal Frenchman from their
    café Pernods
Shouting, "Vive l'Australienne!
Vive Layton who brought her among us!
Let us erect monuments of black porphyry to them!
Let us bury them in the Panthéon!"

(Pas si vite, messieurs; we are still alive)

And when, an undraped Jewish Venus,
You pointed to a child, a whole slum starving in her eyes,
Within earshot of the Tuileries,
The French who are crazy or catholic enough
To place, facing each other, two tableaux
– One for the Men of the Convention, and one puffing
    the Orators of the Restoration –
At once made a circle wide as the sky around you
While the Mayor of the 5th Arondissement
Addressed the milling millions of Frenchmen:

"See how shapely small her adorable ass is;
Of what an incredible pink rotundity each cheek.
A bas Merovingian and Valois!
A bas Charlemagne and Henri Quatre!
For all the adulations we have paid them
In our fabulous histoires
They cannot raise an erection between them. Ah,
For too long has the madness of love
Been explained to us by sensualists and curés.
A bas Stendhal! A bas Bossuet!

"Forever and forever, from this blazing hour
All Paris radiates from Aviva's nest of hair
– Delicate hatchery of profound delights –
From her ever-to-be-adored Arche de Triomphe!
All the languors of history
Take on meaning clear as a wineglass or the belch of an
    angel
Only if thought of as rushing
On the wings of a rhinoceros towards this absorbing event.
Voyeurs, voyez! The moisture of her delicate instep
Is a pool of love
Into which sheathed in candy paper
Anaesthetized politicians drop from the skies!"
(Word jugglery of course, my Sweet; but the French love it
– Mistake it in fact for poetry)

And the applaudissements and bravos
Bombinating along the Boulevard Saint-Germain
Made the poor docile Seine
Think our great Atlantic was upon it.
It overflowed with fright into the bookstalls
And sidewalk cafés.
Fifteen remaining Allemands with their cameras
Were flushed down the Rue Pigalle.

And when you were raised up
Into my hairy arms by the raving emotional crowds
Waving frenzied bottles of Beaujolais
And throwing the corks away ecstatically
(Not saving them!)
It was, my Love, my Darling,
As if someone had again ordered an advance
Upon the Bastille
Which we recalled joyously, face to face at last,
Had yielded after only a small token resistance.

TRILLIUMS AFTER A PARTY

Unlike men I met last night
Trilliums have not tight arses;
Serve neither sullen nor bright
Banter, nor recite verses.
And their three-petalled purses
Are open, displaying gold
For closelipped or passionate
Or those who laughing are cold.

Not one is professional
In the Law or Medicine;
Haphazard they take the hill
Yet let the grasses creep in.
Vision without division
Is sound argument enough,
Proffering the heated fool
Out of exuberance, love.

DRUNK ON McGILL CAMPUS

My veins are full of alcohol
I lie sprawled on the grass
The dying sun warms my face
And warms my bare chest

And the grey buildings
Begin to shake and dance
Books tumble out of library windows
And burst into pure joy

A lovely redhead
Plops a live sparrow
Into her mouth
The world wheels about

Over the restless buttocks
Of the fig-leaved statues
The campus fountain throws
Its cold sunspangled spray

Like a drunken lover
I pull down the sky
To kiss: and where my lips touch
Appears a joyous white star

A TALL MAN EXECUTES A JIG

I

So the man spread his blanket on the field
And watched the shafts of light between the tufts
And felt the sun push the grass towards him;
The noise he heard was that of whizzing flies,
The whistlings of some small imprudent birds,
And the ambiguous rumbles of cars
That made him look up at the sky, aware
Of the gnats that tilted against the wind
And in the sunlight turned to jigging motes.
Fruitflies he'd call them except there was no fruit
About, spoiling to hatch these glitterings,
These nervous dots for which the mind supplied
The closing sentences from Thucydides,
Or from Euclid having a savage nightmare.

II

Jig jig, jig jig. Like minuscule black links
Of a chain played with by some playful
Unapparent hand or the palpitant
Summer haze bored with the hour's stillness.
He felt the sting and tingle afterwards
Of those leaving their orthodox unrest,
Leaving their undulant excitation
To drop upon his sleeveless arm. The grass,
Even the wildflowers became black hairs
And himself a maddened speck among them.
Still the assaults of the small flies made him
Glad at last, until he saw purest joy
In their frantic jiggings under a hair,
So changed from those in the unrestraining air.

III

He stood up and felt himself enormous.
Felt as might Donatello over stone,
Or Plato, or as a man who has held
A loved and lovely woman in his arms
And feels his forehead touch the emptied sky
Where all antinomies flood into light.
Yet jig jig jig, the haloing black jots
Meshed with the wheeling fire of the sun:
Motion without meaning, disquietude
Without sense or purpose, ephemerides
That mottled the resting summer air till
Gusts swept them from his sight like wisps of smoke.
Yet they returned, bringing a bee who, seeing
But a tall man, left him for a marigold.

IV

He doffed his aureole of gnats and moved
Out of the field as the sun sank down,
A dying god upon the blood-red hills.
Ambition, pride, the ecstasy of sex,
And all circumstance of delight and grief,
That blood upon the mountain's side, that flood
Washed into a clear incredible pool
Below the ruddied peaks that pierced the sun.
He stood still and waited. If ever
The hour of revelation was come
It was now, here on the transfigured steep.
The sky darkened. Some birds chirped. Nothing else.
He thought the dying god had gone to sleep:
An Indian fakir on his mat of nails.

V

And on the summit of the asphalt road
Which stretched towards the fiery town, the man
Saw one hill raised like a hairy arm, dark
With pines and cedars against the stricken sun
– The arm of Moses or of Joshua.
He dropped his head and let fall the halo
Of mountains, purpling and silent as time,
To see temptation coiled before his feet:
A violated grass snake that lugged
Its intestine like a small red valise.
A cold-eyed skinflint it now was, and not
The manifest of that joyful wisdom,
The mirth and arrogant green flame of life;
Or earth's vivid tongue that flicked in praise of earth.

VI

And the man wept because pity was useless.
"Your jig's up; the flies come like kites," he said
And watched the grass snake crawl towards the hedge,
Convulsing and dragging into the dark
The satchel filled with curses for the earth,
For the odours of warm sedge, and the sun,
A blood-red organ in the dying sky.
Backwards it fell into a grassy ditch
Exposing its underside, white as milk,
And mocked by wisps of hay between its jaws;
And then it stiffened to its final length.
But though it opened its thin mouth to scream
A last silent scream that shook the black sky,
Adamant and fierce, the tall man did not curse.

385

VII

Beside the rigid snake the man stretched out
In fellowship of death; he lay silent
And stiff in the heavy grass with eyes shut,
Inhaling the moist odours of the night
Through which his mind tunnelled with flicking tongue
Backwards to caves, mounds, and sunken ledges
And desolate cliffs where come only kites,
And where of perished badgers and racoons
The claws alone remain, gripping the earth.
Meanwhile the green snake crept upon the sky,
Huge, his mailed coat glittering with stars that made
The night bright, and blowing thin wreaths of cloud
Athwart the moon; and as the weary man
Stood up, coiled above his head, transforming all.

NORTH AND SOUTH

Time that one night dropped from my mother's womb
uncoiled me to this moment and this place
that I palmtrees might see like immense phalli
naked near fountains and gaily-coloured strangers;
and pigeons, a parody on gulls in public parks

Each eye of mine is full of sunlight and flowers;
my skin is blacker than that of a Moroccan
who exposes his chest to kiss or dagger;
the conches of my ear are lined with bird whistles,
my thick nose smells the good tomorrows from afar

Here is indeed a paradise for pagans,
for gamblers and faggots with slim waists;
the tropical droppings of birds moist as a whore's kiss
miss them by inches, splatter on the stony parts
of ephebes wrapped in the warm air of civic squares

To convince me utterly all that now is lacking
are for Adam and Eve to emerge from that bush;
how astonished they would be to see the generations
idling on painted chairs or making love furiously,
and their surprise would add to the raptures of Eden

Yet I, a pilgrim, have come from the far north
where Heinrich Heine and his compatriots sleep
under tumuli, some more peaceably than others;
and where each dusk without fail a grey ash keeps falling
and settles on wrists and eyelids of the abstracted citizens

Strange bivalve of time that fell from my mother's womb;
by standing erect only I caught the air I needed,
head and straining feet holding the two halves apart;
one day out of wilfulness or fatigue I shall bend down
and feel that dark indifferent bivalve close for ever

Nice, France

387

INVENTION

The water from the sprinkler
has invented the three-leaf clovers
to hoard its pearls in;
the birds with their sharp cries and whistles
have called up the palmtrees from the ground
and made a present of them to the sun;
they fly over their waving tops all day long
like overseers of South American plantations;
buildings and statues
have asked a city to flower out of marsh and stone
and given it fountains where kneeling
with young girls it kisses its sleepy reflection;
the red lounge chairs have invented the green park
and the rich the beggars on the quay
whose tatters fluttering like colorful mediaeval pennons
assemble the hungry pigeons for crumbs
the silent apartment windows toss at them
before closing for ever

And the poem has invented me
to pry it loose from time's lockjaw
and from the earth that is dumb unless I speak
and the wombs of women
barren without the echoes of my voice

Away from the poem that is writing me
the world loses mystery and coherence;
and how inglorious and vain
are all words not in a poem:
like a bride's veil at the bottom
of a manila packing-case
like the shattered geometry of a bee-hive
or the crushed-open pod lying beside its seed
like an unoccupied chair in a park
like brown grass without water
or trees without birds
or empty cisterns where no faces come

When my head is filled with a poem
it is a hand holding another hand in love
it is the womb filled with fruit
it is my little son's arms encircling my neck
it is the sun lighting up the pearls
of all the three-leaf clovers of the field
at a given signal of the sky
it is the beggar resting his head
on a found treasure-chest for pillow
it is the prophet vindicated in his own city
it is the confident sunflower awaiting the dawn
it is myself as I truly am

May time keep me worthy of the poem
that has written me since time began

RHINE BOAT TRIP

The castles on the Rhine
are all haunted
by the ghosts of Jewish mothers
looking for their ghostly children

And the clusters of grapes
in the sloping vineyards
are myriads of blinded eyes
staring at the blind sun

The tireless Lorelei
can never comb from their hair
the crimson beards
of murdered rabbis

However sweetly they sing
one hears only
the low wailing of cattle-cars
moving invisibly across the land

CLOCHARDS

Like wounded birds that fall from a height
in ever-decreasing circles
they've finally come to rest on benches
and in the doorways of old churches;
or like the pitiful leaves of autumn
a sudden wind shoves into a ditch
and passes over, they lie in the unwanted
intimacy of misfortune, only their sordid rags
the fluttering banners of their separate selves

And one wears a cross for an amulet,
his sole covering for the night;
and one wraps himself in a newspaper
which the wind will read for him
through the long, monotonous hours.
It is they who know the hours of the dark
when the auto's spurt and snort in the empty street
puts another stone under their troubled heads;
when the diamond stars appear close, close
and sometimes ungraspable and far away,
and the body weightless yet somehow full of cares

They sleep like flowers in the crevices of streets
whose ragged edges abrade and pain,
making them raise their innocent grizzled heads
through all the periods of the moon;
who like themselves outcast, a poor clochard,
owns the waning night which no one wants.
And in the dawn the birds whistling them awake,
they sleepily brush the dream's deposit
of cold dew from their tatters
while dismay like a thief enters their eyes
at the renewed clamour of appetite and sense
the night had promised them to still forever;
and rising from the grim doorway and bench
they move like birds towards the unwelcoming street
silent and unnoticed as death itself

AT THE BELSEN MEMORIAL

It would be a lie
to say I heard screams
I heard nothing
It would be a lie
to say I saw ribs
like the bones
of beached ships
I saw nothing
It would be a lie
to say I sniffed
the odours
of decomposing crystals
or of bodies
that are left to lie
in the wind and rain
I sniffed nothing
nothing at all
It would be a lie
to say
emaciated ghosts
of little children
brushed against me
and that I reached out
my hands
to touch them
There were no emaciated
ghosts
and my hands
remained in the pockets
of the summer suit
I was wearing
The taste of death
was on my tongue
on my tongue only
When it pierced my neck
I was turned into stone
towering and black
Come:
read the inscription

MUTABILITY

I wanted to say something
    about love and hate
and I heard the waves say:
'Hush, it has been said.'

I wanted to say something about man,
    about woman too
and I heard the waves grumble to the shore:
'It has been said. There's nothing new.'

I wanted to say something about God,
    the Big Tuna
and I heard the green waves roar:
'There is nothing to say.'

I wanted to build a Nineveh tower
    on the plains of shining sand
but I heard the waves menace:
'We shall let nothing stand.'

I wanted to build temples, forums and thruways
    and I heard them hiss
at my feet:
'We shall wash them all away.'

I wanted to take from the sea
    for my beloved, my sweet
a single radiant ripple
but it has turned to water in my hand,
only water.

TIME'S VELVET TONGUE

A white neon sign
reads WINDSOR'S
above the store window
that reflects the blond girl
licking
her ice cream cone
at the corner
of Maréchal Foch and Avenue de la Victoire

Under
the dying stars night
time's velvet tongue
licks her
in the same slow relentless way
and indeed when I look up again
– she is gone!

WINTER LYRIC

Winter knows the good are poor,
that talent goes begging warmth
from ice and snow.
I hear my soul howling in the wind.
How can I write a pocm to you
when you leave nothing for my pen?
There isn't a nib's thickness
between wish and fact, between
ideal and actuality.
If I give my imagination a head start,
you always catch up with me
– especially in bed!

It's almost 3 P.M.
The yahoos in the tavern
are more restless
than usual.
I'd better go home and tell you
how perfect you are.

SUN BATHERS

They will sit all afternoon
    or lie on mattresses, heads propped up,
and watch snapping at the beach the waves
whose exasperation turns always into foam,
finding they have filled their mouths with stones;
these in a cold white fury they spit out
    and chin-nudge down the sloping bottom
to return, their eternal appetite unappeased

Yet this spectacle which is repeated
    over and over and over again
neither bores nor displeases the sun-bathers;
nor does the hissing noise of disappointment
and pain that issues each time from between
the broken white teeth of the waves:
    though indignation and menace are in the sound,
waves are more powerless than beggars on the quay

Yet almost as restless as the waves
    they turn from side to side to capture
the sun's arbitrary rays in the magical
globules of oil they've smeared on their skin;
the sun is untouchable and far away,
not like the sea whose noble appearance
    the noisy proximate waves constantly betray:
they squint malevolently, their faces sullen

For to the sun-bathers
    stripped of all recognizable distinctions,
the anonymity of the myriad waves
is both comfort and community;
and their restlessness, a nice counterpoint to ease
making the idle day still more pleasurable;
    along with servitors bringing their drinks, the waves
are slaves who come and vanish at command

394

But more, there is the satisfaction
	to the machine-conquered lying about
and dolefully attending the sun's focus
in watching the clear, blue-green, aristocratic sea
fawningly kiss their bared toes; to these
there is pleasure in hearing the ever-renewed roar
	of defeat: and this is the subtle drug
the sun-bathers of Europe take hour by hour

COLLABORATION

Side by side, these sarcophagi contain
The ashes of Molière and Lafontaine;
With miser and knave one filled up his stage,
And one set beasts discoursing on each page.
Their pooled resources so fine and sable
Here persuade us life's both farce and fable.

BALLAD OF THE STONES

What if a stone on the beach
could become you
and I flung one into the water
where it split in two

And both of you, laughing,
sat down
and without a word of reproach
enjoyed the sun

And smiled at all the fables
I willingly told
of stones the sun had warmed
and let grow cold

Or of stones a magician flings
far out into the seas
and return as wave-riding girls
by twos and threes

From all the oceans they come
with tresses dark and fair
asking the magician to comb
the pearls from out their hair

He crushes the brightest pearls
the enamoured girls bring
and rising on them high as an Alp
he begins to sing

He sings of lust, of love and hate;
of life, with the strongest breath
till men and women who hear him
ecstatically cry for death

And each girl closes her eyes
and lays her head on the sand;
her body shrivels into air,
her head turns a stone in his hand

The magician rolls the stones on the beach
the flat, the odd-shaped, the round;
all of them are cold and pearl-less
and they make no sound

But when the sun is on them
they wanly smile
and then he thinks of oceans
and glistening limbs for a while

And he throws back his head to laugh
but the stones pain his limbs and his head
so he rises at last to his feet
and commences to dance instead

He dances to the shore of the sea
he dances like one who is mad
and no one who sees him from afar
can say whether he is happy or sad

I end my fable: you rise up to go
but one turns back with a moan
and one of you is here
and one of you is a stone

INSOMNIA

After the bath
you lay on the bed
exposing layers
of beautiful washed skin
we both stared at in surprise;
long strands of hair, shiny and damp
under the yellow lamplight,
fell over your shoulders:
they made two exclamation marks
with your stiffened nipples.

And gently you fell asleep
at my side;
while I, my sweet, stayed awake
all night
who had your uncovered beauty
to think about,
your nipples troubling me
in the night
like two mysterious asterisks.

THE AIR IS SULTRY

The air is sultry.
    So is my soul.

The coffee is bitter.
    So are my thoughts.

The cigaret is stale.
    Ditto my emotions.

There's a filthy hole in the wall.
    There's one in my heart.

It is going to rain.
    The rain can't help me.

My darling has run off with another man.
    Who cares?

I hear her knock on the door.
    She brings me suffering.

She tells me she loves me.
    I tell her I adore her

The air is sultry.
    So is my soul.

WOMEN OF THE BACK STREETS OF EUROPE

Swept to one side by the broad avenidas and boulevards
they stumble into dark, evil-smelling houses
or bend over their *pasta* and *sardinas*

Or you will see them in the hidden lanes and alleys
dressed in black, looking prematurely old,
looking like dry blots the sun has made in mockery

O like birds that have sickened
they gather in the back streets of Mediterranean cities
– a misery from which God takes refuge in churches

It is there they go to seek Him out
bringing Him their arthritic fingers,
their illnesses and wounds to renew His courage and faith

Desperate beauty which the poets have ignored!
And I have heard their suffering God whisper hoarsely:
'Return to your husbands and children, to your aches and
        burdens.'

And I have gone with them up a hill that leads
to the Castello San George where consumptive girls are
        skipping,
and as they skip and dance, dampen my cheeks with tears

ERICH KÄSTNER   (1899-   )

When I met the German poet, Erich Kästner,
he kept belting down one whisky after another,
after which he said to me: 'Women are life,
don't ever forget that.' Though sixty-seven,
he didn't look a grey hair over fifty;
obviously he had enjoyed women – I mean
life, his pessimism a Berliner's
sour note, not to be taken seriously:
hadn't he survived Hitler and the other
gutter commandos who had burned his books?
Anyway, being born just one year before
a century begins gives a man a head start
in this world, an unassailable belief
in his own superiority; he'll smile
ironically and think, 'All this huff and puff,
bloodshed and bluster are useless and absurd:
do its worst, the century can't overtake me.'
He has that cutting edge, you see, of one year.

MAHOGANY RED

Once, a single hair could bind me to you;
had you told me: 'Jump
from the tallest building'
I'd have raced up on three elevators
and come down on my skull;
from the land of wailing ghosts
I'd have mailed you a fragment of skullbone
initialled by other desperate men
who had despaired of ever pleasing their lovers.
Once, pleasure expanded in my phallus
like a thin, excruciating column of mercury;
when it exploded in my brain
it was like a movie I once saw
where the earth is grabbed by the sun
and fried black;
or another ice age arrived on snow
and I danced hot and bare and alone
on a lost glacier,
hairy mammoths circling around me.
Once, I was a galley-slave
lying stripped in all your fragrant ports;
a tickle in my groin
made your skin a torment to me,
and I dived into the dimples of your knees
when you stretched naked and sexy on your bed.
Godhead, the Marxist revolution, History
that is so full of tombs and tears,
I stuffed them all up your golden rectum
and sewed up their sole escape route
with frantic kisses sharper than needles.

Now, without any warning
you are a middle-aged woman
who has tinted her hair mahogany red;
one of your front teeth, I notice, is discoloured grey;
I notice, too, how often you say
'phony' and 'artificial'
and wonder each time if you're not projecting.
Yes, suddenly you are a woman
no different from other women;

402

a little less nasty perhaps,
a little less insincere,
less contemptuous of the male sex,
wistful and dissatisfied in your contempt,
still hankering for greatness, the dominant man,
his flowing locks all the spread-out sky you want;
unfair, conscienceless, your bag of woman's tricks close by,
hard beset, as women in all ages have been,
needing to make your way, to survive,
to be praised immoderately,
to be nibbled by a lover's amorous teeth,
to procreate . . .
vain of your seductive wiggle when you walk away from me,
of your perfect breasts displaying nipples
I wanted to devour
and die choking, their pink tips tickling my throat;
vain of the fiery pennant under your chin
pinned there by your latest lover.

The bulb in my brain
once ignited and kept aglow
by genital electricity
lies smashed to bits.
I look out at the world with cool, aware eyes;
I pick out the pieces of grey glass from my brain;
I hold them all in my trembling hand.
Only a god could put them together again
and make them light up with sexual ecstasy,
but he lies sewn up in your golden rectum
huddled beside History and the Marxist revolution.
It is sad to be an atheist,
sadder yet to be one with a limp phallus.
Who knows
maybe if I had swung and knocked out
your one discoloured tooth
I would still love you, your little girl's grin,
small gap in your jaw
(who knows, who knows)
and not have wanted to write
this bitter, inaccurate poem.

THE WAVE

Look, I said to the shopkeeper,
this is a *bona-fide* wave,
the real thing;
hand me some pebbles
and I'll show you
how it curls and uncurls
making a small splash
on the table
you can hear if you turn off
your TV set

Take a good look, I begged,
you can see
it still has some weeds
in its mouth

Weeds? Who wants weeds?
said the shopkeeper,
get rid of them!

But this is a unique wave,
I continued,
complete with a streak of moonlight;
if you bend down and look closely,
you will see it;
and though it's a single wave
detached from the others
it still has its rotatory movement
intact
– do you see how it climbs up
on its shoulder
and throws itself down on its face?

Big deal, sneered the shopkeeper,
making a move to go away

But just think, I pleaded,
you can have a wave
all to yourself;
there isn't another like it
anywhere in the world;
look, mister, if you take it
I'll throw in a single cloud
I've got here in my glass case
as well as a ripple of air
a big wind left behind
when it turned a corner last week
on its way to the open sea

Wave, cloud, and ripple of air
all for the price of one

Nah, said the shopkeeper,
me and my wife like clean water;
take your dirty wave
and throw it back into the sea

CRISIS THEOLOGY

To this pass has Christianity come:
There is no God, and Jesus is his son

PORTRAIT DONE WITH A STEEL PEN

I've seen him work to start a quarrel
between two men not over-friendly
and then his lips are a thick rubber band
holding in place invisible poisonous weeds
— a bouquet for each! And he'll smile
showing his few good mended teeth
when someone takes the proffered weeds and sniffs
and wheezing sends a spray of snot across the room

O his smile is innocent enough,
good-natured and tinged with sadness:
you might say malice has turned to melancholy
now his point has been made and human nature
shown up again for the shabby thing
he'd always known it was

A nice game to play if one knows
how to play it, and he does

And like himself his poems
are disjointed, big with hands and feet
that are out of place
— graceless. Lurching like his body
they sprawl or wander across the page
uncertain which way to move, up or down,
this way or that: the drunk's irresolute stagger

He is ten provinces of the Canadian pleb;
formless, lacking a centre of control,
the unitary discipline of the soul
that makes for freedom, power, nobility;
and the capital of his frail dominion,
lemon-pale, the colour of oysters I've seen
in Prince Edward Island, nodding sometimes
crazily like a funny-face balloon
with smile constant as a Nipponese spy's
or lolling from drink, fatigue, or malice
is the uneminent eminence
where foreign thoughts enter and leave
and diplomacy accords a recognition
but not beauty, certainly not distinction

Lanky like John A. Macdonald and like him
lecherous, vulgar, a politician
his lunging shadow falls between the coasts,
his animated spittle on desperate coteries:
those fantastic literary polyps that feed
on news of poems or poets and where reputation
is raised or lowered like a kite
handled by a critic in a classrom chair
or three lost souls in a prairie café

And like the father of our country
he welds together the scattered colonies
of the spirit and gives to fragile
alienated souls dominion over sugaring
and supermarkets. Then his body
with its peculiar lope, its slither and heave
like that of a vessel on Lake Erie
seems moving towards a wider ocean
with only the sky's luminaries for guide
or towards a tranquil basin sunny
with peace and palm-trees, and going inland,
with tall weeds which he plucks by the armful
leaving awkward love-notes among them
containing genuine lines of poetry

GRATITUDE

I healed a man of muteness
and the first words I heard him say
were: 'You ridiculous old man
get going, get out of my way!'

I healed another of blindness;
he laughed out loud and said:
'Mister you have such an ugly face,
get lost, drop dead.'

I cured a youth of deafness;
he put a hand over each ear
and said with a loud snort
'Say nothing, mister, do you hear?'

I taught an ancient cripple
to walk without a crutch;
he looked at me angrily and said:
'Walking has been praised over-much.'

I showed an ignoramus
how to write simple poems;
now I overhear him murmur:
'The old fool still uses rhymes.'

FAIR MUSIA

Musia, the world that calls you fair
Knowing your eyes, your lovely hair,
Was yet astounded when it heard
How justly you deserve that word:
For the dazed youth whose ailing heart
Never could have survived your art
Had you allowed a single stare
Blabs you spared him and buttoned up
Your pert blouse to the very top.

BEACH ROMANCE

Rubbing oils
on herself
she pulls out
a pocket mirror
to take a long look
at a face
that asks
if it is becoming
sufficiently
tanned and sleek
to attract
one of the male flies
buzzing about her breasts
buttocks
and exposed patches
of raw skin
and when he will alight
to inject
the sweet venom
of love
into the receptacle
prepared for it
to round out
the contour
of her belly
with another fly

409

AN OLD NICOISE WHORE

The famous and rich, even the learned and wise,
    Singly or in pairs went to her dwelling
To press their civilized lips to her thighs
    Or learn at first hand her buttocks' swelling.

Of high-paying customers she had no lack
    And was herself now rich: so she implied.
Mostly she had made her pile while on her back
    But sometimes she had made it on the side.

Reich she read; of course the Viennese doctor.
    Lawrence – his poems and novels she devoured;
Kafka at the beginning almost rocked her
    But as she read him more she said he soured.

Swedish she spoke, French, Polish, fluent German;
    Had even picked up Hindi – who knows how?
In bed she had learned to moan and sigh in Russian
    Though its rhythms troubled her even now.

A nymphomaniac like Napoleon's sister
    She could exhaust a bull or stallion;
Bankers had kneeled before her crotch to kiss her
    And ex-princes, Spanish and Italian.

And all the amorous mayors of France-Sud
    Impelled by lust or by regional pride
Would drive their Renaults into her neighborhood,
    Ring her bell and troop happily inside.

And pimpled teen-agers whom priests and rabbis
    Had made gauche, fearful, prurient and blind
Prodded by Venus had sought her expert thighs:
    Ah, to these she was especially kind.

And having translated several Swinburne lines
    She kept the finest whips she could afford
To be, though most aristocrats brought their canes,
    Ready for some forgetful English lord.

We saw waves like athletes dash towards the shore
    Breaking it seemed from a line of green scum;
We saw the sun dying, and this aged whore
    Noted how it gave clouds a tinge of rhum.

Engaging was her mien, her voice low and sweet;
    Convent nuns might have envied her address.
She was touched by the bathers below her feet;
    I, by this vitality sprung from cess.

And as she spoke to me on the crowded quay
    And reminisced about her well-spent years
I mourned with her her shrivelled face and body
    And gave what no man had given her: tears.

FOR THE RECORD

This cultivated bourgeois detests me
since I will not die – not yet!

He thinks poets should not live
beyond twenty-five;
they also should be firebrands of integrity
to be extinguished by some crook's brine.
My resolve
to outlast philistines and brutes
disturbs him

Cut down young, romantically unfortunate:
that's how he'd choose
to have the poets
as he gaily describes a profitable transaction
and rumbles some lines of Mayakovsky
over a plate of goose.

NATIONAL VIRTUES

In Munich
I met a German
who told me
that as a consequence
of Hitler's
'final solution'
he could no longer
hate Jews

And a Cordoban
assured me, that he,
personally,
had no feelings
about pierced bulls,
one way or the other

While an Italian
from Bologna
his skull glistening
with hair oil
informed me
he had promised the Virgin
to give up pinching
the bottoms
of little girls

The virtues
of the Frenchman
I have not yet
been able to discover

412

PIGEONS

When it begins to drizzle
the pigeons fly to the boughs of trees
where they sit quietly,
pretending they are birds of doom:
wet crows in a charcoal illustration
for a Gothic fable.
Purest illusion!
for with the first beams of light
from a repentant sun
they shake wetness and theatricality
from their tails
to alight once more on grass or gravel
in a fussy search for food; pigeons
are always hungry;
or is it insatiable greed
makes them ceaselessly prod the earth
with their pointed beaks,
their ridiculous slender heads
sawing the world
into two equal and severe halves,
one for each suspicious miser's eye
to take notice of
and disapprove

413

ON THE QUAY WITH MY MOTHER'S GHOST

At the far curve of the basin
it is all beautiful, all magical
for the mist has silvered the luxury apartment buildings
into remote fairyland castles

Turrets, fluttering pennons
and the pale trees outlined sharply
under a cloudless blue-grey sky
pilgrims climbing towards some cathedral
I can imagine but cannot see

It is the silver haze
magical, transformative

O if only my mother were alive
that I might show it to her

Look, I would say to her
this is what I saw when I was a boy
this I daydreamed all day long
Now look,
just as I imagined it!
the gulls, the castles by the remote, forgotten shore,
the silver haze
– a fairyland into which my boyhood
went walking
in search of a trumpet that was never blown

Listen, listen, someone is blowing it now
and surely that's my captive boyhood
waving at us from behind that pennant,
each flutter erasing a year from my years

O happiness!

And so I sit all afternoon
my head turned towards enchantment,
imagining a superbly arrogant princess
in her jewelled gown
dreaming of me when she looks away from her turret;
while below my feet
glisten the well-oiled bodies of the sun-bathers
and from the commonplace air
a balloon or beach ball
occasionally descends on a hairy belly
or a sunglassed stare
which my mother's ghost remarks
even more sardonically
than I

PRESBYTERIAN CHURCH SIGNBOARD

How amazing it is that the Prince of Peace
Who loved the birds, the little lambs that totter
Should be served by ministers with names like these:
The Reverend Doctors BUTCHER and SLAUGHTER

415

GYPSIES

It is only in Europe
I have met gypsies

Beggars with a history!

No one knows for certain
where they've come from,
these pagan mendicants
who dance and make love
on the unquiet graves
of European civilization;
and not only on its graves
– on its concert halls, theatres,
libraries and laboratories;
and those who refused
the closer embrace
of its crematoria,
on its crematoria

A colourful Lazarus
he will not leave our doors

An uncircumcized Mordecai
he measures the doorposts
– are they high enough for scaffolds?

At my approach
under the arcade
of the Avenue de la Victoire
this young gypsy
pinches her infant son
to make him cry
and holds out to me
her practised hand and frown

416

We need her
waiting there for us
under the arcade
of the Avenue de la Victoire;
she tests whatever
remains of Europe's heart
made frigid in the ovens
of Auschwitz,
the interrogation cells
of Treblinka

And she will outlast
her persecutors
who will go down
to dust
under her outstretched
begging arm,
her piteous frown

She will outlast us all
for she is a kind of poetry;
free as the imagination,
irresponsible

Dance, gypsy, dance
on the graves of Montmartre and Montparnasse;
play, gypsy, play
in the German, Greek, and Spanish
cemeteries

Still, I think of her infant son

At twenty-five
in the middle of some feast
or love-tryst
will he suddenly
begin to cry

For no reason,
for no reason at all?

MAMMOTHS

What, there are still communists!

    Yes, shaggy-haired
survivors
from an Ice Age:
the Thirties

    Mammoths
with broken tusks,
let them roam
the plains
of Europe
and America

    In Russia
the species
long ago
became extinct
leaving behind
no trace
except a single
skull
preserved for show
in a glass case

LOOK HOMEWARD, ANGEL

Just across
the Café de Lyons
where I take
my nocturnal cup
of tea and lemon
(avec infusions)
is a shop
displaying ladies'
apparel
– stockings, bras,
all sorts of panties,
soft slip-ins
and kimonos –
and a blazing
neon sign
which reads:
MONTREAL

What a lovely touch
of home!

SPECULATORS

There is a speculator
in Canada
who buys up snow:
whole valleys and mountains
covered with it,
and forests of evergreens
that wear their white capes in winter
as if they were Sisters of Mercy
racing towards some disaster.
I've even seen him dicker
for an ice-floe somewhere in Alaska
merely questioning the seller
about possible cracks and fissures:
the size and exact location of the ice-floe
didn't matter.
He once told me he'd like to buy
the frigid air above the snow
but can't find anyone rich enough
to sell it to him;
when someone as enterprising as himself
offered to deliver
a million tons of the stuff
he put finger to nose
and shook his head:
the price was too high;
besides, what proof
could the vendor offer
that the air had pressed against the snow
long enough to make it consistently cold
at least to the extent of one mile
both in length and depth:
so the deal was off.

I asked him what he was going to do
with all the acres of snow
he had accumulated
and he said something about Fort Knox
and minting a new kind of snowflake
or selling it to a ski resort
at a special discount
if they raised the Swiss flag
on three of their most popular slopes.
Why the Swiss flag? I could never find out:
he didn't look Swiss; more like a Turk, I'd say.
It was when I saw him
looking at some ice-cubes
in a glass
which someone had just drained
of lemonade
and opening his Moroccan leather wallet
to extract his business card
that I decided
his ambition to corner the market
on ice and snow
had to be thwarted.
I threatened to pour
the hottest sands I owned
in the Gobi and Sahara deserts
if he acquired so much as another snowflake.
This made him furious
and we came to blows.
Now they let him make all the artificial ice
in the place
and I've been warned
never to let myself be seen by him
carrying electric pads
to those who need them
and certainly
never with a kettle of hot water
in my hand

APPARITION

Thinking of you, I could not sleep

You came into the tenebrous room
like moonlight
and sat on the chair like a pool of light

I was too awed to touch you

I waited for you to speak
There was a sudden flicker
(of amusement? distress?)
and then you addressed me
as light moving swiftly
from chair to table
to lie folded there like a white napkin

At last I broke the black silence
(was it I who spoke?)
The light stirred like some live thing
and fell on the wristbone of my right hand

That is how I know
it is you who came into the room

The light shimmers on my white wristbone
which throbs as if it were a pulse
It is you for whom it throbs
though my heart has stopped still

FREEDOM

I said it
before
but with desperation, tears
(just like a poet)
fist clenched white
and with raised voice
— so I did not mean it, after all

Now I say
'I am free'
and scarcely whisper the words
yet the walls of an entire city
tremble and fall

STREET VIOLINIST

Someone told him to buy a violin
and pretend he was a musician
down on his luck, he'd get more sympathy
and centîmes that way: scrape on the heart
strings and you open the purse. Of course
he plays the same high note over and over,
knowing no other; still, his beggary
is now tricked out in the dignity of art;
and you might say, too, he has become
a sort of street-corner specialist
who gives the one violin note he plays
such a resonance of human distress
no meaner evidence of hardship or defeat
can quite so movingly express

RUINS

The sun lies sprawled out on the Aegean
as if high on marijuana
or a punchdrunk old soak
who keeps cuffing her with hot wet fistfuls
each time she tries to move from his embrace

And I've seen the astounding Acropolis
where it stands on a hill, white and unforgettable,
looking down on a lot of crummy Athenians
who may have splinters of marble in their souls
but no harmony, no harmony at all,
no beauty of figure and face, or of speech

Money money money money money money money
and pleasure, Philebus,
making men and women weak as piss
the Acropolis in ruins
Delphi in ruins
Olympia in ruins
Knossos in ruins
the Greeks, every sharp-trading one of them,
in ruins
the English visitors in ruins
bringing with them the unmistakable smell of decay
so familiar to the left nostril of history
and the French, Italians, Germans, and blond Dutch
ruins, all ruins, coming to look at ruins,
coming to stare at the hole in the ground
where it all began

FOR MISS CÉZANNE

Last night I dreamt
        of one of your canvases;
the figures, obscure and innocent,
had stripped and slipped off
to be promptly arrested for indecent exposure
and smoking pot;
        also for stealing packets of chewing gum
from drugstore counters that suspected nothing.
Your whole disorderly world,
        messy with life –
the bourgeois' nightmare, the civilized man's
despair –
jiggled crazily under my blessing
twin-branched arms, all ten fingers
lit up like chandelier crystals
        washed by whisky:
and waiting
                waiting
for the feel of your heavy flesh,
for the sadness, gayety, surrender, tenderness
and Being final as a root
which of all loves men have known
stretching in a luminous black line
to Eve's last, most radiant ringlet
you alone bring and give.

REPETITION

Each morning I go to the same place;
my chair, green and clean, is expecting me
directly under the bright familiar sun
and the park, prodding the flowers and birds,
receives me like a friend, the trees bowing gently

The palmtrees look like upended erections;
I try to imagine what disaster might be found
to have overtaken the males of Ethiopia
for it seems they all have been shot from the sky
with the tips of their black phalli stuck in the ground

I read my wife still loves me, there's money for cake,
nothing to get my pee in an uproar about;
what's more, my few remaining teeth are sound.
So to hell with dreary Absurdist plays!
Grown wise with the years, I'll join in the shout

For whatever it is that people are shouting about.
I'll repeat carefully the lies people want told,
tell the plainest girl she has the face of Helen of Troy;
let the pigeons crap on the three fountain virgins
their nipples look softer for the white mould

Ah, sweet smell of lechery, of steamy scrotum
and crotch; colorful wings bring it to my nose
and as if from Noah's ark I see the Nicoise
two by two, wine fermenting in their bladders,
crawl from my mother's barrel of herrings to flirt or doze

Still, the spectacle does not altogether please;
something is amiss, an abyss is lacking to shove
it all into, to see what comes up first:
herrings or sunflowers or the black phalli of palmtrees.
What I'd like to overhear is an avowal of love

One statue might immoderately make to another;
that would be different, that would be news!
I'm tired of seeing the world go by on its well-oiled joints,
of all this repetitive, ignoble, useless pother.
It's the sameness that finally disappoints

LIGHT

When I half close my eyes
I see illuminated, short spikes,
projectiles of sunlight, strike
the naked body of the sea

And narrowing them still more, it is
as though I saw long, golden needles
tattooing on it the sky's royal insignia
— look at that patch of indigo!

Lastly the sun's semaphore I see flash
which no swimmer will decode
but is meant for the eyes of certain fish
waiting for it at the bottom of the sea

EUPHORIA

They go past me
the newly arrived traveller
looking for the mythical hotel
the earnest Dutch tourist
reading a paperback on the French Revolution
his skull is stuffed with guillotines
the young mother following him
holding her child by the hand
a retired couple
their faces are bland and serious
a beggar whose shuffle
cuts the morning sunshine like a rusted knife
a woman making the well-cared-for park
wheel about her invalid husband
a troop of girls on the way to the conservatory
camera-fiends, sunbathers, fairies
and friends their delight in each other
enveloping them like a sheet of light
and I want to reach out
to caress them
my heart is throbbing gladness and love
but they will not stay
and I must address my inhuman cries
of affection
to the birds on the sparkling freshly-watered grass
who scorning my shouts
fly off
making luminous concentric circles in the air

PILGRIM

What am I doing here?

I loathe the capitalists
I detest their corrupted slaves
even more
women are hysterical idiots
whose holes smell of herring
poets plant roses on the tops of dunghills
(bravo!)
their famous striptease
in the tiled washrooms of the rich
no longer interests me
all men seek power
if saints and ascetics, over themselves;
over others, if ordinary Joes
statesmen are a fine blend of the two
like certain tobaccos;
admirable companions, truly,
but treaties like flags fade
and where is Metternich? Guizot?

Nature? I'd scrub my ass clean
with that mouldy blanket of stars
except for possible star-splinters coming loose

Tell me, someone:
where am I going?
what am I doing here?
where are my pilgrim feet taking me?

Luckily
I have a wily brain
money in the bank, one or two friends;
or men knowing my true sentiments
would shoot me at once

CONFEDERATION ODE

Like an old, nervous and eager cow
my country
is being led up to the bull
of history

The bull has something else
on his mind
and ignores her;
still, dazed by her wagging tail, in good time
he must unsheathe
his venerable tool
for the long-awaited consummation

Certainly it will be the biggest
bang-up affair
within the memory of centenarians,
and seismologists have been alerted
everywhere
to record the shocks and tremors

Emissaries
are fanning out to advise
younger and older statesmen around the globe:
take note, finally our brindled Elsie
is mating history

For everyone coming to watch
this extraordinary event
there can be standing room only
for himself
and a single bag of overcharged peanuts

Poor dear
what will she do
the day after
when she looks in a pool
and sees
the same bland face,
the same dull wrinkles between the horns
and the relieved bull
even more indifferent than before?

QUAY SCENE

The old French beggar
touches his beard
humbly
His smile releases
two stumps
that are black and friendly
and his simple gaze
is that of a child
expecting some favour
for good conduct
or for no reason whatever
Once upon a time
he saw angels descend
from heaven,
their immense silent wings
laden with plums and quince
but not now: Now
he is old and hungry
and hurt
because the Nice bourgeoise
and her husband
sunning themselves
on the quay
shrink into their chaises longues
and stonily
give him the back of their necks
Poor thing
unaware
after so many years
of touching his beard
humbly
and smiling
to the back of fat necks
that he suffers
from the most dreaded disease
of all:
poverty

BEACH ACQUAINTANCE

His eyes twinkled like blue salts
his torso was tanned and lithe
he was a young man
with a crop of white hair
or an old man
with a young African body
It was good
to lie side by side on the beach
and see the oils frying
on his muscular body
He brought the sun closer
made it burn more fiercely
'What have you learned
from seventy years?' I asked him

He turned over on his back
and addressed the sun:

'Only the strong are free
Life is a white fever
of carbon that rages
in beautiful girls and garbage;
let it rage for ever
I revere heroes and saints
and offer the many too-many
an affectionate contempt,
to slaves the back of my hand
Also I never read the poets;
they malign the world
because they are impotent
and call their St. Vitus dance
ecstasy
Women are mystics
that semen tranquillizes
The sea, the sea roars
but is never noisy
I love its cool folds
Death, mon ami, is a good life's
last surprise'

432

He smiled and jumped to his feet
with the quickness of a child
'Now let us take our swim'

TO A BEAUTIFUL UNKNOWN GIRL

All morning I struggled to write a poem

I thought of my childhood
that had rolled like a button under the bed
and was lost forever

Of the armless vituoso
who lit my wife's flaming cherry jubilee
with his nimble toes

Of my mother dying in the hospital

Of girls walking towards
all the beaches of the world
with NO PARKING printed on their rear ends

Of God finally unmasking himself
in a public square like Zorro

Of pebbles that sang arias
from my favourite operas
whenever I dropped them into the sea

Of love which I had forgotten to take out
from the drawer where I keep my neckties

But when the beautiful unknown girl
came towards me
holding the French poodle in her long graceful arms

I threw away my imperfect lines
what was the use
she was the poem I had wanted to write

433

NEW YEAR'S EVE

In Times Square
my girl and I
join the enormous, dark crowd
standing hushed and expectant
in their annual devotion

Their deity:
not change or flux
but unchanging, abstract Time.
I see one or two kneel in prayer

I see hands tighten
as if clutching one end
of an eternal skipping-rope:
how some will make the new year jump!

A couple kisses shyly

Several youngsters blow whistles

A drunk smashes a beer bottle

But the hushed thousands
fall away from us
like a dark, silent runway
for the old year's flight;
in a few seconds
it will take off
for the oblivion of history

I, too, touched
by the pathos of the moment
kiss my girl

As the two hands
of the illuminated clock
freeze into one,
the crowd expels
the new year
from its lungs
with a sharp cry

And at once shatters
into lonely individuals
suddenly aware
of the long pin
the cold impassive clock
is maniacally tap-tapping
into their skulls

A SONG ABOUT WOMAN

I put all that I knew
      about woman
into a pearl-lined shell
and flung it into the sea;
but a wave rose up like a fist
      and seized it
and hurled it back to me.
The waves stood up like a chorus
      and I heard them hiss:
'We have monsters enough in our deeps
without this.'

I put all that I knew
      about woman
into an air-tight box
and shot it into the sky;
but someone behind a cloud
      put out a hand and flung it
back to the sand and rocks;
while a cloud muffled his words
and the sky hung like a shroud
      his words came down as rain
and the rain was thick as curds.

I put all that I knew
      about woman
into a jewelled urn
and buried it in the ground;
but at once the grasses parted
      and flowers began to turn
and the thing that I had buried
      came up without a sound.
'Fool,' said a voice full of mirth
'she is perfect, my lovely daughter!'
Then still were the lips of earth.

THE HUMAN CONDITION

Hope for the human race?

I hear a talented novelist
a sensitive, beautiful Jewess
exclaim:
I believe in the sanctification
of life.
I believe the six million died for us.
Their deaths bought us time.

Her eyes, dark lovely, glow
like those of Miriam the prophetess
(Quiet, everyone
a kind, imaginative human being
is meditating):
Did twenty million kulaks perish?
They massacred my forbears in Odessa.
Stalin was a very great man.

I believe Mao
is the greatest man in our century.
He's going to eliminate the whites
like bleached flies.
We're guilty of evil.
We've made a botch of things,
a mess.
Let the Chinese come.

She also tells me
that being Jewish
she believes in the dignity
of the individual.

FOR MAO TSE-TUNG:
A MEDITATION ON FLIES AND KINGS

So, circling about my head, a fly.
Haloes of frantic monotone.
Then a smudge of blood smoking
On my fingers, let Jesus and Buddha cry.

Is theirs the way? Forgiveness of hurt?
Leprosariums? Perhaps. But I
Am burning flesh and bone,
An indifferent creature between
Cloud and a stone;
Smash insects with my boot,
Feast on torn flowers, deride
The nonillion bushes by the road
(Their patience is very great.)
Jivatma, they endure,
Endure and proliferate.

And the meek-browed and poor
In their solid tenements
(Etiolated, they do not dance.)
Worry of priest and of commissar:
None may re-create them who are
Lowly and universal as the moss
Or like vegetation the winds toss
Sweeping to the open lake and sky.
I put down these words in blood
And would not be misunderstood:
They have their Christs and their legends
And out of their pocks and ailments
Weave dear enchantments –
Poet and dictator, you are as alien as I.

On this remote and classic lake
Only the lapsing of the water can I hear
And the cold wind through the sumac.
The moneyed and their sunburnt children
Swarm other shores. Here is ecstasy,

The sun's outline made lucid
By each lacustral cloud
And man naked with mystery.
They dance best who dance with desire,
Who lifting feet of fire from fire
Weave before they lie down
A red carpet for the sun.

I pity the meek in their religious cages
And flee them; and flee
The universal sodality
Of joy-haters, joy-destroyers
(O Schiller, wine-drunk and silly!)
The sufferers and their thick rages;
Enter this tragic forest where the trees
Uprear as if for the graves of men,
All function and desire to offend
With themselves finally done;
And mark the dark pines farther on,
The sun's fires touching them at will,
Motionless like silent khans
Mourning serene and terrible
Their Lord entombed in the blazing hill.

VIGNETTES

1

He's impotent
    and takes his revenge
by saying of each girl
he meets: "She's promiscuous!"

2

He's a connoisseur
    — of men and women, that is;
with age, his taste improved
but people, he found, did not.
    Now he has a score
of Botticelli pictures
he scrutinizes again and again.

3

The opinions of mediocrities
    are predictable
as the reflexes of a cockroach.
Told that the famous poet
    is a bohemian
he reviles him for his indolence
    and poverty;
Told that he's hard-working and rich
    he sneers at him
for abandoning his ideals!

4

Rarely
    do we see
a man and his wife
    both fat:
one feeds on the other.

MYTH

if the light in Greece
insists on truth
why did I meet
more liars there
than elsewhere?

the tradesmen lied
the landlord lied
the clerks at the post-office
lied
all Greek officials
I ever had dealing with
lied
now that I think of it
no one holding a cup
of black Greek coffee
in his hand
(really Turkish:
see what I mean?)
spoke a true word
– not if he could help it

I suspect
the whole thing
was a unique invention
of some nimble-witted Dorian
to outsmart
competitors in olives or corn,
some rival
for the tight ass of a boy

a myth so
imaginative
it puts in the shade
all that fiddle-faddle
about wood-nymphs
and Bacchae,
the lies gossips
still repeat
about Helen of Troy

HE SAW THEM, AT FIRST

He saw them at first, from a distance

    some with their limbs in boiling excrement
    some who were stung incessantly by insects
    some who danced on fiery bricks
    whose explosions under their soles
    made them keel over into cauldrons
    of boiling water from which they emerged
    with horrible grimaces on their lobster-red faces
    they heatedly told one another were smiles
    some whose bodies bubbled like over-heated tar
    and lustful women whose vaginas were nests
    from which mice scampered out from time to time
    to dry themselves before the burning bricks

He saw commissars, fatbellies, asslickers, frontmen,
    chippies, peddlers of dope; and coming closer,
    he saw some who were pinched, some manacled, some
    whipped by devils, some with their heads stuck
    in pails filled with ice-cubes as if they were
    bottles of champagne: the more shameless among them
    begging pity for the wounds and mutilations
    they displayed

In the heaving, ever-dissolving, ever-congealing courtyard
    where a brisk alternating wind raised and lowered
    the flames like a thrifty housewife her gas jet,
    he saw groups whose members pelted one another
    with shit and rotting offal that scorched the hands
    reaching down to seize it

He approached and saw one that appeared to be female
    and drew her out of the circle of excrement-covered
    figures, catching and holding her reeking arm
    in its half-movement of violence

He said: let me trace your features on the hot sands
with this glowing splinter I detached from
a burning prison wall. As he bent down to begin
his self-appointed task she threw herself on him
and cried joyously: 'I love you!' Without looking up
he muttered to the crackling sand, 'And I, you.'

The fires were suddenly everywhere extinguished
and the gloom was rolled behind the silent furnace
taking the tormented denizens with it. A clean
fresh wind scented with far away seas blew
through the emptied vaults; a man and woman
were lifted like crazy petals the wind
puts down in a field where magisterial leaf-laden
trees give shade. I saw them
stretch out on the grass and embrace, the flowers
curling around their wrists, marrying them;
a purling, cooling stream ran past their feet
singing their epithalamium.

NIGHTMARE

In a recurring
nightmare

A masked woman
with a hoarse voice
holds a gun
to my head

And whispers in my ear:
your poems to be destroyed
or your son

And I tell her
without a moment's hesitation
to shoot me

443

THE WORLD

First and foremost
there is the enduring
pleasure of cruelty;
there are insults
women use for their sex
and for men,
and there is avarice
egotism, callousness;
and there is slavery
in one form or another
– inevitable slavery;
and beauty
a bad habit
poets can not unlearn

Alas, I no longer trust
even the poets

Like children
who tantalize
with a pretense
of treasure
their closed palms
contain nothing

OLYMPIA KAPUT

the Americans with their cameras
the French with their *Guides Bleus*
the Germans following their guide
    from ruin to ruin
(will they never learn)
and a lone Olympian shirtless
sunning himself on a slab of stone
before these sad embarrassed columns
denuded of their glory
(they should have been left
where they were found,
their secret forever buried with them)
till an outraged attendant
shouting demotic Greek
and the relentless jeering of the cicadas
drive him from his place
– as it happens, where once were crowned
the naked athletes of Zeus!

CHANGELING

In my arms
you become again
a Russian

Germany
your neat one-and-a-half room apt.
in West Berlin
your work for the newspapers
drop in quiet folds around the bed

Your pubis
is a warm granary
in the white bareness of your body

I watch the gradual return
of your homeland
in the midnight blooming of your breasts,
in the transformation
of your mouth and chin: the primness
all gone

Your laugh
is a sunlit Ukrainian wheatfield;
your kisses are music
coming unexpectedly from behind
closed windows

More than half your life
lies in ruin

As summoning the lust
of a young Tolstoy
and sentences
from our favourite Russian
authors
I drive into you again and again

FOR THE STINKER WHO CALLED ME
AN APOLOGIST FOR NAZI CRIMES

FOR PETER LUST

I would like to take him and beat
the living daylights from his eyes,
who loosed the deadly spirochete
that lives on mob-approving lies

May another spirochete bring
to his brain rot, to his skin crust;
and his blackened tool, a loose string,
mock for all time the name of lust

GAMES

One afternoon
the wealthy Hungarian
actress
who had lost her parents
and husband
in Bergen-Belsen
and Dachau
came home
to find
her seven-year-old son
playing Hitler
with some dyed hair
he had found
on her ivory comb

ON THE NAMING OF STREETS

In this city
beautifully inserted between sea and hills,
    streets running one way
are named for celebrated composers;
those intersecting them at right angles
    after victorious generals

So you get a queer feeling
if you stand some bland afternoon
    at the intersection
of Rue du Maréchal Joffre and Rue Meyerbeer
or, let us say, Gounod and Clemenceau,
    the last-named, I know, not strictly
a military leader but as head of state
and nicknamed the 'Tiger' leading the country
in its bloodiest war: Maréchal Foch (intersecting
with Rue Berlioz) his right-hand tool
    for converting at a terrific rate
lively Frenchmen and Germans into pieces of flesh
    hanging from barbed wire and parapets

The composers: what do I know about them?
They wrote music. What else is there to know?

N.B. The nationality
of the music-makers varies: German, Italian, Austrian
but the successful maréchals and générals
    are, naturally, all from one country

Well, you might by straining your neck
at the corner of Rue Rossini
just manage to read the plate which says Boulevard Gambetta
named for another resolute activist,
    this time of the Franco-Prussian war;
and you'd get the sort of feeling, I suppose,
that you might from looking at a flower
and having the pistils suddenly go off in your face:
    don't wince, I punned for a purpose

    Well, then, finding myself at the corner
of Rue du Maréchal Joffre and Meyerbeer
    I thought at first it was the joke
of some minor official with a twisted sense of humour
(some frustrated poet or librettist at the City Hall)
but now thinking on the matter calmly
    I'm not so sure

    It might be a Frenchman's belated attempt
to heal the infamous Cartesian split
    between gross matter and spirit;
a violent yoking of the two
by means of architecture and town planning;
a way to bypass or negate or simply play down
the regrettable chasm between two realms
    imperious French logic decrees must be kept apart

    Or is it perhaps a wry concession
to the necessary fact of our being here at all
    in this terrifying yet perfect universe,
an acknowledgement carrying with it no hint of human approval
that somehow under the blandest of skies
    war and music are intertwined,
the crunch of the antelope's shoulder
between the tiger's teeth
giving the drums their ecstatic final roll,
the tears of the soldier's orphans flowing
    into unforgettable melody

449

It is, after all, death which makes art imperishable

But here I am at the intersection
of Avenue Georges Clemenceau and Rue Paganini
and I must choose which street to take to the beach and the sea;
either one will get me there ultimately since the shoreline curves.
    Ecstasy of creation or destruction?
Both, it seems, are needed in the wear and repair of galaxies;
the parade under the Arc de Triomphe
    no less than notes throbbing with human love and despair;
both have their heroes and saints.
I'll toss a coin in the air and see.
    It's Rue Paganini. Good!

SIGHT SEEING

When the distinguished Israeli
visitor
was asked by the guide
what he most wanted
to see
during his stay
in the Federal Republic
he replied
after only a moment's
delay:

'German cemeteries'

INSECT BLOOD

One mid-day
I saw an ordinary bug
stretched out
under a dollar bill
and heard him say:
Nothing can hurt me now

I saw a dung beetle
cover himself with a ten dollar bill
and heard him say:
In my cave I have
all the things I want;
delicious charcuterie money can buy

I saw an ugly moth
curled up in a fifty dollar bill;
his eyes blinked as he said:
Egotism pays off, my lad;
it's eat or be eaten in this world
Love is the name of my favourite spice

A scorpion I saw
with eyes like ice,
crouched under a hundred dollar bill
and heard him say:
This crisp note makes everything I do right
I earned it by hypocrisy and dishonour

Then a Chinaman
in shiny black boots
came down
on bug, beetle, moth and scorpion
and I heard the dry crunch
and spurt of insect blood
against the crisp paper

WESTMINSTER ABBEY

I entered Westminster Abbey

    and walked through the maze of chapels
    and stood below the stained glass windows
    and strode past marble busts
    of philanthropists and admirals
    and trod over granite slabs covered with inscriptions
    whose meaning was instantly clear to my alive eyes
    and I expected the slabs to open like trapdoors
    after I had read the inscriptions
    the way garage doors open when the electric beam is cut
    but the trapdoors did not fall open
    and I did not see Eternity that afternoon

And there was a stink

    and I saw the royal chapels, any number of them
    from Edward the Confessor's on
    where the kings and queens of England
    lie reduced to piles of dust
    and I touched the caskets
    and concluded they were indeed strong enough
    to prevent ashes from blowing away

And there was a stink

    and I saw Queen Elizabeth's chapel
    which also contains the queenly deposit
    of her sister, Bloody Mary,
    and I ruminated six inches from their sarcophagi
    that between the two of them
    these ladies had dispatched thousands
    through the trapdoor that leads on to Eternity

And there was a stink

and I saw the pompous niche
the Earl of Buckingham, the favourite of James I,
some say his bum-boy,
had cosied up for himself and family

And there was a stink

and I saw statues of great orators and statesmen
whose devastating rhetoric
was heard only by themselves
for the crowds moved on dumbly
to stare at some other approved name

And there was a stink

and I saw the Poets' Corner
where a bust of John Dryden almost faces
that of the dunce he savaged with sarcasm and insult
and busts of Burns, Southey, Coleridge, Johnson
as well as a centrepiece
made from the imagined likeness of Wm. Shakespeare
and they looked even more vapid and silly than the rest

And there was a stink

and for the first time in my life
I saw clearly what was meant by the English Tradition
how it is a slice taken out of Death
and made homey and negotiable like currency
a way of increasing real estate values
by squeezing caskets, urns, busts, memorials
into every last available inch of space
and I also saw that this can go on for ever
as long as the supply of famous corpses doesn't run out

And there was a stink

and I saw how the Englishman
is not passionate and grand and mystical
about Death as the Spaniard is
but sentimental, prosaic, and therefore matter-of-factly
seeks to profit by its existence
as he does from lucky deposits of coal and iron
in his right little, tight little island

And there was a stink

    and how shameful, I thought, how unfair
    to the dead who after lives of guilt and evil
    had earned their right to oblivion like everyone else
    to be put on display for curious tourists
    smelling of travellers' cheques
    and floating their democratic banalities where the air
    moulders and is heavy with pathos and death

And there was a stink

    and how I wished for a conflagration to raze this place,
    for a flood to wash into the oblivious sea
    slabs of granite, urns, busts, and memorials
    whose lettering only three-eyed monsters might decipher
    while the smaller fry, for a lark,
    played hide-and-seek among the opened caskets,
    pillars of ash rising by day and by night
    and making lovely iridescent bubbles for them
    to bounce off a tail or fin

And there was a wink

    and I saw the practical English
    had stationed pious policemen everywhere
    to keep fire and flood out and Death in,
    and I bent down to listen
    to Thomas Hardy under my feet
    who informed me in a low confidential whisper
    that all the insurance documents
    (since life is a tissue of ironic accidents)
    on this curious indoor cemetery
    this sprawling profit-making mausoleum
    are religiously kept in some other vault
    remote from here

Where there is no stink

FOR MUSIA'S GRANDCHILDREN

I write this poem
for your grandchildren
for they will know of your loveliness
only from hearsay,
from yellowing photographs
spread out on table and sofa
for a laugh.

When arrogant
with the lovely grace you gave their flesh
they regard your dear frail body pityingly,
your time-dishonoured cheeks
pallid and sunken
and those hands
that I have kissed a thousand times
mottled by age
and stroking a grey ringlet into place,
I want them suddenly
to see you as I saw you
— beautiful as the first bird at dawn.

Dearest love, tell them
that I, a crazed poet all his days
who made woman
his ceaseless study and delight,
begged but one boon
in this world of mournful beasts
that are almost human:
to live praising your marvellous eyes
mischief could make glisten
like winter pools at night
or appetite put a fine finish on.

MODERN GREEK POET

In the Aegean night
we drank cold wine
and sat where we could see
the white Acropolis
shedding its useless radiance
like the shattered plinths of a star

And I wasn't the least bit eager
to see any of his poems
until he told me
how in the late civil war
he had single-handedly
killed twelve guerillas:
the fallen apostles he called them

Then I begged him
to show me
everything he had written

OIL SLICK ON THE RIVIERA

Cowboy in black shirt, black hat, black tie
it rides the waves bucking like a bronco
and will not be thrown.

Let them arch their backs and go suddenly limp;
let their white manes toss wildly,
the froth fall from their mouths; though their fury
is unspent and never-diminishing
it is useless. Nothing
will ever unseat this superb, imperturbable rider.

Or from here is it chimney smoke I see
wind and wave have deflected?
A wavering net strung out along the margin
of the bay
to catch bits of paper and wood, weeds and ferns?
Or is it a funereal graph
for the drownings of vessels and people at sea?

Ah, but the green waves are stubborn, unyielding;
yet no less is the oil slick:
cool as a commissar, dark and crafty as the Georgian
it bides its time, knowing that history will always pardon
whoever has the patience and will-power to only hang on.

THE SWEET LIGHT STRIKES MY EYES

The sweet light of heaven strikes my eyes,
strikes the oiled bodies lying small and sensual on the beach
    and the blue-grey water of the Mediterranean
as it unrolls itself wave after wave
    upon the shore in bolts of translucent silk.

Five children, five glorious cherubs
float on the waves, swirling and twirling on their inflated tubes;
    and their excited cries as they fall with the waves and rise
rise piercing and joyful above the clamorous spray
    that gives again and again its white huzzas to the city.

And I see how at each end of the long promenade
the white buildings drop from the hill's summit
    into the sea like a light, bright waterfall;
while jet planes curving with the bay's glittering margin
    sweep over me unerringly to their target below the sky.

On the beach the graceless scavenging pigeons
insert their grey, probing beaks between the stones
    or for my laughter, like Japanese warlords in a film,
accomplish an archaic ritual of courtship or war,
    the males fluffing out their neck feathers and strutting.

Surely a piece of Eden broke off and floated here
and I must look for the scratched names of Adam and Eve
    under that girl's thighs or use her fanned legs for compass;
surely suffering and evil are merest illusion
    when such colour and sounds overflow into eye and ear.

The waves push the long afternoon shadows before them;
wind, sun work against each other for my maximum pleasure,
    and the sails holding the serene fullness of a good poem
are blue and white. God, the sweet light strikes my eyes;
    I am transfigured and once again the world, the world is fair.

EPIPHANY

In vain
the marine police fish for the body
with long poles

On the beaches and quay
the disappointed faces
resume their restless vacancy

And in a flash
the hopeless predicament we're in
becomes blinding clear to me

MODERN LYRIC

The corn rose where their skulls were bashed;
    Rye and barley too.
Where blood had made its own gutters
The fields of timothy flourished,
    The tall wheat grew.

So sweet a place it was for love
    I pulled my girl down;
The grass was thick on which we lay
Between bushes that were our grove
    And hid the sun.

I held her fair head in my hands,
    I kissed her closed eyes;
Her blood's pulse beat under my own.
I slashed the traitoress' neck veins
    And there she lies.

LOVE POEM WITH AN ODD TWIST

Knowing
        that for as long
as I love you
   I shall stay
          merely a poet,
a babbler & word-spinner
   content to describe
or deride
       the bloody acts
of brave men
(Homer was my ancestor)
         my self-revulsion
twisted into dagger
   or religious text
(which? let vanity
       or opportunity determine)
I've bought
     pistol
& black holster
   from an ex-Nazi.
            For target
I've nailed
     a blown-up photo
of Nasser
     to an appletree
& each time I fire
   I shout, "I don't love
you": meaning
     you

PRELUDE

Like desperate guerillas
wave after wave of white mice
storm the beach and disappear
among the stones and pebbles

The weaker ones
retreat in confusion
hissing their bad luck, the steepness

At a distance
a reminder of yesterday's oil slick
glowers at me like a swastika;
nudged by a used condom
it elongates into the grim shadow
of a puritan
and backs away

A swimming girl laughingly
tosses
the floating rubber
on the back of a white mouse
scampering towards the shore

She straightens herself
in the water
and pulls up the wave
at her feet
like a turquoise slip

Coming towards me
she holds her breasts
as if they were brown puppies

TO WRITE AN OLD-FASHIONED POEM

To convince myself I could still do it:
write an old-fashioned, pre-Castro poem
    with figures of speech, nostalgia, and sensitive notations
on natural phenomena, beauty, love (young or middle-aging)
or mystical yearnings for the blood gouts of the spurting Christ,
    that mythical God-centred haemophiliac,
I slowly like Gray's ploughman made my way to the park
where I could observe chairs dozing in the noonday heat
or rocking themselves to sleep; chaises lounges, red-canvassed,
gathered in small insurrectionary groups at corners,
and the pigeons thinking they were made of my mould
    or poets like me crapping over everything
but more especially, as the accumulating evidence showed,
    on the moustache and stiff upper lip of Albert I.

I sat down, feeling my years all over,
and hoped despite the wear and tear on my testicles
a green tree was growing inside me and birds, other than pigeons,
would visit it and, nesting, sing among the long-leaved twigs;
    and I invented a replayable delicious fantasy
in which Algerian poetesses adored me and came away with me
    because they loved the colour of blue
and my eyes were true blue except where the whites showed through
– but that was all right because they didn't care for freaks.
And I felt great, great, for the leaf-lighted twigs
    were dropping their colourful odours in a blaring
noon hour overture which the delirious wing-wonderful birds
snatched up in their beaks and smeared over everything
in the park except the bearded palmtrees towering
    tall and majestical over me
as the rabbins of my long ago far away innocent childhood.

And I reflected, hell, for old time's sake
    and simply to prove I could still do it
and to make our nervous age feel good again,
let me describe, let me annotate
like a medieval scholar who has just regained his sight
the lawny grass in the centre of the public park
    how it smells, how it tickle-cools my instep,
how the murderous French children pull it up by the roots
and the barbered poodles inelegantly shitting on it
spot it with numerous tiny baskets of green-gold blades,
while the young mothers wheel themselves around
    in their infants' perambulators, the sun
vanishes like a yolk behind the eggwhite clouds
breezes flake and spume across the sky;
and the ancient Nicoise ladies opposite me
    sit more quiet than small noonday birds,
their wrinkled skins delicate as garlic peels
and their thin legs tucked under them like memories.

SOAPFLAKES

In Paris I heard of an elderly woman
    who used to go to the marché municipale
to stand in front of a triperie
    where she would wonder aloud what
the tongues, livers, and kidneys
    of the illustrious statesmen & diplomats
might fetch at current prices
    and whether they would prove delicious
as the calves' brains she saw
    neatly wedged in the white & washed tins.

Taken away to the loony bin
    during the Sinai crisis
she saw millions of soapflakes
    descend on the heads of De Gaulle and Kosygin
and form white wigs that were irremoveable
    – that's when she screamed.

463

MARCHÉ MUNICIPALE

In the empty market
    coolness spills out
from vineyards
    gathered in boxes of grapes;
the rumour of orchards,
and pears full of an indisputable dignity
that lie like jaundiced dowagers
    in their white wrappers;
and from freshly washed tomatoes
that flash in the surrounding gloom
like the neon signs of lost American towns
you speed past on rainy nights
    on the way to nowhere.

It is a coolness
    making herrings smell more rank;
in which the ripe colour of bananas astounds;
potatoes, a visible skin affliction of air,
lie mute, lie sullen in their earthy bags;
and the slow mysterious decay of olives
    filling the deserted aisles
with its black sensual irony discomfits
the pragmatic vegetables in their stands,
    countermands
the imperial fiats of pineapples.

And the stillness is such
    that waits for iron weights or a box
to shatter; or a child hidden
in a cupboard expelling his breath
and saying, "Ah, Ah" making it appear
    silence had spoken;
or a film with no commentary
showing machine guns and rifles

fallen out of
the huge blistered hands of destiny
sands are burying; even the muzzles
that with a last malevolent squint
    at the sun
sink into a darkness and silence
more vast, more final than Pharoah's kingdom.

QUEER HATE POEM

I went out looking for philosophers
    and found only prudent men

For poets:
    and found only romantic cripples

For teachers:
    and found only egotists

For saints:
    and found only sheared wolves

For heroes:
    and found only discriminating murderers

I went out looking for you, O woman,
    and found only myself.

465

THE NEXT TIME DOES IT

I

The old taboos
are falling

Eins

Zwei

Drei

There's a lot
of good food
running around
on
two legs

II

Don't worry, darling
I won't let them
eat you

I want you
for myself

III

If you're starving, mister,
see the mayor;
he had a large family
and might have
some food
to spare

TAMED BIRDS

Feet readied, not the fierce murdering beak,
  Grey and graceless, the domestic pigeons
Swoop, no, flap down between the sunbathers
That roll or lie ruined on the beach stones,
Their grotesque bodies blackening in the sun.

These tamed birds are like the Europeans
  Among whom they strut or pick up refuse:
Mediocrities, fearful of danger.
From love the cloying destroying caress
They seek; and ease, not risk and adventure.

Imagine a hawk suddenly let loose
  Among this unheroic scavenging flock;
And beaching their long boats under the bland skies,
The cruel Norsemen with glittering sword in hand:
How sweet would sound the unavailing cries!

THE LARGER ISSUE

My girl
  complains bitterly
that my head
          is so taken up
with politics
  I give no thought
to the lovely parts
with which she enticed me.

"How can I think
  of them"
          I tell her
with a rueful smile
  "when I have
the Gulf of Aqaba
  on my mind
and the Suez Canal?"

TRIBAL TIC

I know some poets
so envious of my fame

that at the publication
of each new book
of mine

they hopefully
count the lines
of my poems

gratified
if they are as brief
as this one

IRISH LUCK

Here's a lucky man!

Here's a man to be envied!

None of his friends
has the heart
to tell him he's Irish
but not
witty
        only
in and out of his cups
afflicted with garrulity
and mouth-rot

A SORT OF AFTER-DINNER SPEECH

With the sensual materialism
of a female
she smiles, winks at the guests
around the open-air restaurant table
and rubs her husband's shirted pot

What's hubby doing at the moment?

He's being delivered of an apocalyptic vision

He's seeing water turn into blood,
fresh wafers into stinking carrion

In their homes,
from boredom
couples embrace each other with shining
knives

On the streets everyone
wants to be headsman;
people queue up and take turns
but the line never grows shorter

As a merciful deity
tempers wind to the sheared lambs
a vast self-disgust
readies men and women for their destruction

Blood rains down from the skies
for the sun is a boar
whose head has been sliced off

A general's brains
is being auctioned
in the Place de la Concorde

Hubby perorates: the wife tenderly
strokes his pot and smiles

He ignores the metaphysical refutation
in her cynical fingers

IF WHALES COULD THINK ON CERTAIN HAPPY DAYS

As the whale surfaced
joyously,
water spouted from his head
in great jets of praise
for the silent, awesome
mystery
he beheld between sea and sky.

Thankfulness
filled his immense body
for his sense of well-being,
his being-at-oneness
with the universe
and he thought:
"Surely the Maker of Whales
made me for a purpose."

Just then the harpoon
slammed into his side
tearing a hole in it
as wide as the sky.

LIKE A MOTHER DEMENTED

Like a mother demented nature caresses
her children before she chokes them to death;
she raises tall palmtrees and whirlwinds to crack them:
only by continually devouring herself does she endure.

Out of her immemorial dung come flowers and stars,
come gracious ladies with tiny troutbones between their teeth
or goose-fat on the tips of flirtatious tongues
– with animal perfumes on their cool adulterous wrists.

At a later hour, the gracious ladies fall into the earth
where graveworms nibble all day long on their delicate parts,
unaware how fallen breasts and vaginas once gave birth
to mediocre poetry, to ecstasies and sighs.

For you, my sweet, you and me, the human race entire
she invented to watch this tragic and strange affair
for who wishes to play Hamlet when the gallery is bare?
Mind, Mind was in the mind of that performer!

Now when lightning splits the high arrogant oaks
and mountains rise and fall; or lions and tigers prowl
or crippled poets run and win the coveted laurel:
man, her darling pervert, sees and notes it all.

But the cost, the cost of this ghastly privilege
is unendurable guilt that we dredge and dredge
as horrorstruck we find our condemned selves on the stage
beside her, nature's most murderous tool and accomplice.

Love, I kiss your navel and my X-ray eyes see
fisheyes wink in your dissolving entrails,
and when I write my lying poems know I am using
an anodyne from which the fastidious man recoils.

FOR MY TWO SONS, MAX AND DAVID

The wandering Jew: the suffering Jew
The despoiled Jew: the beaten Jew
The Jew to burn: the Jew to gas
The Jew to humiliate
The cultured Jew: the sensitized exile
    gentiles with literary ambitions aspire to be
The alienated Jew cultivating his alienation
    like a rare flower: no gentile garden is complete
    without one of these bleeding hibisci
The Jew who sends Christian and Moslem theologians
    back to their seminaries and mosques for new arguments
    on the nature of the Divine Mercy
The Jew, old and sagacious, whom all speak well of:
    when not lusting for his passionate, dark-eyed daughters
The Jew whose helplessness stirs the heart and conscience
    of the Christian like the beggars outside his churches
The Jew who can be justifiably murdered because he is rich
The Jew who can be justifiably murdered because he is poor
The Jew whose plight engenders profound self-searchings
    in certain philosophical gentlemen who cherish him
    to the degree he inspires their shattering aperçus
    into the quality of modern civilization, their noble
    and eloquent thoughts on scapegoatism and unmerited agony
The Jew who agitates the educated gentile, making him pace
    back and forth in his spacious well-aired library
The Jew who fills the authentic Christian with loathing for himself
    and his fellow-Christians
The Jew no one can live with: he has seen too many conquerors
    come and vanish, the destruction of too many empires
The Jew in whose eyes can be read the doom of nations
    even when he averts them in compassion and disgust
The Jew every Christian hates, having shattered his self-esteem
    and planted the seeds of doubt in his soul
The Jew everyone seeks to destroy, having instilled self-division
    in the heathen

472

Be none of these, my sons
My sons, be none of these
Be gunners in the Israeli Air Force

VILLAGE FUNERAL

They look
            as if death
came on them
                performing
a shameful act;
                an undignified one
like nose-picking
                and turn away
uneasily
        from each other's glance.
They move stiff & listless
                    in a role
unsuited to their talents
        or boring in its familiarity,
only the chief mourner
                    behind
the polished coffin
                walking well-rehearsed,
her face
        wearing its tragic mask
with confidence & concern
                    to the end.

AUTOPSY ON ABERFAN

A black mountain fell on them and children died.
The small white coffins were lowered side by side
Like innocent seeds into the common grave:
Could sorrow save man, such sorrow ought to save.

But such is the ill perversity of man
A foul inferno of hate is Aberfan
Since the human heart unfroze around the world
And buried it under a landslide of gold.

Men who drank their friend's health now fight in the pubs;
Mothers, like angered cows, strike each other's dugs;
And from one comes the sinister human cry:
"Why should your children live and my own child die?"

TALK AT TWILIGHT

Night
slides down
the smooth, immense
tooth
of day
like firemen
down a pole
and everywhere
stamps out
the garish light.

My love's voice
crackling
under my ear,
I smother it
in a blanket
of silence
soft
with tenderness
and irony.

MEDITERRANEAN CEMETERY

The leaves on the ground
were hot, sere, and dry
and the smell
was just right
for the time of day
and place:
invitation and menace.
Warm and smothering as bedclothes
cool as cerements
it came up from the earth
in gusts,
in gasps and spasms,
parting grass and flowers
on the graves
and holding the tombstones
in a trance so heavy, so deep
the stirring of a dry leaf
sounded like a reproach
to the summer air
that had stirred it,
an appeal for care and decorum,
when I beheld
standing on a mound
a doll
in Andalusian costume,
its painted head
leaning against a tombstone.

END OF THE SUMMER

   Already the sun burns less intensely;
its deepest passion is for other skies, other lands;
wedged between two clouds
it seems embarrassed by its sudden loss of power.
The foam now whitens my melancholy
and even the waves speak in a voice not heard before:
more tumultuous yet sadder
like people who shout at each other
at the end of a love affair.

   It makes me think
of quiet Mediterranean cemeteries I've known
to see the sunlight limp across the beach
stuffing black leaves of shadow between the stones:
of old women with white skins
and fields of despoiled windflowers.
Where's its force, its fiery heat?
Is this the July monarch that reigned here? This slave
to a calendar, this enfeebled lecher
with not one good squint, one amorous gleam
left in its red eyes?
Slowly the sun mounts the stone steps of the Plage
and stares at my bronzed chest and arms
like a woman failing to recognize
her former lover.

PEACEMONGER

After our love-making
my Greek girl wipes the sweat
from my loins;
then she brings out chilled cucumbers and wine
and setting these before me
commands me to drink and eat.

Why doesn't everyone live
loving and carefree as we do
she wants to know,
a wrinkle appearing
on her forehead
tight as an unripe fig.

When I tell her
not all men are as lucky as I,
she says to lure them
from the battlefields
she would give her small, satisfying body
to all the armies of the world
– even those of Nasser and Hussein
or the despised Algerians.

When I explain laughingly
that the chief attraction
is the chilled cucumbers and wine,
the wrinkle deepens to a frown.
"Ah, that presents a problem," she says;
and my merry Greek wraps me around her,
spilling the white wine.

SONGS OUT OF SEASON

1

Instead of being jolly
The poets voice their melancholy,
Repetitious as a polly
Trained by human folly.

2

My mistress frowned:
"The heart propels
And the head keeps back.
Lay me out for dead
When the other way round
The head counsels go
But the heart says no."

3

The vital man is he who kills
Who lives with pain and danger;
Blood's his proper food, not cereals
Some Babe loved in his manger.
The flashing eye, the ruddy cheek
Are gained by chewing up the weak.

4

I have a friend who speaks of Grace
As if he knows its secret place
And like a sunlamp dimmed in space
Can switch it wholly on his face.

5

"A great god invented art;
All else, a wilful demon:
They cannot be torn apart,
They are not two, but one."
This is what a hermit tells
Desolate under the sun.

478

FANTASIA IN BLACK

The sun passes over me
like a mad steam-roller no one owns
and lays me out like a miniature asphalt road;
by noontime it is a glinting razor
that shaves me thinner and thinner
till I'm the page of a book fire-blackened
or the facial skin of a Harlem negro
stretched out tight and bereft of features
– no, a sheet of glistening carbon paper!
A gull, a gust of wind lifts me
from the fauteuil I've sat in all morning
and lets me flutter down
on the corrugated roof of Plage Ruhl
where I fit over the rolls with perfect adhesion
and wait for someone to begin typing
my heart into the world's knowledge
or for me to move like newsprint on rollers
out into the luminous margin of the sea.

TO THE RUSSIANS AT THE U.N.

Comrades – cancer rot your well-oiled tongues!
They should grow black as the lies they speak
And like sick stems on which webs are hung
The infection spread to larynx and cheek.

As the Sicilian bull first roared
With its inventor's flesh and wild cries
So around this great globe men record
How you burn to nothing in your own lies.

July 1967

479

THE BEST PROOF

Love your neighbour
and labour daily
    at proving
how much you love him

By making yourself
so powerful
    nothing can ever
tempt him to injure you

KAMERAD

With clenched fists they shouted: "Long live Stalin!"
The soldiers chuckled; nevertheless they fired.
While back at the farm or at the Kremlin
The Vohzd, to savour the joke alone, retired.

ARABS

The world's last poets
in love with hyperbole and disaster:
    eloquent romantics
Inshallah, malesh, bukra
In the beginning was the word
    which, prepotent,
exorcises tanks and planes,
annihilates machines and skilled mechanics.

Ah, my word-intoxicated brothers,
    for your faith
going down to defeat, to misery and misfortune
with the sad fatalism
    of a Verlaine,
how can I not love you:
you who cling so beautifully
    to a tradition
that refuses to turn lathes for you
or operate motors and drills;
you who pave the floors
    of your dark hovels
with a mosaic of dreams
proud lovers, poets, scholars, and astronomers
tread upon in all their remembered brightness.

The 20th century
ticks in all the ominous corners
    of your unswept courtyards:
"you are not contemporary, go away"
and in your defeat
    I see my own
as destiny picks you up
still muttering to the indifferent air
"Inshallah, malesh, bukra"
    and like one of Omar's chessmen
puts you one by one silently away.

HAIKU

The sound of a wave

Falling on the shore

Is heard once and heard no more.

POET AT SINAI

Corpses fingering blood-stained triggers
seem to the poet a grim charade
who sees the silent, bloated figures
lying like balloons in a parade.

Crushed tanks: their oil bleeding into sand
that a wild molecular frenzy
changes into dark hieroglyphs; and
outlines of a desolate beauty.

Arms raised to salute the victory
by sightless soldiers that have no breath.
Let the victors rejoice; he only
tells them of the cardboard smell of death

HERACLITOS

For years
            I taught myself
the wholly impractical art
      of arranging words
on paper

And gave
            a respectful hearing
to sentimental utopians
      poets among them
as well as metaphysicians & moralists
discoursing on the human
      condition

Forgetting
            nature
plays favourites
and gives only
      to those who have:
the weak
            she pounds
into the earth
                  to learn there
her lesson
      from worms & moles

Forgetting
            she's a deaf-mute
who's never   heard
      and who never
speaks
            of conscience & justice

Though
            wearing an enigmatic
smile
      she will allow
for a season
      the over-sensitive
            to mention them
in passing

THE NEW SENSIBILITY

Never mind
beating out your exile, Ez:
that's literary hogwash,
vintage quaintsville

A more efficacious
epigram
for stopping the mouths
of tormentors
is a bullet in the head:
it opens a hole
and closes the matter forever

Tamed bears
toothless tigers
caged lions
defenceless ghetto Jews
(Polacks to Nazis in Warsaw circa 1941:
  nab them, nab them, they're Jews!)
and poets
who dish out the familiar idealistic crap
always make the murderous crowd
slobber
preparatory to prodding them with sticks
and pouring gasoline on their cadavers

The up-to-date poet
besides labouring at his craft
should be a dead shot

Do you hear me, Old Man?
a dead shot
sending the bullet
winging like a finished stanza
straight between the eyes

That's the new poetry
minted June 1967
in Tel Aviv and Sinai

I thought
I should let you know

LESSON FOR TODAY

"Acquit yourself like a man,"
    said the grey-haired poet to his son;
    and with a wry smile gave him
    a bomb, a bowie knife, and a gun.

DOROTHY PARKER (1893-1967)

I read you when I was a younger man;
Your poems, your stories, and your articles;
And recently a sketch that came to hand
Gave me again the fine familiar thrills.

Your mockery was both gay and bitter,
Your revenge on a world that made you sad;
It was your knife for an ancient tumour:
Men being mad, you said that men were mad.

Well, death let you make your jests. Now his own
Has quite surprised you by its calibre
And left you speechless. Good-bye, dear woman.
No more witticisms from you. No more.

MERITED

For having said of the cattle he ruled:
"Fools, with their mouths open!"
Stalin
merits having the heat reduced
10°F.
every ten years.

ON THIS FAR SHORE

Far from the great city I love and hate
and summer suns split open like a hive
I hear the hum of its petty schemers,
their soured brats, their mistresses and wives.

And the brutal cries of hunger and love
more crude than an exhibitionist's prick;
and foulness that like an escaping gas
issues from the defeated and the sick.

Boy-lovers, typists, thieves, professors:
they jostle each other in restaurants;
a delicate poet sits at a table
fancying he knows what each mortal wants.

He weeps for them and begs all-seeing Jove
to regard him, to rain down luck on his head;
a chick enters, he feels a hard-on stir
and hang between his thighs heavy as lead.

The cynical whores of Stanley Street meet
in the calm shadows of the Y.M.C.A.
But no, these come only when night falls:
now they sleep and snore ill-luck away.

On this far shore, friendless, I think pell-mell
of those whom I would teach and cannot reach
and of one who in her own element
swims ever silent as a mackerel.

I look up at the sky where poetry is;
above my head a helicopter groans
and a youth with fierce black corkscrew ringlets
parachutes a Torah on the small stones.

YET WHAT IF THE SURVIVORS

Yet what if the survivors had wished
to see their families all wiped out:
the hated, tyrannical father
red-necked and forever bullying;

The competitive older brothers
and scheming sisters, the feared rivals
that pushed one aside with kicks or smiles
to stand under the eyes of mother

Giving her gaze as to no other
– the lucky ticket with the right signs;
yet she too baffling the heart with hate,
numbing the ego with affection.

What if she revoked her love and frowned?
Capriciously cursed instead of blessed?
Or one had sought the warmth of her breast?
Ah, the mind, the mind's a dish of worms!

Herr Hitler, were you the tool, the hand
huge as hate that ended all their fears;
their sinister, most secretive wish
bristling on your clipped, absurd moustache?

And the indigo tattooed on arms
the exact number they would have slain
had they but means equal to desire?
Sad orangutans are men who know

They're killers, the knowledge siring guilt
only further killing can benumb;
and the ape that walks erect has made,
Schikelgruber, the whole world your tomb.

FOR THE CAUSE

"I want the world perfect," the fanatic cried,
 and did his bit for next moment he died.

THE GRAVEYARD

Lord, I understand the plan, the news is out:
I kill him, he kills me, change and change about,
And you ever in the right; and no wonder
Since it's no great matter who's up, who's under.
Teuton or Slav, Arab or suffering Jew –
Nature, Justice, God – they are all one to you.
The lion breeds the lamb and the antelope
As evil breeds good; darkness, light; despair, hope.

And though your scheme confounds theologians' wits
All come and go sired by the opposites;
And they decree: he who slays and he who's slain
Leave on your excellent world no crimson stain.
The tragic, warring creatures that here have breath
Are reconciled in the partnership of death;
And death's akin to art, and artists please
To the measure they have stilled the contraries.

Energy must crackle on a silent urn,
Nothing catch fire though Jerusalem burn,
And the lion poised on the poor bok to spring
Hold in his furious jaws no suffering.
Motion and rest, love and hate, heaven and hell
Here cease their Punch-and-Judy show: all is well.
There is no pain in the graveyard or the voice
Whispering in the tombstones: "Rejoice, rejoice."

ELEGY FOR STRUL

Shall I be maliciously funny, Strul,
and say you look like a display of glassware
on crisp hospital sheets as white as yourself?
You who were once a barrel-chested
Mephistopheles
tempting a boy
to follow him down a pedlar's road
with adventure stories
of money and success;
a whoring, roaring bull of a man
that kicked up his heels
in my mother's kitchen
and filled our ears
with strange Balzacian tales
of priests and nuns:
better known in the villages, you boasted,
than Jesus himself
whose girls you fucked and afterwards tucked
a cheap medallion into their raw hands.

(But you were no cynic.
  Life, you said, is a feed, and a fart;
  nor did terror make you a hypocrite.)

I hear sounds tumble out
from your cancered throat
and I bend down to your perishing mouth
to catch the dreadful whisper:
I lived like a fool, I am dying like one.
There are tears in my eyes
for you, Strul
– ogre of stinginess I once hated so much
but not now, lying there and dying.

(Where's the booming, unmalicious laugh
  that belied the meanness
  that made you run like a madman
  switching off lights everywhere
  and leaving your wife's guests in darkness?)

Now I see only your wasted physique
time and bugs have diminished
and the fantastic vitality
it once housed
ebbing into the surrounding space
minute by minute,
a mere pulse on the pillow . . .
a flutter . . .
and then you are still for ever,
only the wan tubes in your veins stirring
and catching the quiet light from the window.

THE SKULL

Out of my wrecked marriages
disappointments with friends
the rime time desposits
on heart, imagination

And earth's magnetic pull
downwards to the grave

I want to write poems
as clean and dry
and as impertinent
as this skull

Found by me
outside the small boneyard
at Mithymna

That perched on a cliffedge
stares
and grins at the sea

491

PROTEST

The church bell clangs
the men and women at once put on
the smiles they've been told
to wear for the occasion
the children get ready to pelt
the great man with flowers
the fat black-bearded priest
walks peaceably beside the mayor

While the Aegean changes colour
they patiently wait

At the agora, however,
the procession will end
and the butcher has hung a solitary
pig's head in his window;
how can the official when he speaks
be kept from seeing
the sly and bloody face
on the black hook

Surely he will have to stare at it
all the time
he's explaining the new constitution:
the great improvements it will bring
to the villagers of Mithymna
called out to cheer him

ON SEEING THE STATUE OF SAPPHO
ON THE QUAY OF MITYLENE

You look, Sappho,
like one of your own virgins
who has just been told
an off-colour joke
– such a simper

Not at all
as I imagine you
my loving, dark-skinned girl
with yellow hair
and a hand darting
into a man's tunic

No smarter are the citizens
of Mitylene today
than when you showed
yourself in the harbour
to sailors and merchants

Or to the soldier
whose cloak was dyed purple
and was Eros, you said,
on his way down
from heaven

Immortal poetess
you wrote of love
as it no longer is,
of desire without shame

I who have done the same
greet you with the sibylline words
you once sang:
"Dead, I won't be forgotten"
you can have no complaint

493

But I must go

Aphrodite
has taken care to have
a girl waiting for me
in Mithymna
with soft hands
and softer mouth

She's a sensible girl
and will not mind
if I say the first libation
is to you

Between our raptures
we shall think of you
this night

FISH

Over the dark and silent water
the fishermen
light their lamps

Silly fish

They think it is the moon
and are caught

Severe and bitter are their
disappointed mouths

494

FOR AVIVA

I am at the beach
eating oil-soaked tomatoes
and fish

And drinking retsina

You know the place
you know the hills, the sun
the Aegean
                    indigo
just about now
I will not describe them for you
you have seen them

Whatever is in your head
is in mine also

We are made indissoluble, love,
by such images
and by love

FAREWELL

I said to her: "I
no longer want
to make poems
out of pain

I want
            the years
left to me
to be peaceful
as boats
in a quiet harbour

495

As even
as the beat
of the sea
on the seashore

Farewell"

CREATION

The pregnant cat
rubs her distended belly
against my leg

She moans and stares at me
with simple cat bewilderment
and cannot have enough
of stroking and petting

She arches her back
like a sick voluptuary
to make me extend the caress
I began at her eyes

Saying, and I translate:
"I have earned my moment
and place in Creation;
soon I shall litter life
on this cold dumb ground"

But why suddenly
does she scratch and bite
my stroking hand?

And with so much fury!

496

NEANDERTHAL

I know a man who

when there's a fly
in the room
that he could kill
with a fly-swatter
or the newspaper he's reading

carefully closes
all doors and windows
and sending everyone
out of the room
shoots it full of insecticide

He likes to watch
the fly's dizzy interrupted
fall to the floor

and the last agonies
that go on for minutes and minutes,
the wings useless

THE PIT

I tell it like it is,
man

However excellent you are:
as sage as Solomon,
brave as Charlemagne

And possessing many talents

In the end
you will be gulled
by a woman's insatiable
vulva

POMEGRANATES

Thank you, John and Julie
for the pomegranates

That was nice of you

In the heat
one of them split
right down the centre;
the other didn't

They reminded me
of two sisters
I once knew

I OWE THIS TO ST. PAUL

To the Greek girls
        of the village
standing in a circle
like dark Persephones
and full-bosomed Demeters

Who dare not be seen
talking to a man
if not properly affianced
to him
        with dowry
and exchange of gifts

Though I have gray hair
        and crumbling teeth
and my mid-century ass
drags on the ground

I am Apollo
        and young Hermes
rolled into one

I have only
        to turn around
to look at them

And they start
                squawking
from shyness
like assaulted chickens

SOURWINE SPARKLE

At the exhibition of "Erotica" the faces of the people
who came to stare and conceal their smirks were more
interesting than the explosive genitalia. Pictures and
people seemed to bear an astonishing resemblance to
each other, the men's faces shiny and stretched with
egotism or drooping and wrinkled with failure; the
faces of the women, horsy or vacuously round but
always smug – for this was the female's sanctuary and
achievement – the coldcreamed hollows and creases begging
to be rubbed away by the magical touch of the
extended phallus. In the eyes of both sexes, a terrible
lewdness as if their possessors had just been initiated
into a burdensome secret and were dying for someone
to blurt it out. Yet if that happened how deflated
they would instantly appear. For it is this impure
knowledge, the residue of many unhallowed nights,
which keeps the bags of themselves blown up and
armoured for the day's humiliations. If sex is the wine
of life, as I think it is, in which the ego bathes
and floats and swims in its nectar light and poises
itself joyously between exaltation and extinction,
if it is the unalloyed, self-intoxicating expression of
egotism – the animal flesh with its odours,
secretions and excretions demanding that it be kissed,
caressed, patted and fondled, that is, admired and loved –
what I saw on the faces of the people who crowded up
to the diseased phalli and hairy, black-pit vaginas
was the skin of a wine that had gone sour,
a sourwine sparkle.

FOR JULIE

Hearing you sigh:
none has written poems
for me

I gave up disputing
with a eunuch
about passion

And turned from my
malevolent letter
to regard carefully
your face and form

Surely you live among the blind
or among unlettered people

Or where you come from
envy-stung castratos
have at last enacted
the incarceration of poets

What man
feeling desire stir in his veins
would not praise your lips and eyes?

Lucky is that one
who holds you each night
in his raptured love-lock!

HILLS AND HILLS

For Aviva

The hills
remind me
of you

Not because
they curve soft and warm
lovely and firm
under the Greek sun

Or flow
towards the horizon
in slow limpid waves
fading away mysteriously
at the edge of the sea

So that I can only
surmise
their being there
beyond my gaze
and stare into the grayness

But because
a long time ago
you stared at them
as I am staring now

OEDIPUS

The island Greeks believe
to kill sightless kittens
brings bad luck

(Who would strike blind Oedipus dead?)

So they leave them
to starve behind hedges
or in a fosse

If you're not careful
you can hear their soft whimpering
in the fields

Then you must take
all the bad luck
on yourself!

IF EUCLID WERE YOUR ANALYST

Man
is the only animal
that finds pain sweet:
of others preferably;
his own,
if he's a modern masochist

He is also
the only animal
that extols and creates
beauty – consciously
Ergo: art
is the enjoyment
of cruelty
without the infliction
of pain. Q.E.D.

503

STORM AT YDRA

Blow, blow hard,
Aeolus:
you ask no man's leave

Spit great mouthfuls of water
over the boats
whining like tethered horses,
and crack your long, green fingers,
Neptune, on island walls

Cleanse me, gods,
of the insincerity
learned in cities

Batter the christian lie in my soul;
wash out tolerance and wisdom,
fill my mind with power;
even as you flood
the spaces between the quay's
pavement stones,
pour ecstasy into my breast

Ah, sullen gods,
hurl, heal me with your tempests

BOUDHA NATH

I have come from a far place to see this:
A changing village in the Himalayas,
Peasant women bending over green shoots
Or chopping away at the soil beneath;

When I look up I see a golden temple,
Gautama's face, huge and high, on four sides,
Eyes blue, his nose twisted like a question mark
(Watch out, for Big Boudha is watching you!)

Naked children, ecstatic or crying,
Dogs, taxis, cows, flies, droppings, and a boar
Someone has caught and brought down from the hills,
Leading him to laughter and a quick slide

Into death, blood sluicing from the temples
And shattering with its universal noise
The sunlight and this false religious peace;
While an image nags me with the last gouts

That trouble the matchless crimson circles
Below the butchered head, the Boudha eyes,
Of that foul beast the darkened cities loose
Which only the best or the worst can ride.

ELEPHANT

Until yesterday I knew nothing about elephants
    except their slowness to mate;
this morning, in a Nepalese village, while I sat out
    the rain in a wayside shrine,
a riderless elephant slowly made his way
    towards one of the ancient trees
lining the street and there began to scrape
    his immense slate-coloured flank
against the rough, knobby bark of a similar greyness
    and toughness; forward and back,
forward and back, as if bent on sawing down the tree
    with one side of his belly;
keeping somehow as much of a clown's sad,
    self-conscious dignity
as humiliating circumstance might allow,
    yet his bull posture
plainly spelling it out: blows, ridicule, men's
                        displeasure

    are wind beneath his ears;
nothing will drive him from this ecstacy rotundity
    and gratuitous weight
make proportionate to his itch, this rapturous blare
    under his vast hide unwrinkling
like a flower.

Look at that wise, old sybarite!
    The creaking tree says it
for him, and the leaves of the tree
    like multiple green tongues:
"A-ah" "A-ah" "A-ah" until the birds
    nesting or resting among them
take it up and translate it into song;
    unhurriedly, methodically
like an old woman washing herself in the morning
    he does the other side of his belly

which now hangs like a big, grey globe of the world;
        then comes the turn
of his nolessitchy behind though his absurd tail
        fouls his sexy stripper's act;
and lastly that of his hind legs, each time making
                                    me think
        he has three of them.
He moves his head to let me take in the roguish humour
        in his eyes, the ironic
and quietly exultant smile of someone who has learned
        the necessary art
of converting irritation into pleasure
        and giving a final flick of his tail,
a disdainful yet gentle "that's it" or "that's all
                                    for now"
        lumbers off as mysteriously
as he came, leaving me with this poem.

NIGHTFALL

We have taken the night
like a Persian black cat
into bed with us;
your fingers stoking my body's heat
are the glittering red
glassware of my childhood,
are scents suddenly
remembered and pungent;
dark rivers flow under your hair
as under remote bridges.
I feel with my hands
the cool rain bark of your limbs.

Afterwards lying on our backs
like pillowed sovereigns
we decree space
and allow thought and the room's objects
to separate us;
abstract and personal
we turn
in the round cavity of sleep

ENDS

There is of course
personality

Animals have it too

If you stare
long enough
at a flock of goats
you will notice differences

Or at cows:
one cow's more bovine
than another;
another swings her tail
with nuances of inflection

At sheep, yes, at sheep
and the lambs
Jesus was gentle with

And there is also the mouth
and the large intestine

MODERN MIRACLE

There was a Lazarus who dead, rose
And warmed his members with food and drink;
You, Charles, a greater miracle show
For your dead mouth sweats, you live yet stink.

508

FOR JOHN SLAVIN'S BIRTHDAY

I greet you, John Slavin,
on your twenty-ninth birthday

May this day be favourable to you
and all the days to follow

May you live like Moses
to be one hundred and twenty years,
and older – if you want to

And by then be more knowledgeable
about politics and Plato and Rilke
translations
and all the other matters I have in vain
laboured to instruct you

But remain
as compassionate, eager, honourable,
endearing, and full of talent
as you are now

With your adoring, ever-beautiful Julie
to comb your hair
and smooth a towel tenderly over your back
to keep the furious sun from hurting you

THE SMELL

Try as hard as he might
to be a hero or perfect lover,
the smell of dung
always pursues him

He is dizzy with running;
yet run as fast as he can
past temples and fruit trees
when he stops for breath
the smell is always beside him

On his knees or standing
he prays to the Holy Virgin
to intercede for him.
What's the use?
She too smells: two thousand years
of dysentery

Everything smells of shit.
It surrounds him like a fog
surrounds the lights of the sea-coast;
even the gardens and lanes
are smeared with it,
especially when there are golden sunsets

Nothing defends him
from the monster
burrowing in his nostrils
like a bloated worm

If he buries his head
between the perfumed breasts
of a woman,
he begins to gasp for air
as if he had fallen
into an open latrine

Merciful God
is there no help for this man?
His affliction is greater
than that of lepers
or those shaking with palsy

Do you hope to pull him
to you
by his nose?
Is the smell your divine hook?

Give it up, Old Man of the Sky.
He has smelled you out too

You, before all others;
you, the first whiff
that came out of his trouser leg
and made his nose
go like a rake over everything

JASMINE, ANYONE?

Leprosy had eaten away
four fingers and half his palm

Like a neckband studded
with wet, fragrant pearls
was the *gajra*
he held out to me
on his rotted thumb

I had to be careful
where I placed the coin

COUNSEL FOR MY STUNG LOVE

My darling,
when your friends out of envy
    with your delights
puncture your skin
with the needle
of their self-dissatisfaction
and afterwards further rub
    the inflamed region
with their insincere apologies,
accept tranquilly
    their inevitable humanity
as you do the hungering bite
    of the mosquito.

Let your intellect grow.
I would have you turn away
    from the imperceptible
red lump of spite
they have raised on your arm
to consider
the grand impersonal processes
    of nature;
the stars and radio galaxies
and the amazing quasars
that emit no visible rays
    and are remote
from the earth, my stung love,
    nine million light years.

THE COMING OF THE MESSIAH

For patriotic reasons, or for socialism or nationalism
people curse one another
torture, maim, eviscerate, kill;
and strike down little children, even babies
They do all this
because they are themselves cursed,
they have had an evil spell put on them
and must act out their parts;
the regional costumes and weapons
were long ago selected for them
and the deaths they will accomplish
were long ago willed as their doing
It is they and no one else
who must compose the firing squad
destroy that town or city
sentence that spy to death by garrotting
unreel the fine-meshed net of hate
and hang canisters on every loop
to explode at the lightest touch

We shall come to love by and by
over heaps of burnt corpses
over the mutilated bodies of children
through destroyed homes where only the doorposts remain
We shall come to love
when ashes and rubble heaps are the black divisions
on our compass
but not now, not yet

We have not suffered enough
we have not killed enough
we have not maimed enough
we have not massacred enough old men and women
we have not amputated enough limbs of young men
we have not blinded enough infants in their cradles

There are still regions on our planet
human blood has not made wet
valleys and mountains that have not heard
the sound of human groans and wailings
forests that have never witnessed
human treachery and human vindictiveness
sunsmitten gorges that have not echoed and re-echoed
with the searing cries of hate and triumphant carnage

The Messiah will come
only after every inch of earth has been stained with human blood
only after every lake, river and sea has been polluted
with the corpses of butchered men and women
only when the air is made thick with the moans of victims
expiring with indignity and extreme pain
only when all nations have tumuli of slaughtered humans
on which he can step as he makes his way to his seat
on the highest mountain

The Messiah will come
when the maimed and mutilated, the weeping and suffering
in all lands, in every valley, mountain, and plain
agnize the universal heritage of evil,
turning curse into blessing,
and redeemed,
embrace joyously their common tie,
their bond and brotherhood
in death, in dying

515

BRIEF DIALOGUE BETWEEN NEGRO FATHER AND SON

What's dat in yoh hand, son?

A switchblade.

What yah want dat foh, son?

To carve myself some human dignity.

RIGHT CONDUCT

One can be
hypocritical
with eunuchs and castratos

Or truthful
and say right off the bat:
I hate all dead things

I have grey hairs
and still have not found
the right way of behaving

FISHERMEN

When I wish to make myself perfectly happy
—as happy as when I was an ignorant boy—
I hurry down to the village harbour
to hold in one gaze the sun scarcely above
the horizon, itself a wall of soft flame
and the small brave boats that have been out
all night moving towards the stone pier
stately and slow and magnificent as the ships
of Columbus; O for all their blue solemnity
I think they are bursting to signal us
the great news: "It's been a good haul!"

I have seen fishermen unload their catch;
they are silent with exhaustion, perhaps
with reckoning up their gain. There are still
boxes to fill and broken ice to sprinkle
over the fresh gray skins of the fish
glazing like the eyes of many many-eyed
Arguses crushed and glistening between the crystals;
and the torn nets strung out for mending
when the crates of fish have been nailed shut
—to be freighted to the maritime stomachs
of Athenians waiting for them like ravenous fish.

I like the rhythm and unhurried skill,
the humour and dignity of fishermen.
These are men; they do not have to unravel
Danes and Germans to disinter their dead selves.
Bibliothèques are for the soul-sick, for whoever
have swindled themselves of risk, companions,
the communion of sun and sea. In the monster cities
they are doomed; alas I can summon no pity,
no affection for them: they choose their hell.
Deep and irrational as the sea itself
my joy returns with the fishing boats at dawn.

THREE ON A PARK BENCH

Always, of course, excepting
the exceptional few
women are repulsive mammals
without souls;
and after parturition
and the raising of offspring
have no occupations
for mind or spirit:
none

Observe well, my son:
at fifty
a woman's body
is misshapen and sexless
(a sack of spuds,
some grosser than others)
and her face
is either a blob of painted flesh
or it resembles warped leather;
at sixty
it is a warp in the void

Why in the world should that dapper
middle-aged Frenchman,
scented
and obviously pleased with himself
put down his serious papers
stimulating
his manhood afresh
with muggings, rapes, and battles
and look at their horrendous faces?

THE SAD MADONNA

I was thinking
of the primordial energy
that had imagined my life
from the first cry of pain
to the solace of milk
and after of satisfied vanity
when a gypsy stopped me
under the Grassi arcade
of the Avenue de la Victoire

The sad madonna
was holding her copper Christ child
in famished arms
that suddenly became
uncoiled snakes about to strike,
the hands darting at my face
like forked tongues

I remember now
the sun
had just gone behind a cloud
and that I stood transfixed
dividing the crowds
as if I were another column

HIS HOLINESS IS RIGHT

I went to the slaughterhouse

It's true

Man
is an animal
              different
from all the others

HERO OF BABI YAR

You made sausages and you survived

The Hitlerites made in Kiev
a desolation,
flinging the corpses
into the deep ravine, Babi Yar;
then came the turn of the Bolsheviks

You escaped both plagues

"The world is big," you explained,
"and a sausage-maker will never be lost."

Poets turn shit into poems
and plaster them on slaughterhouses:
but the smell comes through

Ah, that smell:
it takes blood and plenty of guts
to manufacture it;
also hacked flesh

Wiser than Plato and Christ,
more truthful than any poet who ever lived,
you turned horsemeat into sausages
and sausages into gold

There should be a monument to you
in every big city of the world

CLIMBING HILLS

Dictatorship, oppression, fear
what have they to do with me
who sit on a Greek stone by the roadside
staring at the hills ahead and to come,
at the almond and fig trees on both sides
and sometimes straight at the sun
that pins my shadow to the ground
like a burly and invincible wrestler?
Here is peace, the sounds of birds
and insects, sometimes of the wind
but none for too long or too loud;
I am as free as an anarchist
cancelling his self-imposed regulations,
as a nudist when I take down my pants
to ease myself behind a hedge

Here are no doors to knock down,
no persons to placate with smiles
or favours; and I can imagine
all my detractors lying under the blackened
stones of the village cemetery
with all the inscriptions chiselled by me.
It is a good pleasant world, I lack
for nothing. In my mind as I squat
I've wiped out Kosygin and Brehznev
and given the outnumbered Czechs
two hundred divisions with which
to drive the Russian louts back
to the stables they were let loose from,
and before the last grunt I complete
the morning's lofty inspiration
with an amnesty for all the Greeks
in all the prisons Papadopoulos
has made especially large keys for:
he himself has palsy and cannot hold
them, and the secretary to whom
he entrusts them is an underground

spy in the pay of Papandreou
—I mean Andreas, the one with loads
of higher degrees from American
universities and not an ounce
of all-necessary political horse sense

But what's that to me looping my belt
and getting ready to take all those hills
I studied on a map but didn't know
were so numerous or so high?
Still, as long as I can mount them
walking alone with the lantern show
of good and evil only dumb shadows
in my head I don't mind how many they are.
Hills are so sane, so honourable
with the sunlight straddling them,
and won't suddenly rear up to throw you
into a ditch; hills don't set traps
either, are not treacherous and will not
accept bribes to tell lies;
I've never known one of them ever
try to deceive me or to menace my welfare:
a neighbour threatened to kill my child

So I like hills, especially with gravelled
roads running through them; and I can say
for roads what I just said about hills;
they seem made for each other,
like some old couples one meets up with
before one's too old himself and lucky:
particularly this morning with a soft
breeze at my back and the sun holding
in reserve his full strength until I reach
the village at the top of the last hill.
After that I'll sit with a bottle of retsina
and think of Kosygin and Brehznev again
and of Papadopoulos whom I left way back
several turns and hedges ago
and of a world as tranquil and lovely
as the hours when together with the sun
I mounted these radiant hills.

ONE LAST TRY AT A FINAL SOLUTION

So the Russian soldiers
tore their blouses and wept
fine, passionate fellows that they are
when they saw Auschwitz
on a carefully controlled tour of inspection

And even the cautious Czech officials wailed

And the Polish communist leaders
let out a terrible howl of sadness (in Polish)
that made the ovens quiver

And the Bulgars cried and unashamedly displayed
their deepest Bulgarian sentiments

And Tito himself was seen blowing his handsome nose

As arm-in-comradely-arm
whimpering and blubbering and dabbing handkerchiefs
to their red tearing eyes

They gave the Syrians and Egyptians
bullets, land mines, tanks, hand grenades, machine guns
poison gas

To finish the job

June 1967

NEPALESE WOMAN AND CHILD

Poets have easy tears
for what they imagine
is your predicament:
tears but no solutions

And Switzerland exports
like wristwatches and cheese
nice-smelling, intelligent women
to teach you their unhappiness

Demagogues with cold eyes
advance on your crumbling doorstep
to amplify your belch
into a peal of thunder

Time doubtless has griefs stored up
for you dazed and gross as the earth
and your tiny son that hangs
like a black pendant under your chin

Smoke your hookah forever
and give suck to your baby
O perfect symbol
of stupor and fertility

TAJ MAHAL

Was it the wise architect
or the grief-maddened emperor
who knew
                    beauty lies
in the perfect symmetry
    of death and Eros?

ATTACHMENTS

Friendship
means gifts, letters,
constant obligation
and concern

And compromise,
those small adjustments
we make for acceptance
and praise

Enemies
are attachments
without burdens

FOR THE GIRL WITH WIDE-APART EYES

My girl waits for me
with soup and wide-apart eyes;
she too has hankerings for immortality:
this morning I left her
inventing the figure
of a cosmonaut
on a crowded beach
– doubtless he was looking for her!

The sea is gentle this morning
(it has not yet read the newspapers)
and gives only the most restrained send-offs
to the stunted borzoi
scrambling towards the shore;
later it will roll
from the lidded shore
like a huge inflamed eyeball.

I pull words out of my fountain pen
and stare at the beach girls
in their bikinis,
scrupulously hiving
the passion they generate
in my loins;
when I return for my noonday meal
I'll offer it to my talented girl
and lay my poems
before her wide-apart eyes.

THE BRIDGE

Do you call me
   to you, Daphne,
sweet-smelling, wanton
Daphne?
   Shall I take
this hoary, battered gull
as a messenger
           you sent
to let me know
   you are sitting
on your perfect
         ass
out on the patio
rubbing oils
       into your skin?
I smell your scented hair
and my erection
         measures
the Atlantic ocean
stretching
     from here
to where
    you are frolicking
and warming up
  under the sun,
        your ever faithful
lover.
    If
I can detach it
from my crotch
      and get
some fairy on the quay
to hold it
   while you grip
the other end
  I'll hurry
     my sweet, over
into your waiting arm.

529

THE WAY TO GO

Envy, lust, my rare-scented queen,
    rule men's lives; lust declines
for time and use turn the love-muscle flabby
but envy takes a man right to the grave

Surviving I note wrily in the noblest
    it troubles me like wens
and deep pitmarks on the face of a woman
once loved for her beauty

I pray my last days on earth be mad
    with sexual desire
so that virgins scatter at my coming
like timorous pigeons and sparrows

And when I die, die my Love
    with a lascivious image
in my head: my hand slowly
ascending your hot uncovered thigh

HOLOCAUST

Each morning he finds at the sink myriads of tiny
brown insects – a mass of virile pencil dots
merging and diverging. Where did they come from?
He stares at the unanswering marble top and
surrounding tiled walls. By contrast with the
restless insects they seem more inert, more than ever
mere philistine matter. Momentarily he warms up
to the skirmishing armies massed on the rim of the
sink, the abyss. His daily ontological lesson.
Nothingness hell-bent for nowhere. Godlike he
observes for a few moments this ridiculous parody
on human existence, sponge in hand. No angel parts
the ceiling to shout, "Hold!" And with one rough
sweep he wipes away this living smear of fig-jam
(including one or two artists and philosophers
who have separated themselves from the frothing
brown mass) and restores to the marble top its
cold ironical surface.

NOCTURNE

A mosquito
stings me
awake

My eyes
open
on the dark
pillow

My first thought
is of you

SEDUCTION

I said: "I am too
complex
to love you
wholly

without misgiving
without holding back

I am too old
for innocent love-play

and passion
such as you
young and lovely
make blaze in strong-thighed
men
half my years

In your presence
they discharge
and must run home
like children
to their mothers"

You laughed: "I prefer
your similes
to their useless semen:
much good it does me!

Come, put your head
on my breasts
firm as quince apples

don't be obstinate
and shifty

As for holding back
do
do just that"

CLEAVAGES

A lively Nicoise
fat, fifty, fun-loving, and well-fucked
(Rubens would have delighted to paint her)
starts throwing pebbles
    into the cleavage
of her companion
and soon the two women
their paunchy limbs and faces pink
    from the afternoon sun
are making each other's bosom
    swell bigger and bigger

Not since I was a child
    have I heard such laughter

Seeing them play like this
how can I maintain my hostility
    to the human race,
        keep my gloomy thoughts?

If I had a pink-flushed cleavage
like theirs
I'd join them

ISRAELIS

It is themselves they trust and no one else;
Their fighter planes that screech across the sky,
Real, visible as the glorious sun;
Riflesmoke, gunshine, and rumble of tanks.

Man is a fanged wolf, without compassion
Or ruth: Assyrians, Medes, Greeks, Romans,
And devout pagans in Spain and Russia
— Allah's children, most merciful of all.

Where is the Almighty if murder thrives?
He's dead as mutton and they buried him
Decades ago, covered him with their own
Limp bodies in Belsen and Babi Yar.

Let the strong compose hymns and canticles,
Live with the Lord's radiance in their hard skulls
Or make known his great benevolences;
Stare at the heavens and feel glorified

Or humbled and awestruck buckle their knees:
They are done with him now and forever.
Without a whimper from him they returned,
A sign like an open hand in the sky.

The pillar of fire: Their flesh made it;
It burned briefly and died — you all know where.
Now in their own blood they temper the steel,
God being dead and their enemies not.

AFTER AUSCHWITZ

My son,
don't be a waffling poet;
let each word you write
be direct and honest
like the crack of a gun

Believe an aging poet
of the twentieth century:
neither the Old Testament
nor the New
or the sayings of the Koran
or the Three Baskets of Wisdom
or of the Dhammapada
will ever modify or restrain
the beastliness of men

Lampshades
were made from the skins
of a people
preaching the gospel of love;
the ovens of Auschwitz and Belsen
are open testimony
to their folly

Despite memorial plaques
of horror and contrition
repentance, my son,
is short-lived;
an automatic rifle, however,
endures
a lifetime

DIVINE GROUND

On sidewalks, streets, in lovely ancient parks
Cowdung and human excreta abound,
But the names of the Brahman who sees and marks
Are Pure Light of the Void and Divine Ground

BUGS

Whenever
I see bugs manoeuvring
on the kitchen floor
with bits of food or paper
sticking to their bodies

I have a resistless desire
to crush them
under my foot

Only if they have bright colours
will I spare them

POSTSCRIPT TO EMPIRE

Behind Connaught Place
shops, buildings, houses
look like platoons of exhausted soldiers
after a forced march in the sun

And at the intersection
of Parliament and Viceroy or Parliament and Curzon
Hindus, seeing me, speak only English
—just like the Fr. Canadians back home

And the manager of the hotel where I stay
wishes to know when Memsahib is coming,
and certainly the editor of Times of India
is a re-incarnation of Steele or Macaulay

And a sign at the famous Aryan temple
sternly prohibits the passing of urine
on the premises; also Christians
and Moslems on all the holy days

And each night dark-skinned young men
detach themselves from the shadows
to whisper old perversities in my ear:
their voices are soft as the tread of pumas

And the nights, black as India ink,
are filled with the cries of vanquished conquerors,
of gods and beasts and men become like beasts;
I listen and do not know what to think

For in the intense white light of day
the bicycles that lie neatly sprawled in dusty lots
have the air of bicycles that are waiting
for the *Wille Zur Macht* to mount them and ride away

THE FINAL PEACE

I lift up my arms
to pluck tranquillity
from the hills and trees

I scoop it out of the sea,
letting the silver-white coins
fall back into the sea

I want nothing in my hand
but water and sunlight
– a fist cannot hold them

Why should I contend with anyone?
Surely Death is his enemy
as he is mine

SILENT JOY

Remembering
St. James street, Sunday mornings
– a vast empty cathedral,
my footsteps echoing in the silent vaults

rooms on quiet afternoons, alone
or with one I loved deeply

shadows, cool and long, in hot lanes

insect-humming cemeteries
and light dripping from vines
in globules of rose, of pale-green

I am so utterly filled
with joyful peace and wonder,
my heart stops beating

Friends, I stare at everything
with wide, with sightless eyes
like one who has just died

LEAVETAKING

Good-bye
fields, waves, hills, trees
and fairweather birds whose blasts
woke me each morning at dawn

So that I might see
the early sun

Good-bye, Sun

I am growing older
I must instruct myself to love you all
with moderation

May you be as kind
to the next poet
who comes this way
as you have been to me

When you see him,
give him my felicitations
and love

NAIL POLISH

Seeking for the murderous self
a concealing and sweet perfume,
one will rush to a synagogue
another dissect a small poem

Or loving himself, a good man
in jest will split a stranger's thighs
then give back with tender moist look
the grin on his mouth as he dies

And some will strike for a frail cause,
proudly burn or unfurl a flag;
amuse dying soldiers in wards,
make love to a love-diseased hag

Who can for truth or justice kill
are the earth's enamoured movers
and they who babble of sweet love
over the bones of their lovers

An obsession with a nice scent
unknown among nature's great laws:
yet what men call good and evil
is but nail polish on their claws

ETERNAL RECURRENCE

Even that leaf as it falls
Will one day fall again
Be sad, be gaily crimson
And flutter while a bird calls

And the bough on which he sits
Lengthen into the dark
While my staring eyes mark
How between the trees your shadow flits

And in my mind image of your face
Vain and angry as you said
Your words and turned away your head:
They will come again, the pain and grace

A million years hence; and from that bough
The same bird calling,
The same crimson leaf falling
And I writing and weeping – then as now

THOUGHTS OF A SENILE REVOLUTIONIST

Ah, if only I knew
for certain
whom to blow up
with my billion megaton
bomb

So that Justice be done
So that Truth may prevail

END OF THE WHITE MOUSE

I do not know what Chinese dragons eat
but *vipera russellii* in cages must be fed

On the soft mat of vipershit, godlike,
without compassion or malice
the famed nutritionist
released the white mouse
— cotton fluff with bright pink eyes —
and for a second only
the poor albino
turned to us his bewildered pink eyes
then shifted and ran around the cage
— the dancing, prancing little show-off;
ran with the heady stuff of life
in his ridiculous tiny wishbone legs,
at times raising himself against the glass cage,
standing there, white, like a splayed bat,
then fluttering off into the flecked shadows,
a piece of cambric in a sudden lift of air

Stung,
the white mouse reared up,
swayed and wobbled like a diapered infant
— the death quiver in his small buttocks —
then fell like a furred stone,
the four legs stiffening with eternity

The unhinged viper
swallowed him head first
and the last I saw of the mouse
was a poignant good-bye flick of his tail,
the soothing peristalsis
ending only when he rested
in the middle of the viper's length:
a pleasant, elastic, cosy bubble
lulling as the Madonna's lap after the Annunciation

And I broke into laughter
for this absurdity
and for the mouse's juices soon to begin
running the length and roundness of the viper,
for the flesh and fragile bones commencing
their inevitable transformative cellular dance

I laughed
as might any well-disciplined Zarathustrian
in this godless epoch
but that evening after I'd sown grass seed
in the round bald spot of my lawn
neatly circular as Caesar's empty pate,
restored the earth and watered it carefully,
suddenly when I was resting on the doorstep
I felt a tremor in my head and frame
as if a whole world had moved inside me

CONSIDER THE LILIES

My colleague
humorous to the end
bawdy and unresigned
was buried today in Winnipeg, Man.
— cancer of the brain

At the burial service
the Anglican minister,
his cultured voice innocent
of irony,
praised the dead man's devotion
to art,
his lifelong delight
in all manifestations of growth

543

LAKE SELBY

Definitely it's not polluted
since no germ would wish
to be found dead in it,
and also it's absolutely
safe for you and the kids
for however far you walk
into its lukewarm wetness
wavelets sedulously suck-suck
at your hips and navel: believe me
it's hardly worth trying
to drown in it; you'd only
be found sitting on your bottom
and the lake's, rope around
your neck or ankle,
stone heavy in your lap

My son who is six flatly
refuses to swim in it
though wind and water
drive him crazy with joy,
especially water;
he calls the stuff squishing
through his toes 'sea food'
and wants none of its sliminess;
as he describes it
it's so many vile fingers
clutching clammily at his heels
he has to kick at furiously
before they will release him
sputtering with rage
and spitting out mouthfuls
of tepid lakewater and weeds

Yet the townsmen summering it
in stolid painted cottages
that each year tighten
around the lake like a noose
plunge into the shallow water
with cries of delight and gusto
ha-ha-ing to one another
and trying a hundred-and-one tricks
to amuse the less venturesome on shore;
for hours and hours I watch them
pretend they're bouncing porpoises
leviathans and comical octopi
or cruel-mouthed sharks
to make their beached wives and progeny
wave admiringly and praise;
afterwards, scrubbed clean of grime
and slime, smoking their pipes
they will sit and stare at the lake
which moon and silence have changed
into a silvered apparition
or some lost and perfect island
rising slowly to enchant them
between the dark elms and pines

HOMAGE TO ONASSIS

It's only right that you should have gotten
The president's lady, my lovely Jacqueline;
And not some poet: weakling . . . clown . . . buffoon

Women love strength and sniff all weakness out,
Nor have they any patience for the lying shout:
Only the Greeks knew what it's all about

Consider Thucydides and Plato
Who knew all about culture but also
Never to let it rot a man's marrow

I tip my glass in homage, giant runt
Who standing handsome and tall on your mint
Make small men turn their heads away or squint

And revenge themselves with those obscene jests
History awards to all its poor outcasts.
I, however, extol your grubby fists

And your gutter-lessoned philosophy
Of love through might; knowing he's truly free
Who can decide whether kings stay or flee

And have only simple unending praise
For the Renascence boldness and blaze
Of your strong life: happy tailing, Onassis!

YOU AND THE 20th CENTURY

On the one hand, dear girl, there's
this brutal stinking 20th century;
on the other hand there is you
or rather your incredible sapphire eyes

Let me do some rapid mental arithmetic:
the big wars one and two, some smaller ones,
Auschwitz and Vorkuta, of course Hiroshima,
revolutions, massacres, executions and – Stalin

And as companion piece though lacking
the Georgian's consummate hypocrisy, Hitler;
such two you may be sure will never again be seen:
not even History can repeat her masterstrokes

Though once again the merciless pinheads are loose
in the streets, man-loving idealists are sniffing
human blood; the weak resenting their weakness
dividing neatly into demagogues and murderers

It's a familiar enough story, God knows
who uses the same old ploys to push us on
to meet the Messiah, i.e. death of course
who alone brings peace, redemption from lies and murder

I endure both what I know as memory
and as learning as well as the day's outrages
hustling us inescapably into vulgarity and serfdom
because not otherwise can I know your beauty

Yet, love, when I see your incredibly lovely eyes
wise as an old woman's, bright with mischief,
it seems I can pick up the day as calmly as a child
picks up a forgotten toy from his littered floor

FOR NATALYA CORREIA

You possess the sturdy elegance of a cannon
and move always with the authority
of someone about to capture a city

Are indisputably beyond the vanity
of attention and compliments
like famous statues fixed in permanent triumph

Who in aloof approving silence
or unending melancholy disdain
regard their admirers at the crowded base

If you dispense anger or annoyance
it is as if doing so you establish
the existence of those who provoked them

And entertain each day those certainties
acclamation and gratified desire foster
in a voluptuous and talented woman

I admire wholeheartedly the egotism
with which you half stretch out on your couch
like a glistening female sealion

And pour without my permission
wine from my wineglass into your own
fanning with delighted self-absorption

The smoke curling about your impressive head
or jab ebony cigaret holder into space
as if to poke chrysolites from their hiding place

MEMO TO MY SONS

Remember, my sons,
   man is an animal
who has a soul:
different from giant reptiles
hawks
and repulsive monsters
              in forest
and sea
he wants to kill
with a good conscience

Speak softly
   to this queer beast;
soothe him, soothe him

TO THE PRIEST WHO KEPT MY WIFE AWAKE ALL NIGHT, FARTING

Some use a primitive gong, others a bell:
This devout priest does equally well
To call his parishioners to early Mass
By loud, insistent trumpetings of his ass.

FREE EXPRESSION

Having picked out
from among many
a German
with cold blue eyes
and yearnings
for a long prick
in his rectum

His ex-mistress
like a reformed whore
hot for virtue
nightly shoves
her index finger
up his moistened asshole

To please her Bavarian
still more
her free mornings
are given up wholly
to finger painting

550

OHMS

ohms
is such a beautiful word

soft as marshmellow in the mouth
as a lover's sigh

hearing it for the first time
in Physics 6
I was electrified

it was like my first kiss
my first piece of ass
but cleaner purer

since then I've loved ohms
passionately
especially ohms of resistance

if you try to say the word
in anger
or vindictively
you can't ohms is pure poetry

bellow it
it comes out a muted cry of pain:
the sound the universe makes

yet poets have written
about owls yes about owls many times

nightingales snakes daffodils bridges
graveyards
but not about ohms

therefore I've written this poem
and now wish to add only this:

ohms is immortal
chaste and lovely as a rainbow
it will delight our seed
on Venus Jupiter Mars

when the great Florentine
even he
is gibberish to their ears

RECIPE FOR A LONG AND HAPPY LIFE

Give all your nights
to the study of Talmud

By day practise
shooting from the hip

GREY MORNING IN LISBON

September

the Castello
on one of the seven hills
is massive and bleak:
a disgruntlement of stone

yesterday's gladness is gone

from fountain and flowertrees
rooftiles
civilized park
even the police helmets
parading
under my alert three-storey eyes

the city reveals her grey stumps
and shiny store teeth

I do not listen
when wrapped in shawl of dull fleece
with slowed-down pulse
and lustreless eye
she begins to recount her history

553

LAURA CUNNEYFLOW

returning from her summer travels
– an event annual
as ploughing & seeding –
Laura at once tells me
of the men who tried to lay her,
of their near-triumphs and failures
– and of their triumphs!
I listen to her
entranced
since life-loving
middle-aged chicks
wall-to-walling
in plush vacation hotels
on the beaches
of Nice and Havana
have much to teach
a melancholy poet

chemically pure redhead bubble
in the ceaseless senseless
biological froth
Laura Cunneyflow rich
and riggish
mistfully remembering
the vast innocence
of her lovers
in four continents,
their endearing romanticism,
is a portent
on whose entrails
the future has already
begun to move

EROS

So expertly did he teach
his Jewish mistress
the art of love-making

that now
when she goes down
on her newest lover
– a much-troubled Austrian

he moans with ecstasy
and babbles
                    he no longer
sees his father's polished
boot
        pressing for gold
in the bone-rubble
of Belsen and Dachau

SATAN IN UTOPIA

here in Inishmeer
fights start
not because of race
(all are Aryan)

not because of religion
(all are Catholic
and go to church
Sundays without fail)

not because of communism
(all are too poor for that)

not for politics
(all vote as the curate
advises them to)

or rival nationalisms
(all are Gael
and tourists with foreign
money are welcome)

or because some are free
and some are slave
(all are in equal bondage
to soil and climate)

but because
one has a field
with flatter or rounder stones
or more honourable ancestry
or can drink two quarts of whisky
without a belch at the end

or owns a cow that yields
more milk or shit or brown hairs
or smells better

see, they've had their pints of **Guinness:**
now watch the fists fly

listen to those Irish curses

GOD IS LOVE

Fifteen minutes after the hurricane
had mauled the coastal town, uprooting
elms and telephone poles that now lie sprawled
like mired drunks in avenues and lanes,
the young minister gathered up his fold
at the whitewashed roadside cross unbroken
miraculously above the caved-in homes
and cried triumphantly: 'See, God is Love!
He has only larrupped us for our sins.'
But an injured whore eyeing His stricken Son
soundly bleeding paint on beams of wood
sneered aloud to her transfixed neighbour,
'The Lord sure knows how to care for His own,'
and scanned the mob for an amorous customer.

FANATIC IN SAN FELIU

They said it wouldn't rain
after the 21st of June
in San Feliu.
It did. It rained every day.
And oftener.
They said I would find
and finger
multitudes of young girls
with tight butts
and tits like pistols
cocked to go off in your face:
lies, the fantasies
of incarcerated lechers.
They said there would be festivals
every day, beginning
with the day of my coming:
to date, a Spanish sparkplug
exploded in the empty street
– nothing else.

Someone – was it you? –
hijacked
the crowds, the fierce and arrogant
Catalan dancers,
the cruel women with dazzling **mouths**
and whisked them off
to a neighbouring town
where everyone is making love
to lascivious girls of fifteen
– banners and streamers
are everywhere
and people all night
are drinking and singing
in the festooned squares.

Now under this soaked awning
beside an abandoned aquarium
full of crawling baby lobsters
whose rubbery black eyes
I imagine moles
on your lifeless breasts
are only some empty chairs
and myself,
a lonely fanatic with images
of your white faraway body
and corrupt mouth
to torment him this rainswept
cold evening
while the high and swelling wind
howls with his terrible sickness.

DIONYSUS IN HAMPSTEAD

Springtime's greensickness squirrels
and insects roiled soiled coiled
in cycles of propagation and death
tender blossoms of apple rough winds staple
to the heavy false odours of lilac
and dung my neighbour's disciplined lawns

I shout hooray for everything that dances
wild songs fucking birds and beasts wild words
an Australasian waving her gay pirate's flag
of pubic hair her snakelike arms writhing
over breasts and crotch O Florentine whores
with gestures of great lewdness and beauty

The wise and the just are too solemn
under their long shadows they do not dance
at the weddings I hear in the grass
at the mock funerals I hear in the leaves of trees
and hedges sunlight trims with golden razors
they do not leapfrog in ancient cemeteries

Who am I to explain sovereignty and flowers
who forever am thinking of silent unseen cracks
music makes till all walls fall in slowly
dissolving dreams of the migrations of birds
and terrorists the bad poets of this century
laying their heads like bombs between a woman's **thighs**

On a rock surrounded by alligators and goats
I sit shedding invisible blossoms like dreams
over quiet archipelagos and Africas
more content than an old astrologer
who belches from a surfeit of stars and charts
till heaven's sceneshifter arrives and
covers the earth with a bloodstained shroud

560

NO CURTAIN CALLS

They came called by the best Samaritans:
the street waited for the gay sparks
to dance out of the window
                              run along
the roof, dance dazzle and with bright upthrust
doom with blaze . . . . ah-h
          INSPIRED POET CATCHES FIRE
Heavy-booted and ponderous
they raise retractable red engines to now
no more than a thin curl of smoke
a cigaret whisper in milady's ashtray
– a frail contemptuous yawn of tired air

Nozzles on shoulder, helmets
shiny and embarrassed
                         they peer
over readied axes
like burly enormous cats
                         and watch
helpless and alert
the last disappearing mouse
flick a famished tail of smoke
under their valorous distended noses

While the street
                 silently hissing
the poor show and fake build-up
(standing room only)
will not disperse
                  but waits hopefully
for a flaming Alcibiades
                         preferably smashed
(to please the hard-to-please critics)
to come leaping from the house
and stumble at their feet

561

ARAN ISLANDS

Dun Aengus

High walls . . . of stones;
man-humbling cliff and shattering sea;
ramparts:
trenches of stone, fierce four of them
and in-between
prehistory's barbed wire, *cheveux de frise*
. . . of stones.

Enclosing a mist.

Gone are the defenders;
gone, they who attacked.

Nothing here:
only mist
and blue-grey stones.

Cliffs of Moher

At last, as in a dream,
I've come to the cliffs
from where God hurls down
His enemies, every one.

Rat-faced cunning mercers
with a rat's delight;
all, all who are dead of soul,
male and female.

See, their polls open like flowers
on the black rocks below;
their brains dance with the foam
on a green wave's tow.

Kilmurvey

Low are the hills, a mere rise
in the ground, grey with stones and green;
Stand anywhere and you can trace
outlines with your new-found eyes
of stone fences delicate as lace:
Stand anywhere and you can be seen.

KILMURVEY STRAND

An old man walks barefoot
in the water his trousers
rolled up to his knees
and his hair is white
as the foam is white He
bends his shape to hear
the seagulls crying overhead
and scatter the fragments
of cloud floating in the stilled
pools he wades into between
the rocks
         In the vortex
of his happiness he revolves
like an uprooted plant in
a small remote whirlpool lend-
ing a small dignity to its suck
All his years are pebbles under
his feet Sands on the fine hairs
of his blueveined calves

The waves pick up
sand and brown mice
sometimes huge black rats They
do it over and over
one more time till doomsday
with the same patient roar
of admonition but the mice
and black rats keep dissolving

One white cloud then another
each nudging the other
over humps lustreless aeons
of hills have reared

I kneel on the strand
and notice things unhelpful
for myself at fifty-seven
still capable of hope
and anger No thought of mine
pushed from behind but appear-
ing as if from nowhere like
a bird solitary and sudden
in a sky One
had not noticed before

PAUL VERLAINE

It's when he's drunk
that he knows he should never be married
or have children;
what has he to do
with the conversation of wives
or the chatter and nosepickings of children?
he should be a cloud, a forest fragrance
a startled fawn, at one
with the elemental force
that makes a plantain leaf
fall to the ground
or a peacock spread its tail to the sun

INISHMORE

I've not been here long enough
to know you I am still an intruder
on your silences though my woolsweater
and face are known to them as I sit
this mild midday on one of your multi-
tudinous flat stones and to your flies
less plump than those of Richelieue
your sheep gulls bad weather vegetation
lonely horses and stone fences unrolled
collars at sundown of black lace enclosing
mist and mist and fields of stones hostile
and humble like the severed heads of slain
Goliaths or dragged here to their last
resting place all who ever looked on the snake-
curls of Medusa

        And scour my mind
for farewell words farewell gesture in-
evitable and sad as funerary inscriptions
under Celtic crosses or cowsplatter
in and about Dun Aengus fort whose unhomered
heroes fought and killed and were killed
with cries of gulls mingling with their own
outlasting them
carrying their death screams
in their throats and beaks as elegy
as harsh requiem down the winging centuries
and whose ramparts and *cheveux de frise*
raise up the ghosts of Guderian and his hard-
driving tankists, Mongomery bereted and ailing
dictating his victories

        To find in it
perhaps because your name is so lovely
image of woman I met briefly and briefly
made love to in an Irish castle ruined
and empty by a deserted wayside the surface
of whose soul I scarcely touched but whose
embrace neither fullfillment nor promise
is a secret ache and turbulence

YESTERDAY

where did yesterday
go

what happened to it

everyone in the world
including myself
saw and felt yesterday
yesterday

it did something to all
of us

changed the world
in so many countless ways:
changed mountains fields
bullocks geese ripsaws carburetors
even swamps and foxholes

probably changed the whole universe
by several equations

now it is gone
as if it had never been
its sway for a day
ended

I feel it must have lingered
by the ocean
for the fraction
of a minute
before plunging in

and if I dived in now
I'd come up
holding yesterday
in my hand

EPITAPH FOR A POET

I sang of thighs
I sang of breasts
I sang of shoulders
soft and black as soot
white and soft as cloud
and of curved lips
from which kisses
fell like rose petals
or flew like birds
wilder and wilder
I sang
as I grew older
and my loins wrinkled
like the forehead of a sage

JULY 21, 1969

Rightly have poets called the moon a woman:
Once penetrated, all her mystery's gone!

FOR ANNA

You wanted the perfect setting
for your old world beauty, postwar Hungarian:
a downtown Toronto bar sleazy
with young whores pimps smalltime racketeers

remembering boyhood Xmases in Elmira
plus one poet pissed to the gills
by turns raving or roaring like an acidhead
then suddenly silent like the inside of a glass

I'm sure you placed him there as camera
as incorruptible juror or witness
but who can give report of a miracle?
having seen it what struck dumb can he tell?

and to whom? they who pressed around you
were converted and left off dreaming of murder
or rape in public parks/some cried for happiness . . .
they outside or riding the subways will never believe

Now I know everything which happened
that night was your creation/you invented
it all by cupping your elegant proper hands
then letting the night escape like a black moth

that shattered the fantastic radiance of your head
into a thousand glints and scintillations
transfiguring bottles whisky glasses even the leers
on aroused Canadian clerks fingering their wallets

and making me run after you to discover
whether you are a woman with blood and orifices
one may after all love and if the answer is yes
whether you will warm my aging limbs as a lover

FROST AND FENCES

Something there is that doesn't love a wall:
Is that what the American poet said?
His heart might break to see fences of stone
As if to prove him liar after all

Or was it dark hate and contradiction
Infested these islands with honeycombs
– Grim trenches military and man-tall
And looking as if they were eternal

Or perhaps an obstinate kind of spite
Akin to pride or feeding off its flame
Grew these ramparts like a calloused skin
And wrapped this seed of Adam safe within

No matter: things of marvel and delight
Survive, time-calcined, their creator's death
Though they seem insubstantial as a breath
And such nonsense as won't deceive a child

Or make a man who has a solid head
Point to the fenced fields with their crop of stones
And cry: 'I praise only what my eyes behold'
As if he thought they'd hear him and applaud

DIONYSIAN REVELLER

When I've had lots of wine and love
I am a god and speak like a god;
then I curse all the passionless worms
that slide their fearful, grey forms

Over this astonishing earth; let them dissolve
like rain into the sought-for mud;
let their worm eyes explode from a sudden
unlooked-for glimpse of God!

THE STRAIGHT MAN

In the doom
of his freedom
man
vertical man wars
with the horizontal.

For what? A nearer
look at sunspots?
To be all stiff
with rectitude,
the upright man?
At best, patch . . . botch . . .
Christ on a crotch?

Ah, for fantasies
time distills
out of the slime;
bubbles, nothing else,
the intellect looses
from our genitals
and death proves
foam or scum.

571

PLEA FOR MY LADY

You won't let me kiss you?
Me?

Lady, you must be joking!
Lady, you must be mad!

Who put the agony in my lips
as though they had sucked
for a thousand years
on a prickly pear?

Who taught them
to want yours
with such a fever?
On crowded thoroughfares
of the city
I feel my mouth pulled
towards wherever you are.
Mariners need a compass.
You are my lodestar.

Of what use are my hands
if you won't let them caress you?
My arms, if they can't embrace you?
O my whole frame's
become a piece of useless junk.

The season that lovers
and worms wait for
is here
but your disdain
has sewn up all my senses
with invisible threads.

I'm blind to green buds
dead to lilac smells
deaf to all birdsongs.

I can't, O lady, even hear
my own cries
wilder than those Abelard
shrieked
that wild night
they plucked out his stones.

Lady, let me have your lips
Lady, let my hands caress you
Lady, let me embrace you
O lady, lady, lady, lady

ABSENCE

Love,
I make a silence
out of your name
and dip
my hands into it

AS SEEN THROUGH A GLASS DARKLY

Armoured
archaic
and looking
like a man-of-war
in a naval museum
– an old furious dreadnought
manoeuvring into line
in, say, a famous forgotten film
about imperial England

One crimson, cruising
lobster
on the aquarium floor
finally settles stiffly
alongside another

Each moves with slow deliberate
courtesy
keeping temper and pride
under admirable control,
like a retired major-general
I imagine escorting
his youngest daughter
to the theatre box

Nevertheless
for all their upperclass formality
lobsters
in a restaurant aquarium
remind me vividly
of communist and socialist friends

Could it be it's their colour
– a half-boiled red?

574

No: rather
it's the appearance lobsters
in their safe cubicles give
of a rectitude overstressed
because unnatural,
of party earnestness and conviction,
of seeming – that's it! – too self-conscious
exponents
of Kant's categorical imperative

While whatever-one-calls-them,
their feeding filaments,
make small currents of water
and insignificant
bubbles
that break
on coming to the top
without the expected pop

I CAN SLEEP BESIDE MY LADY

Wolves mutilated my lady
her glory dripped from their tongues
and flamed upon the snow
O they rolled her naked body
where the ditch received her limbs
like a woman's powdered crease

But green and velvet was the night
and all her lovers
were marooned in the movies
while the lovers of her lovers
gossiped about sparrows
in the Northeastern Lunch

I who might have saved her
watched instead
her bright blood spill on snow
I who might have saved her
was hungry for the whisper
of her matted hair

And all the houses kneel
like bloated nuns in prayer
around my love they kneel
remote as David's ships
or sway like weak and fasting saints
as she lies bleeding there
from her damaged fingerprints

O rabbis and angels
and lovers marooned
forever in lost movies
when wind and wolves have had **their fill**
I shall unstitch the clawmarks
from my lady's lovely flesh
I shall sleep all night
beside her bruised and glistening **body**
on a lonely hill

ENTRY

He was a Jew with a faked identity
card;
the ghetto was in flames, its puny defenders
scattered, dead

As he crossed the emptied square of the now
silent city
and looking up saw the great
black cathedral of Warsaw
the immovable stars overhead
he was caught suddenly
in the murderous crossfire of nazi and partisan guns

He hugged the bloodstained rubbish and stones
and laughed into the dark at how
an impersonal death by a willed or stray bullet
made one at last a human among humans

THE BROTHERS LAZAROVITCH

my brother and I share the same
memory of a slum

it's a recurrent memory
linking Montreal and San Francisco

if I throw an ever-so-light pebble
into its gossamer moment
it bounces now one way now another,
his or mine: until
the pebble has stopped rolling
and become a fixed grey point
from which memory uncoils
like a garden worm after rain
I can't tell

sometimes as I run past him
I see him stooping furtively
to pick it up and put it in his pocket
which still smells of lemonseeds and roses;
just like him I think
and begin to tremble
for his pocket
also contains my boyhood eraser and penknife

I know he uses
my eraser to rub out the Void:
the penknife has become a switchblade

when he flashes the open blade
in the sunshine
it leaves a trail of blood bubbles
in the shimmering air
and his mouth goes soft like cowplop

it's then I remember
he pushed me down the cellar
and as I sank into the dark hole
held up a photograph of himself

in the dark
his shiny white teeth
are all the light I want

EPIGRAM ON A.J.M. SMITH

He wrote two lines of immortal wit:
his best poem, and I inspired it!

FOR SOME OF MY STUDENT MILITANTS

history
is not
        histrionics
or hysteria: it is the strict
verdict
        when you are safe and quiet
in your graves
                your children
and grandchildren's skeletons
crumbling beside you

it is reality
                as you could never
see it: its uncompromising purity
no longer raddles your sanity
nor does its intense white light
blind you
                as it passes over
the arrogance of militant lies
like the sweep of a flashlight
                in a cellar
or the long electric finger
from a lighthouse tower
                        over heaving waters
listen:
history is reality
dressed for the occasion;
it is the Messiah
        we all pray for
and reject

now your arms silently at your side
and your mouths stilled forever
you may receive its judgment

there is no appeal
children
for the round bound eye of the camera
is not the eye with which God sees you
580

AFTERNOON OF A COUPON CLIPPER

My sister who weekly clips hers
Owns a pair of golden scissors
Which are light but strong. They combine
Utility with a rare shine.
'Course she won't say where she got them;
I fancy it was Rotterdam
Though, where she went for last year's trip.
Me? I've often seen her go clip,
Clip, same as you might with a pair
That never ate into a share
Or ran around a trim coupon
Quick as a whore with nothing on.
And yet my sister has her irk
And care—sometimes her fingers jerk!
I've seen the scissors leave the rut
And make a most improper cut.
It's odd, that's when I like her best.
Her great spirit triumphs. Modest
In her failure, gallant, resigned,
She shows such bravery of mind
That I, standing beside the bed,
Adjust a pillow for her head.
Ah my Senora! See her lean
Easily back and fix the clean
Legs of her marvellous golden boy
With their fine exquisite taper
Astride a well of stiff paper;
With carmined lips that smile, adore
She assaults her Toreador
And in each scooped-out buttock she
Can make a mouth so prettily
Two rosy rectums there I see
Or with soft and amorous sigh
Will gently stroke each tapering thigh.
O from this sport her head does shake
With so much force she stays awake
And all night long must pray for rest:
A golden cross upon her breast.

OSIP MANDELSHTAM (1891-1940)

I once did an hour-long TV show reading
from your *Stamen* and *Trivia*: out there
were my compatriots who had never before
heard of your name and pain, your nightmare fate;
of course the impressario spoke impressively
about your stay in Paris where you mastered
the French symbolists, your skill as translator
(what pre-Belsen Jew hadn't promiscuously
shacked up with five or six gentile cultures)
the Hellenic feeling in your prose and poems
– to be brief, he filled in the familiar picture
of enlightened Jew ass bared to the winds

But when that self-taught master symbolist
il miglior fabbro put you on his list of touchables
that was the end; you perished in the land waste
of Siberia, precisely where no one knows and few care
for in that stinking imperium whose literature
you adorned like a surrealist Star of David
you're still an unclaimed name, a Jewish ghost
who wanders occasionally into enclaves
of forlorn intellectuals listening
for the ironic scrape of your voice
in the subversive hum of underground presses

I know my fellow-Canadians, Osip;
they forgot your name and fate as swiftly
as they learned them, switching off
the contorted image of pain with their sets,
choosing a glass darkness to one which starting
in the mind covers the earth in permanent eclipse;
so they chew branflakes and crabmeat gossip make love
take out insurance against fires and death
while our poetesses explore their depressions
in delicate complaints regular as menstruation
or eviscerate a dead god for metaphors;
the men-poets displaying codpieces of wampum,
the safer legends of prairie Indian and Eskimo

582

Under a sour and birdless heaven
TV crosses stretch across a flat Calvary
and plaza storewindows give me
the blank expressionless stare of imbeciles:
this is Toronto, not St. Petersburg on the Neva;
though seas death and silent decades separate us
we yet speak to each other, brother to brother;
your forgotten martyrdom has taught me scorn
for hassidic world-savers without guns and tanks:
they are mankind's gold and ivory toilet bowls
where brute or dictator relieves himself
when reading their grave messages to posterity
– let us be the rapturous eye of the hurricane
flashing the Jew's will, his mocking contempt for slaves

THE GARDENER

he lives life without fuss
or explanations
              cutting grass, trimming
trees and hedges
              an octogenarian's soundness
in all his motions

half-French, half-English
of the two solitudes
he's made one large tranquillity
of acceptance
             and has never listened
for the bitter songs
wounded self-love hums
                 in the ear
of impotence and defeat

wanting no man's pity or compassion
least of all
        of poets pandering
to their own weakness
            only
the remaining strength
in his seven good fingers
               disease
hasn't twisted
        into black unfeeling claws
and the bite of a solitary tooth
standing firm
        in his jaw
like a weatherbeaten nail
for his smile to hang on

SHAKESPEARE

My young son asks me:
'who's the greatest poet?'
Without any fuss I say, Shakespeare.
'Is he greater than you?'
I ho-ho around that one
and finally give a hard 'yes'.
'Will you ever be greater
than . . . a splatter of lisped S's
and P's . . . ?'
I look up at my son
from the page I'm writing on:
he too wants his answer
about the greatness of Shakespeare
though only six and carefree;
and I see with an amused hurt
how my son has begun to take on
one of those damned eternal fixtures
of the human imagination
like 'God' or 'Death' or 'the start
of the world'; along with these
it'll be with him the rest
of his life like the birthmark
on his right buttock; so as though
I were explaining God or Death
I say firmly without a trace
of ho-ho in my voice: No, I'll never
be greater than William Shakespeare,
the world's greatest poetic genius
that ever will be or ever wuz,
hoping my fair-minded admission
won't immediately blot out
the my-father-can-lick-anyone image
in his happy ignorant mind
and take the shine away
that's presently all around my head.

That unclimbable mountain, I rage;
that forever unapproachable star
pulsing its eternal beams from a far
stillness onto our narrow screens
set up as Palomar libraries and schools
to catch the faintest throb of light.
Damn that unscalable pinnacle
of excellence mocking our inevitable
inferiority and failure
like an obscene finger; a loud curse
on the jeering 'beep . . . beeps'
that come from dark silence
and outer galactic space to unscramble
into the resonant signature of
'Full many a glorious morning' or
'The quality of mercy is not strained'
or 'Out, out, brief candle . . .'
NO poet for all time, NO poet
till this planet crack into black night
and racking whirlwinds EVER
to be as great as William Shakespeare?
My God, what a calamitous burden
far worse than any horla or incubus:
a tyrant forever beyond the relief
of bullet or pointed steel . . .
What a terrible lion in one's path!
What a monumental stone
in the constrictive runnel of anyone
with an itch to write great poems
– and poets so cursed beyond all
by vanity, so loused up in each inch
of their angry, comfortless skin
with the intolerable twitch of envy!

Well, there's nothing to be done
about that bastard's unsurpassable
greatness; one accepts it like cancer
or old age, as something that one
must live with, hoping it will prod us on
to alertest dodges of invention
and circumvention, like the brave spider
who weaves his frail home in the teeth
of the lousiest storm and catches
the morning sun's approving smile;
Anyhow there's one saving grace:
that forever smiling damned bastard,
villain, what-have-you is dead
and no latest success of his
can embitter our days with envy,
paralyze us into temporary impotency,
despair rotting our guts and liver;
yes, though the greatest that ever wuz
or ever will be he's dead, dead,
and all the numerous flattering busts
keep him safely nailed down
among the worms he so often went raving
on about when his great heart burst
and all the griefs of the world
came flooding out. His ghost may wander
like Caesar's into my tent
by this rented lake, and I'll entertain
him; but he must also stand outside
begging for entry when I keep his volume
shut, and then he's out in the cold
like his own poor Lear. And – well –
there's my six-year-old son
who says of the clothes flapping
on the clothesline: 'Look, they're
scratching themselves,' or compares
his mother's nipples to drain-plugs
he says he wishes to pull out, or
tells me the rain is air crying
– and he only four at the time;

and though I swear I never told him
of Prospero and his great magic
asked me the other day: 'Is the world real?'
So who really can tell, maybe one day
one of my clan will make it
and there'll be another cock-of-the-walk,
another king-of-the-castle; anyway
we've got our bid in, Old Bard.

THE HAUNTING

Why without cease do I think of a bold youth
    national origin unimportant or racial Peruvian
Russian Irish Javanese he has fine clear eyes
honest smiling mouth a pat for a child's head
talks to old women and helps them cross the street
    is friendly with mainliners anarchs and nuns
Cote St. Luc housewives their ruined husbands and brats
optometrists sign painters lumpenproletarians dumping
their humps into coffee cups plotting revenge
and clerics who've made out of Christ a bearded faggot

From the rotating movement of a girl's beautiful
    buttocks he draws energy as from the sun
(O lovely revolving suns on St. Catherine street)
and from breasts and perfumed shoulders and hair
Picadilly Wilhelmstrasse Fifth Avenue Rue St. Germain
    the suns go rolling on luminous hoops pinwheels
handsprings and somersaults of desirable flesh
the bold youth with wide-apart happy eyes
stepping lightly over blossoming asphalt graves is running
after them touching a child's head smiling to old women

Why don't I ever meet him face to face?
    sometimes I've seen him stepping off a bus
but when I've caught up with him he's changed
into a bourgeois giving the two-fingered peace sign
or a poet shouting love as if it were a bomb
    on damp days into an office clerk smelling of papers
is he somebody's doppelganger? an emanation or
shadow I see taking shape near a plateglass window?
who is he? he haunts me like an embodied absence
and as if I had lived all my life in arrears

INDEX OF TITLES

INDEX OF FIRST LINES